# LIBERTY
## Life, Billy, and the
## Pursuit of Happiness

by Liberty DeVitto

"When I play, I give all my energy; my entire being goes into it. I go into a 'drummer's high.' I feel like I become part of the drum. In the studio, after I do a take of a song, I get so engrossed in it that when I listen back, it's like I am listening to a different person—like it's someone else playing the drums. It feels like I am listening to something that someone else had done."

**-Liberty DeVitto**

# LIBERTY
## Life, Billy, and the Pursuit of Happiness
By Liberty DeVitto

Edited by Joe Bergamini

Design and layout by Rick Gratton

Executive Producer Rob Wallis

Cover design by Mike Hoff

Cover Photo: Leland Bobbé

www.lelandbobbe.com

Photo credits: Lissa Wales (p. 174), Jim Houghton (p. 146), Rick DiAmond Photography (p. 210), Nicole Sweet (p. 239), Kevin Curtin/Curtin Call (p. 234), Andy Gilmartin.

All other photos courtesy of author's personal collection.

Original manuscript edited by Dr. Simon Mills

**View an additional online photo gallery at:**
**https://hudsonmusic.com/liberty/**

I dedicate this book to:

My mother and father and all my family who came before me and will come after me. I hope I didn't disappoint you.

My children: Devon, Torrey, Maryelle, and Mae. My love for you has depth I can't even comprehend.

Billy Joel, for sharing the ride of our lives.

My wife, Anna, for saving my life and putting up with the shitstorm that is Liberty DeVitto.

# Contents

## ACKNOWLEDGMENTS

Dr. Simon Mills. This book is in your hands because Dr. Mills insisted. I spent sixty years creating the stories and writing them down, and he relentlessly crafted it into this book. Watching him do this is what I imagine it feels like when I play on his songs in the studio. I help mold those songs with my drum. He "Millsed" this book with his fingers.

Nice work, Millsy
        -Lib

Thank you to Paul Quinn for keeping things legit.

Thanks also to Sandra Castillo and Holly Payne for all the help and for encouraging me to write.

Thanks to Liberty drums, Sabian cymbals, Evans drumheads and Pro-Mark drumsticks for their years of support.

Thanks to Rick Gratton for his wonderful design and layout.

Thanks to Joe Bergamini for helping me say the right things the right way.

Thank you Rob Wallis for believing in my work a second time.

# Foreword

Liberty DeVitto provided the power that drove our song arrangements and live performances for thirty years. While I was writing the songs for eight of my twelve original song albums (*Turnstiles* to *River of Dreams*), I relied on his particular enthusiasm for those songs to motivate the energy that brought them to life and made them stand out as recordings. I will always be indebted to the musicians I worked with over all those years, but Liberty's drumming, along with Doug Stegmeyer's stalwart bass guitar, propelled my music into another dimension, far beyond the acoustic limitations of my piano-based songwriting.

In this book, Liberty has detailed not only the history of how those songs were arranged and performed, but also how we brought that music around the world with us, along with all the craziness that accompanies musicians with a dedicated mission to "leave it all on the stage." We were a merry band of brothers for many years and over many miles, and despite whatever personal or financial catastrophes eventually befell all of us, we were as much a family unit as any other relationships we had formed during our lives. And, like our other families, we inflicted hurts and wounds on each other—never intending to cause lasting scars.

Reading this book has brought a flood of warm memories that I had long since forgotten, and which I now regret having allowed to lapse into shrouded history, along with other timeworn milestones of my past.

I relied mightily on Liberty's approval of the material I brought to the band, since his rhythmic foundation emphasized the rock 'n' roll ethos I was striving for beyond the melodic parameters that came so naturally to me as a student of classical piano.

Liberty and I have reconciled and reclaimed the friendship that we felt for each other all those years ago. And I am a better man because of that.

But this is not my story—it's his. And it's a marvelous insight into the trials and tribulations that many drummers have had to deal with throughout the rock 'n' roll era. Keep this in mind when you hear the songs and recordings again that you first heard when you were very young—and remember that we were so very young then too.

*Billy Joel*

March, 2020

# Prologue

When you are involved in a phenomenon like Billy Joel, you really don't think about what you're doing. It's like being in the eye of a storm. You're not aware of what is going on around you. We were just a bunch of guys having the time of our lives. Writing has reintroduced me to the music I helped create. A doctor who operates on a patient is just doing his job, but when he comes face to face with that now-well person, he sees them in a different light. My musical past is like that. Through my writing, I have met the music in a new venue.

I met Ringo Starr during his first All-Starr Band tour. When I was introduced to him, I said, "If it wasn't for you, I wouldn't be doing what I'm doing now." He replied, "At least you're not blaming me for it."

Why would anyone want to become a professional musician? I am successful because I worked my ass off to get where I am. I wanted it so bad, I couldn't conceive of doing anything else. I guess I really can't do anything else; it's a spiritual calling for me— as it is with most musicians. I just don't have a choice. At one time I surrendered to the reality that I might be playing weddings for the rest of my life. I came to terms with that and accepted it; as long as I could play, I'd deal with it. I gave up all after-school "activities" to rehearse. I gave up girlfriends and fiancées, gave up buying expensive things, and sacrificed job security and health benefits. I never had a steady schedule; my hours went from when someone wanted me until they were done with me. I never had stock options, sick days, or vacation time. I had work or no work.

As a drummer, I cannot play solo gigs. Most musicians are freelance artists, really. I am self-employed, but still dependent on someone else to hire me. I met my wives through my music and I lost them partially because of it. I missed out on my middle daughter's birth; I missed out on my kids' first steps, recitals, and graduations. I'd listen to my daughter playing violin via speakerphone on the road. I made friends through my work, only to find that they disappeared when the gig was over, or when I quit partying. I have no choice but to constantly watch what I say and be careful of who is around when I decide to talk about business. I have heard my words repeated many times behind my back after confiding in a "good friend." Despite all of this, I still have the greatest job—and life—in the world.

I get to do what I love: create music and perform in front of some of the largest crowds ever assembled. I am blessed with a talent and a love for something I consider to be spiritual. I have a connection with millions of people I have never met nor will ever meet, but we all have something in common: the music. I went from sleeping in a dresser drawer in a one-bedroom apartment in Brooklyn, New York when I was born to sleeping in suites at Four Seasons all over the world, from Australia to the Soviet Union to Japan. I have played in countries where people do not even know the language in which the song is sung, but the music moves them. I have performed in places that American artists wouldn't entertain the thought of traveling, like Cuba and Russia. I have shaken hands with an American President, a future King of England, sports superstars, the most high-profile actors ever, musicians I idolize, and the sick children who are part of Make-A-Wish—and organizations like it—who let me to be a part of their short lives. These are my greatest experiences.

But there also is a dark side that runs parallel with and sometimes intertwines with the light side; a side that often challenges me and my drum. Erica Jong said, "Everyone has talent. What is rare is the courage to follow the talent to the dark places where it leads." I like to walk into a dark room and see how far I get without running into something. I like the way my skin tingles and my energy is lifted. In my darkest hour, my drum and my love for music were there to light the way, and I have had the courage to follow.

We are all moved by music. We cherish something that cannot be seen or held. You can see the music notes on the paper, and you can hold an instrument, but there is no life until you hear the final masterpiece. The notes have always existed, but it takes the musician to convince the listener that these are the notes you want to hear in the order that they are being played. Each musician plays their part, each writer scripts the songs, but each experience is totally emotionally different. Every person hears the same song, but pulls something different from it. I live for that pull, for that emotional exchange between the audience and the artist. There is truly nothing to compare it to. This paradox has been the most positive and negative aspect of my life, since as far back as I can remember.

This is my life, the life of a musician.

My life has been a good life. My grandparents were Italian immigrants who traveled by boat for months to find more opportunity and a better life in America. My parents grew up poor, but with my dad working two jobs, they were able to give me and my siblings a blue-collar, middle-class life on Long Island, New York. I grew up doing what I love: playing music. I have toured the world more than a dozen times and the records I've played on have sold over 150 million copies. I found that sometimes the "right" decisions can be so wrong in the long run. This is my story: the life of a musician, a drummer, a sideman who maybe gave too much passion to his art, and not enough to the people around him. It's also about the battle between "Liberty DeVitto" and "Billy Joel's drummer." This story is about the American Dream—how I had it and how people benefited from it.

Believe me, I love my life. I wouldn't change a thing.

Well, I might have changed one thing: I might have been in the Beatles instead.

**Our first tour of England, 1977. L to R: Doug, Russell, Billy, me, Richie.**

# 1

# The Billy Joel Band

"When you get sent for, you go in alive and you
come out dead and it's usually your best friend
that does it."
-from *Donnie Brasco*

Playing with Billy Joel was one of the best parts of my life, full of spectacular highs. There were also some pretty desperate lows, but I couldn't have imagined a greater journey. Unfortunately, how it ended wasn't what I would have hoped for. Allow me to explain.

We started out as a blue collar band; we related to the working man.Billy and I both grew up having to be tough in our neighborhoods. In the 1950s, as small boys, we listened to teenagers sing a cappella as we watched the 45s spin on our parents' turntables. On a February night we watched from our living rooms as a musical phenomenon swept America that would change our lives forever. Our "look" and love for music would fall into place during the psychedelic years that followed. By the end of the disco craze, together, we were part of a band that could not be beat. Our second album together would go all the way to number two on the Billboard Top 100, only to be kept out of the top spot by the soundtrack to *Saturday Night Fever*. Every time we played, we put our hearts and souls into it, loving every second and becoming great entertainers. We were a band: Billy, me, Doug Stegmeyer, Ritchie Cannata, Russell Javors, and David Brown (who became a member later, on the *52nd Street* tour).

But let's take it back to the beginning. My snapshot of the early years was best summarized in the speech I gave when the Lords of 52nd Street were inducted into the Long Island Music Hall of Fame.

*October 23, 2014*

> *When I joined the sixth grade band, I could not do the buzz roll in "The Star Spangled Banner." The music teacher told me, "Put the sticks down, DeVitto; you'll never do anything with the drums." Then in 1964 the Beatles showed up on "The Ed Sullivan Show." I pointed to the black-and-white TV, and it was there, in my living room in Seaford, Long Island, at the tender age of thirteen, I said,*

*"That's what I want to do. I want to be in a band with my friends."*

*I never took lessons; I learned by listening to records. Ringo Starr was my first teacher. I would play to Beatles records and learn not only the drum parts, but also the words and how they fit with the guitars and how the guitars fit with the bass. I was learning music. The Beatles were followed by the British Invasion, but as an Italian-American boy living on Long Island, I had a tough time relating to the British musicians. Then, God sent me the Young Rascals. Three out of four of them were Italian: Felix Cavaliere, Eddie Brigati, and an unbelievable drummer named Dino Danelli. Finally I could relate. I emulated the Rascals, especially Dino—he was my second teacher. I was amazed how his drumming pushed the other instruments: the Hammond organ, the guitar, and Eddie's vocals. Dino also showed me that the drummer was capable of being a visual part of the band as much as the lead singer. He had style and grace.*

*In 1967 I was in a band called the New Rock Workshop. We played a club in a Plainview, Long Island shopping center called My House. This is where another band called the Hassles also played, and where I first met an organ-playing singer named Billy Joe. The most we ever said to each other was hello as we passed in the darkness of the club. He sang my favorite song, "Colored Rain," by the group Traffic. This is also where I saw another great Long Island band: the Vanilla Fudge. Carmine Appice played with power like I had never seen before. He hit his oversized drums so hard I could hear them moan.*

*Also in this club was where Russell Javors and Doug Stegmeyer saw me play for the first time, and the thought of the three of us together in a band was born. That dream became a reality with our band Topper. We played a club in Wantagh called the Tabard Ale House on Tuesday night for a percentage of the door and all the beer you could drink. We played reggae; Bob Marley and the Wailers, and Jimmy Cliff. We played the blues; "Hideaway" by John Mayall and the Blues Breakers, "Boom Boom Out Go the Lights" by Bacon Fat (from the album* Grease One for Me), *and original songs that Russell wrote, like "One Arm Man" and "Ugly Lady."*

*Like the Yankees scout for great ballplayers to take the team all the way to the World Series, our drive, musicianship, and sense of humor caught the eye of a piano-playing singer-songwriter who was just barely hanging on to his Columbia record deal. He saw what he was missing in what he saw in us. To complete the lineup, someone was needed who was able to play sax, flute, keys, percussion, and sing, plus understand the insanity of the Topper brotherhood. With his jazz and rock background, Richie Cannata fit like a glove.*

*Before I played with Billy I had toured with Mitch Ryder, the Detroit Wheels, and recorded for Paramount Records with Long Island's own Richie Supa. With the help of others, Mr. Steve Khan and all the great players who have passed, Phil Ramone, Hugh McCracken, Hiram Bullock, Steve Burgh, and Ralph MacDonald, together we made history.*

*Tonight the L.I.M.H.O.F. acknowledges this. We thank you. I am honored to be standing here with my fellow inductees, Russell and Richie. When Doug left us he took a piece of our hearts. Tonight is dedicated to our brother. We called him "the sergeant," "slug," "the eel," and "Doctor No." Douglas Allen Stegmeyer, we truly miss you.*

*God Bless*

Billy himself would probably tell you: He didn't make us great, he saw the great in us. Billy had already released *Cold Spring Harbor*, *Piano Man*, and *Streetlife Serenade*. Doug, Russell, Richie, and I—with Howard Emerson—played on *Turnstiles*. This was Billy's last shot with Columbia Records; if this album failed he would be dropped by the label. Billy had the record deal, but together, by his own admission, we were a band. Billy wanted Sir George Martin, the Beatles' producer, to produce his next record. After seeing a show, Sir George said he would love to produce Billy, but he wanted to use studio musicians on the record. Billy said "Love me, love my band," and passed on Sir George.

The job of producer was eventually given to Phil Ramone. What really sold Billy on Phil Ramone, though, was the fact that he liked the band. As someone used to the slick, dour professionalism of old-time session men, Ramone was taken by the raw, "street" sound of the band and didn't want to change us at all. This was a big relief to Billy, who said, "Every time we worked with a producer, it was like the producer was testing the band and had them under the gun with other musicians, having to prove themselves. Phil liked my guys right off the bat. He heard them play the songs and was totally into it." Phil said, "Don't play any different than you play on the road; be the rock 'n' roll animals that you are." This began the partnership that would change the course of Billy Joel's career. In numerous interviews, Billy had said he didn't like the press addressing us as "backing musicians." We were his band; one unit. Billy wrote songs, played piano, and sang, like Paul and John of the Beatles. I played drums, like Ringo.

At one point Russell Javors and Topper were in line for a record deal with Columbia records. Billy's wife Elizabeth was his manager then, and she had it all set up. Someone pulled the plug on the deal when Billy realized he would be losing his band. I was his drummer as much as he was my piano player and singer. He chose me to help him make his songs into hit records. I gave as much energy to his songs as he did. If he was the father of those songs and the songs were his children, then I was their uncle. I taught them how to walk.

When he had an idea for a song he would run it by his band. He knew if the idea wasn't strong enough, it wouldn't fly when we played it. If his band made the idea swing, he would finish the song. He would call me at all times of the day and night to sing me new ideas. When he finished, there would be a moment of silence and he would wait for my response. If I said I liked it and thought it was a good idea, he would say, "Thank you," hang up the phone, and complete the song. If I said I didn't think it was a good idea, he would say, "Back to the drawing board" or "I knew you were going to say that. Oh, well," and rewrite the song. That's the kind of musical relationship we had. Someone once asked me if it was like the Lennon and McCartney relationship. I said, "I tend to think we're more like Laurel and Hardy."

During an NYU music school presentation, Phil Ramone was asked, "What made Billy Joel into such a phenomenon?" Phil said, "He wrote great songs and his band came up with great arrangements for those songs." We were a gang; part of a group. All for one and one for all. No one was allowed into that group unless they could put up with our style of humor and sarcasm. Doug and I became more than hired crony musicians; we became Billy's closest friends and would help to keep his "head together" whenever the going got weird. "The guys keep me in line," said Billy in 1978. "If I ever start acting like a rock star, Liberty will come over and go, 'Who do you think you are, you jerk?' It keeps me healthy. I don't like arrogance. The 'I'm a rock star and I'm all punk and I'm great and everyone stinks' attitude. I can't have that attitude with Liberty watching me."

We had fun doing what we did. I'd make Billy crack up by doing something dopey if he needed to laugh. For instance, on the *Turnstiles* tour of Europe in 1976, we met Billy's dad for the first time. Howard Joel lived in Vienna and spoke fluent German. Billy introduced me to him. First I shook Billy's hand and said "Heir Joel," and then I shook his dad's hand and said "No-hair Joel." (He was bald, obviously.) It pissed Billy's dad off so much that he instantly transformed back into a New Yorker and hit me with a big "fuck you" as everyone cracked up. Over the years when I have seen Mr. Joel, the first thing he always brings up is that joke, but God let Howard get his revenge, because now I am bald and he calls me "no-hair Lib," and we all know Billy is as bald as his father was when I met him.

When we played live, we would black out our teeth with Black Jack gum during the intro to "The Stranger" so when the lights came on us, Billy would crack up, unable to whistle. We would find humor in everything. When we went to the Soviet Union, he took me to Tbilisi in Georgia, not to play, but for comic relief because he knew he would be under a lot of pressure.

I was his friend, and I was there to catch him when he fell, laugh with him, and sweat with him; I took deep breaths when he took deep breaths, and I pushed him when he needed to be pushed, both musically and personally. Before we had "wardrobe," I even ironed his stage clothes before the show. (This is just because I actually knew how to iron.) He pulled hairs out of my nose. I made suggestions in his musical and personal life, but never in his business. Others did that, and I guess that's how I got screwed. What the hell, it's only money and this thirty-year journey was like a fortune in its own right.

After thirty years of performing and playing on thirteen platinum albums that have sold over one hundred and fifty million copies, writing and performing the drum parts on twenty-two of Billy's twenty-three top-forty hits, watching him win six Grammys and be inducted into the Songwriters Hall of Fame and the Rock 'n' Roll Hall of Fame, receive a Lifetime Achievement Grammy Award, and tour the world with him twelve times, I was blindsided when I was not invited to Billy's wedding in October of 2004. This is how I found out that Billy was pushing me out of his band and his life.

Relationships sour and familiarity breeds contempt, but when the attitude went from "love me, love my band" to the feeling of "get the fuck out of my dressing room" (not that Billy directly said that), I guess it was the beginning of the end. But I will always have the stories. I believe I'm still standing not because I was a wise businessman, or because I was a "rock star." Financially, I could have done a lot better—many did, and the star has burned itself out. I am who I am because of my family and the good people I have met throughout my life's journey—the everyday people. No rock star has ever given me, or anyone I know, any good advice. How can they? They don't live in the real world. I had an all-access pass to that world and now that the show is over, I always remembered where I came from, and I'm glad to be back.

Ironically, this is the speech I gave at Billy's fiftieth birthday party. I thought this was a good place to share it just to wrap up the "WTF Billy?" part of the book. After all, this book is about me, my drum, and my life. Of course, with Billy being a thirty-year part of my life, the subject had to be addressed, but time heals and we move on.

*My father always told me to work for a tall boss, it makes it easier to kiss his ass. It's been hard looking up to someone who's so damn short. For the last twenty-five years, I've been watching you perform on stage and I've been amazed and proud at how the fans adore you.*

*If they could, they would erect a statue of you in Central Park, but the pigeons would shit on it and I wouldn't like that. The Billy I know is the real Billy, not the performer, I have never seen him happier than when his daughter Alexa was born.*

*But I have also seen him in the ring with opponents that have pulverized him financially and crushed him physically. Still, they could not kill the spirit that is Billy Joel. He gets up, brushes himself off, and moves on.*

*Twenty-five years ago began a career and friendship that has seen fame, fortune, success, failure, wine, women, the blessing of the birth of our children, and the sorrow of the death of friends and loved ones. Now I watch my children grow and as I see their lives taking shape, I pray that they too will find a friend that means as much to them as Billy means to me.*

*May God bless you for another fifty years.*
*I love you,*
*Lib*

We will come back and visit Billy a bit later.

# My Drum-Part 1

Securing its place in history as the oldest instrument known to man, the drums have been popular since time has been recorded. Many historical and biblical books talk about the importance and impact that the drum and its beat have had over time. Many battles throughout the centuries were fought with drummers leading the way. The drums were created as a deterrent to the enemy; the sound of loud pounding meant impending doom, as the sounds of the approaching army could be heard for miles.

In the mid-1800s, during the U.S. Civil War, the drums played a major part in keeping the troops in line and setting the cadence for marching in order and formation. These cadences became the rudiments of drumming which are still in use today. During this time drummers were kept on the front lines, in formation, to inspire the soldiers to fight and die for the cause. It's hard to believe the psyche and intimidation factor drummers held in history. It's also hard to imagine that anyone would be stupid enough to be at the front of a charge against the opposing enemy with just a drum—while everyone else carried a gun. Most of the drummers would fall with their platoons.

The instrument that I play is the drum set, which wasn't invented until 1918, when a snare drum and bass drum were played together by one drummer. As time went on, more drums (called tom toms) were added, along with cymbals. Eventually, someone came up with the idea of having the drummer sit down while playing—thank God. Around the same time, the hi-hat or sock-cymbal was introduced into the set. By sitting, the drummer was now able to use both feet. It wasn't until the 1930s that the drum set took the shape that we know today. In today's drum set, the sky is the limit. Today's drummers incorporate everything from cowbells, garbage can lids, and brake-drums from cars, to electronics and pads that trigger almost any imaginable sound.

**Left to right: Uncle Pat, Uncle Liberty, Anthony, Aunt Frances, my dad (Vincent), my grandmother Louise, Uncle George, my grandfather Ralph, Uncle Fred, and Aunt Mary. Aunt Millie wasn't born yet.**

# 2

# My Family
## *Liberatori DeVitto: Liberator of Life*

Isn't it funny how some things change from generation to generation? Italian families very often name their firstborn son after the grandfather on the father's side, the first daughter after the grandmother on the father's side, the second son after the father, and the second daughter after the mother. This made my youngest brother, Salvatore (Sal), named after my mother's father; my middle brother, Vincent (Vinny), after my father; and my sister, Louise, the second oldest, after my father's mother. Now, if tradition was followed, and if my mother didn't make such a big fuss—and thank God she did—my name would have been Rafael DeVitto, AKA Ralph. Fortunately I was named after one of my father's brothers. His name was Liberatori DeVitto, AKA Liberty or Lib. Liberatori is my full name too.

Ralph and Louise, my grandparents on my dad's side, were right off the boat from Italy. Louise was born on June 29, 1891, to Fortunato and Maria (Ceglia) Fucci. At the age of eighteen, she left her village of Appai, which was just outside of Naples, Italy. She set off to America with her sister to join up with her father and brother, who had already gone on ahead. It had been a long-awaited sight when she first saw the Statue of Liberty; the boat trip across the Atlantic took three months. She arrived at Ellis Island, went through immigration and straight to Brooklyn, New York, where she and her sister joined their father and brother. Louise never saw her mother again.

Ralph was born on June 9, 1883, to Pasquale and Francesca DeVitto, also in the village of Appia. With the promise of a better life, Ralph and his brothers, Gabriel and Pasquale, left for America, leaving their girlfriends behind. For years the DeVittos did not know that this wasn't the whole story: in Ralph's case, it wasn't simply his girlfriend. In researching my family tree, I found the manifest of the ship on which the brothers sailed. There it was: "Marital status: *Married*." Liar. Busted. Confronted later with this information, my dad and Aunt Millie vigorously defended their father in their Italian way (LOUD), with hands flying everywhere. "*The manifest is wrong!*" So I guess it's true, Italians never turn on the family.

The brothers also went through Ellis Island and ended up in Brooklyn. Ralph wound up living in the same building as Louise. When they met, Ralph would flirt with Louise, but she wanted nothing to do with him. She knew he had someone that he left behind in Italy. But as the days went on, being in a new world and starting a new life, they started a new love. Ralph and Louise were married on September 5, 1909, in New York, and had ten children. Their first child, Pasquale (Pat), was born in 1910. He died at three years old. In 1911, Francesca (Fran) was born, followed by Fortuanto (Fred) in 1912, Mary in 1913, Liberatori (Liberty) in 1914, Pasquale (Pat, named after his dead brother) in 1918, Georgio (George) in 1919, Anthony (Tony) in 1920, Vincenzo (Vincent) in 1924, and Carmella (Millie) in 1927.

When Tony was eleven years old, he and his brother Fred ate some bad clams. Both became extremely ill, and soon it became clear that they had contracted typhoid fever from the contaminated food. Fred was in bed in his family's apartment under a doctor's care. He was told that his brother Tony was also very sick, and was staying in the apartment on the floor below. While Fred lay recovering he heard what he thought was a parade coming down the street. He wasn't told until he had fully recovered that his brother Tony had died, and what he heard was Tony's funeral passing the family's apartment.

Back in the '30s and '40s, things were different than when I grew up in the '50s and '60s. Having the name Liberty in the '60s was really cool, with peace and freedom being the anthem of my generation. People loved my name. Some would just change their names to fit in with the times: Joy, Victory, Hope, Peace. I fit right in, no changes necessary.

For my Uncle Liberty, it wasn't quite the same. He was teased that he had a girl's name, since there was a female statue standing in New York Harbor with the same title. This got my uncle into all kinds of fights, so when I was born and my father told his family what my mother and he had decided to name me, they told him he was nuts. They said, "You're crazy. He'll have to fight all his life because of this. He'll hate it". Well, they were wrong. In the music business, you need your name to be remembered, and when I told people mine, no one seemed to forget.

When my father Vincent was a kid, he was hunting rabbits in the cemetery. A cop grabbed him and accused him of throwing rocks at the windows on the subway. (In those days the subway ran on an elevated track, called the 'L.') My father said he was only hunting rabbits, but the cop, who was Irish, called my father a lying guinea bastard and said he was taking him to the station house. On their way, they had to pass Vincent's brother Fred's barber shop, where his brothers Pat and Liberty were standing. After a brief exchange with the cop about what had happened, with Vincent pleading he had done nothing wrong, the brothers convinced the officer to turn Vincent over to them. As soon as the cop left, Vincent's brothers started to slap the shit out of him. He finally broke loose and ran home with his brothers chasing him.

When he reached home, his mother asked his brothers what happened. His brothers said he threw rocks at the subway and broke the windows. His mother took off one shoe and threw it at him, hitting him right in the head. He ran for shelter under a bed, but his mother came after him with a broom and started hitting and poking him with it. Eventually he crawled out from under the bed, ran outside, and finally hid in the basement. After awhile it got dark, and he could hear his mother talking through the dumbwaiter. She was worried that he was out in the cold without a coat. I couldn't help thinking he would've been treated better by the police!

My father was very close to his four brothers. When World War II broke out, all of them, including my dad, were drafted. The Army took Pat and George to the Pacific, and Dad and Liberty to Europe. Fred stayed stateside in the Navy. Dad joined the 101st Screaming Eagles paratroopers because the pay was good. His mother wrote to him asking him to write to the commander to request to be removed from the paratroopers. He told my grandmother not to worry, it's all about whose name is on the bullet. When Uncle Liberty found out about it, he wrote Dad a letter reaming him out. He said, "You stupid son of a bitch, when I get my hands on you, I'm gonna kick you in the ass. Don't you know that's a suicide outfit? You'll get killed in that outfit."

Having lost two sons already, watching five now go off to war was more than a man could handle. Early one morning, Ralph's brother George died from a stroke. George's distraught wife ran into Ralph and Louise's apartment screaming that George was dead. Ralph mistakenly took this to mean his son—not his brother. Crying, "my George, my George," in the confusion Ralph had a cerebral hemorrhage. He lay in a coma for six months, never knowing it was his brother and not his son who had died, and finally passed away himself at the age of 63. Louise now not only had five sons away at war, but her husband was dead.

At this time, Italy had allied with the Germans. A man from immigration came to my grandmother's house and told her that they were going to ship her back to Italy because she didn't have her immigration papers. So she told him, "Give me back my sons and we will go back." They immediately gave her the correct papers for her to stay in America. Sergeant Liberty DeVitto was with the K Company in France. They were on night patrol, trying to locate the Germans, when the enemy opened fire on them. Liberty was leading the patrol and was shot in his shoulder and neck. The rest of his outfit ran for cover while the Germans held aim at him, so that if anyone came back for him they would have been shot. It was daybreak before his company could reach him. He was still alive when they took him to the hospital, but it was too late. He had lost too much blood during the night.

Three months after losing her husband, Louise received a knock on her door in Brooklyn from a military man holding a telegram and saying, "I'm sorry." Uncle Liberty had been the only one of her sons not to come home for Ralph's funeral; now her worst fears were confirmed. My grandmother could never accept Uncle Liberty's death because she never got to see him. My grandmother had lost two sons already: Pasquale (Pat), who passed away at the age of three from unknown causes, and Tony who, as I mentioned earlier, had tragically died at eleven from typhoid fever. Uncle Liberty's body didn't come home until months after the war was over. It was a closed coffin funeral, with only his picture placed on his casket.

When World War II was over, Grandma's three sons came back home to 128 Hopkins Ave in Brooklyn. Dad came home with the Purple Heart that he received when he was wounded by shrapnel during the invasion of Normandy. Uncle Pat got the Silver Star when he was shot in the process of terminating a Japanese machine gun nest. Uncle George was decorated as part of the Military Police in the Pacific. Uncle Fred never left the States. He cut hair in Treasure Island, California, and came home with more war stories than anyone else. Uncle Liberty was laid to rest in St. John's Military Cemetery in Queens, New York, and received a military sendoff.

In 1899, Benedict and Josephina Sardisico had a son on the island of Sicily. They named him Salvatore. The Sardiscos owned a lot of land in Sicily and were considered very wealthy. Eight years later, Josephina's sister had a baby girl. Her name was Frances. She was born in 1908 to Rosalie and Ludwig Perstigiacomo. Salvatore and Frances were first cousins. In 1913, at the age of six, Frances came to America with her parents from Sicily, and settled in Brooklyn. Josephina and Rosalie had arranged a marriage for their children. Salvatore had come to America when he was very young with his father; this is when the marriage was arranged. He returned for some years and at the age of twenty-one, Salvatore left Sicily to come to America to marry Frances, who was now sixteen years old. At the time, Frances was in love with a boy from high school, but because it was arranged, they married when Salvatore arrived in New York. They lived on 8th Street, which is now Saint Mark's Place in Manhattan. Soon they moved to an apartment between First and Second Avenues in Manhattan, where their three children were born. Benedict (Benny) was born in 1924; Josephina (Josephine) on August 1, 1926; and Rosalie (Lillian) in 1929. Frances was pregnant with twins right after she and Salvatore were married, but she lost them when her mother pushed her down the stairs.

The children used to play in Houston Street Park. They would watch the men play bocce and then have delicious meals at Katz Delicatessen, which is legendary in New York today. They lived a block and a half outside of Little Italy. The children were not allowed to go to Little Italy because it was run by the Mafia. When the Feast of San Gennaro was on, though, it was a different story. Everyone, including the Sardiscos, went to the Feast. People came from all over to get a taste of "true Italian cooking." Mulberry Street would be packed with people as they watched children dressed as angels hung from ropes and pulled from one fire escape to another, while white doves were released as a symbol of the Holy Spirit.

Salvatore was a very religious man. He had statues of saints and candles all around the apartment. Josephine got too close to a candle and her hair caught fire. She put it out in time and wasn't hurt, but it left a terrible smell of burnt hair in the apartment. The family was very poor. Salvatore would inherit the land in Sicily, but only after his father died, so he worked hard because he was too proud to go on relief (welfare). Salvatore loved his children very much. He would tell them, "Never cry with a loaf of bread under your arm." They would stuff newspaper in their shoes when it rained to keep the water from coming in the holes in the soles.

Salvatore worked making razor blades in the Gem factory in Brooklyn, making about fourteen dollars a week. He would walk to work over the Brooklyn Bridge just to save a nickel. He also sold dry goods and as a third job he plucked chickens. At the Gem factory the Irish would call him guinea, wop, and grease-ball, but because he didn't speak English, he never knew what they we're saying anyway. Frances, who went to school in America, would tell him what the Irish were saying, and what it meant. He had a wonderful sense of humor, so to get back at them he would play jokes on the Irish. He would unscrew the hinges on their lockers. When the nightshift came in, they would pull on the doors to open their lockers only to have the doors fall off and land right on their heads. Frances was not like Salvatore; she was very mean. She would send the children to relatives in New Jersey when she would fight with her husband. She would beat him, but Salvatore never raised a hand to her.

Frances' high school sweetheart was always around during her marriage to Salvatore. When Rosalie was a young girl, Frances told her that Salvatore wasn't her real father. Rosalie never believed her. When Salvatore's family in Sicily heard of this, they were going to come to America to kill Frances.

When Josephine was twelve years old, she hated her mother so much that she was disappointed when she found out her mother lived through a gall bladder operation and was coming home. One time, Josephine didn't want to eat escarole and macaroni, so Frances put Josephine's face in the dish. Frances would crack you in the face if you looked crooked at her. She smashed a grapefruit in Josephine's face and would constantly beat the children with a wooden spoon. Josephine looked crooked at her mother once and Frances put her in a freezing hall right in the middle of winter. All Josephine was wearing was a slip. Josephine was so cold that she begged her mother to let her back into the house. Rosalie was crying, but her mother showed no mercy. Josephine loved her father. Salvatore had a wonderful sense of humor. He would sit on the opposite side of the subway car and make funny faces at his children and have them laughing. He loved his children. Whether he ever knew the truth about Rosalie is not known, but he always treated all the children with the same love.

In 1944, when Josephine was seventeen, she walked into a room and saw Salvatore crawling on his knees. He was having terrible pains in his stomach. She called the ambulance at once, and rode to to the hospital with her father. When the doctors took him into the operating room, they opened him up and saw there was nothing they could do for him. His appendix had ruptured and peritonitis had already set in. Penicillin might have helped, but none was available; most of it was going to the troops because of the war.

Salvatore died in May, 1944, at the age of forty-five. Frances went on a rampage: men, parties, everything to make up for lost time. She couldn't wait for her children to get out of the house. So, in October, 1944, at eighteen, Josephine got married to James Nobiletti—just five months after her father died. Frances had a party for her daughter at a hotel. After the wedding, Frances took all the money that was gifted to the bride and groom, put all the furniture in storage, and ran off to Jamaica with her boyfriend. Josephine took her fourteen-year-old sister with her. Because Benedict was Salvatore's only son, he was supposed to inherit the land in Italy. When he took a trip there, he told his relatives, "I live in New York now. Why do I need land in Italy?" He gave it to the relatives in Italy. Salvatore's children never saw a penny of money.

I took a trip to visit my mother's family in Sicily right before my mother passed away. My mother asked me, "Were they funny? Did they take you in with love? Did they feed you?" I said, "Yes." With tears in her eyes, my mother said, "Then you met my father."

Me and mom, 1956.

Dad in his NYPD uniform, 1952.

# 3

# Mom & Dad

In 1947, Lou's Ice Cream Parlor on Fulton Street in East New York was the place to get the best egg creams, malts, ice cream sodas, and the best ice cream, in a cone or in a dish. For two 23-year-old girls who sat at the ice cream counter, vanilla was their choice for the day. The girls sat and talked about their lives and their dreams. The redhead, Mrs. Josephine Nobiletti, nee Sardisco, just didn't know what to do with her life. Ever since she changed her name, her life was a mess. She was married to James Nobiletti, but not for much longer. Josephine and her husband were already separated. She was living with her two children and her younger sister Lillian in a three-room apartment on Hull Street. Lillian had lived her whole life with Josephine, even before James left. She had moved out of their mother's house after their father passed away.

Josephine was abused by her husband throughout her second pregnancy, and while caring for her then-elven-month-old son, Frankie. James would tell Josephine he wanted the deposits on the empty milk bottles before he came home from work. Being preoccupied with her son and her condition, she would forget to return the bottles. When James came home from work, the first thing he did was check the bottles. When he saw they were still there, he'd beat her like he had done so many times before. He would then mark the calendar so he could keep track. He would also take the stencil brush he used to mark the cargo at the dock—he was a Longshoreman—and mark X's on all the clean white walls. Lillian was ordered to clean it all off. Sometimes Lillian was also beaten, mostly for jumping in front of her pregnant big sister in an attempt to protect her.

Josephine had her second child, a girl named Anita. James never went to his daughter's christening because he hated girls. He finally left Josephine, but before he left, he said he would make the payments on the furniture that was in their apartment. One day, Josephine and Lillian were rounding the corner to their apartment when they saw the marshals taking Josephine's furniture out the windows. James had defaulted on the payments. With her apartment now bare, Josephine was so thankful for the people across the street, who knew what was going on and brought her a table and chair so she wouldn't have to eat on the floor and could retain a bit of dignity. Things just continued downhill after that.

After unsuccessfully reaching out to the church for help, Josephine began collecting welfare, which she needed to pay her rent. She got a job putting bobby pins on cardboard cards so she could get money to buy food. Someone—Josephine thought it was one of James' friends— wrote a letter to the Welfare Department telling them that she was working. Fearing her payments would be canceled, she immediately quit her job, but it was too late. The welfare payments stopped. With no money and an empty apartment, she reluctantly turned to her mother for help. Josephine hoped she, the kids and Lillian might be able to stay with her mother until she could get back on her feet. After hearing all that had happened, however, her mother coldly informed her that she had sold her house and was moving. Giving Josephine $50.00 for her and Lillian to split, she sent them on their way and ran off to the British West Indies with her boyfriend, leaving Josephine and her family out on the streets of East New York.

Now, sitting in Lou's, eating vanilla ice cream and dreaming of something good to come into her life, Josephine looked up to see someone that looked like he could be the man of her dreams. "Who is that?" she asked Tessie. To her surprise, Tessie knew him. "That's Vincent DeVitto," she said, "He was a paratrooper in the war, and now he works as a welder at the Supreme Steel Company in Queens. Why, do you wanna meet him?"

Vincent was wearing a maroon cowboy shirt with the name "Zam" embroidered over the left pocket. As Josephine looked him over, she felt like she was seeing a real man—not the weak, abusive husband she had been enduring, but a real man. He had the kindest face she had ever seen. "Tess, I want to meet him," she said. Tess called Vincent over to the table and said, "Josephine, this is Vincent DeVitto; we call him Jimmy, or Zam." Everyone back then had nicknames. It turned out that Vincent knew Josephine as "the girl with the red hair," because she happened to live across the street from Vincent's brother Fred and his wife. Josephine realized right away that they were the ones who gave her the table and chair. They became fast friends, and Vincent felt a great deal of compassion for Josephine. He began to give her money to help feed her kids, and he told the man behind the counter at Lou's, "Whatever she wants, give it to her. I'll pay you back."

Lillian was able to get a part-time job, but it didn't help much. Things continued to get worse. Anita, Josephine's daughter, started to develop boils from malnutrition and wound up in the hospital. She tried to contact James, the baby's father, but she couldn't find him. He never saw his kids after he left, and he never sent a dime to take care of them, either. The people from the government child-care services looked for James, but only found that he had left the state. They couldn't touch him or get anything from him. It got so bad that a friend of Josephine's made the suggestion to give the kids to Catholic Charities so at least they could eat. It was the hardest decision Josephine ever made, but she knew it had to be better for her children. She gave them to the church. She had begun seeing Vincent (Jimmy) by this time, and he promised he'd always take her to see her kids.

On a visiting day, Josephine and Vincent arrived at the charity, but couldn't find Frankie and Anita. Josephine asked the female supervisor, "Where are my kids?" The woman replied, "Your husband took them." It turned out that James had remarried. Josephine was shocked and said, "How can he get remarried? We're not even divorced yet!" The woman gave her the name of James' lawyer. Josephine's brother knew a lawyer, so they paid him a visit. It seems that James had put a notice in the paper, "James Nobiletti vs. Josephine Nobiletti." Josephine could hardly afford food, never mind a newspaper, and not seeing the notice, had no idea she was expected to show up in court. Consequently, the court awarded everything to James. (This couldn't happen today because you have to be summoned.) When Josephine asked the lawyer how they could do this, he said, "The kids are better off this way; they have a roof over their heads and food to eat. You can still see them anytime you want. Eventually, you'll get them back." They actually talked her into letting them go.

Josephine and Lillian moved in with the mother of Josephine's best friend, Lucy. Josephine had known Lucy and her family since childhood, and Josephine had been Lucy's "gumada" (maid of honor) at her wedding. Josephine and Lillian had jobs, so they could afford to pay the mother's rent. Lucy's mother sent the young women off to work every day with a banana sandwich; they didn't have much, but at least they weren't starving. Meanwhile, Vincent and Josephine were getting serious, so one day, Vincent's mother, Louise, came to Lucy's mother's house to meet this Josephine. She was hearing stories that her son was dating a divorced woman. Louise's sister, Carmella, had a similar situation in her family and Louise swore she would never let it happen in hers. When she met Josephine she was very direct with her and (in broken English) said,

"Do you go out with my son?"

"Yes."

"You go back to your husband?"

"No."

Louise replied, "Well, if it's destiny, then it's destiny, and you will marry my son."

Josephine was relieved, as it was Vincent's sisters that were harassing her in the streets, because they felt dating a divorced woman was a stain on their brother's honor. When they saw her, they'd spit at her. Vincent's sister Mary warned her, "When you take the subway to work, don't stand too close to the tracks because I'll push you in front of the train."

Josephine and Lillian were so scared when they went into the subway that they walked with their back against the tile walls. On one occasion, they ran into Vincent's sisters at the movie theater. In those days you'd receive a complimentary dish after paying for a movie. Mary told Josephine, "Leave my brother alone or I'll smash this dish right over your head." Vincent's family did not want him to be with a divorced woman. Despite all this, Josephine and Vincent continued to see each other.

Then, one day in December 1949, Josephine found out she was pregnant. She told Vincent and said, "Let's get married." To her surprise Vincent said, "I don't want to get married, it would break my mother's heart." Josephine told Vincent she would have the baby anyway. After a bit of thinking, Vincent came around. "Okay, let's get married." Josephine's Uncle George told the girls, "I'll find you a furnished room near me, and you can come and eat by me and Aunt Ida." Josephine and Lillian moved out of Lucy's mother's house and moved into Mrs. Fadell's apartment building right across the street from Uncle George and Aunt Ida. Every day they were sent three meals, cooked by Aunt Ida.

Vincent and Josephine married on June 19, 1950, at a Justice of the Peace in New Jersey. Nothing changed with Vincent's family. Josephine was now seven months pregnant, and Vincent's mother would not allow him to stay overnight with Josephine. He had to return to his mother's house every night to sleep; he still obeyed his mother's rules.

On August 8, 1950, at 7:30 AM, in Kings County Hospital in Brooklyn, Josephine DeVitto gave birth to a boy, Liberatori (Liberty) DeVitto. Vincent was thrilled, but continued to remain at his mother's house. Lillian, Josephine, and Liberty stayed in the one-room apartment together. The room was so small that the way you stood up when you got out of your bed was actually how you spent most of your day. It was so small that the dresser was built into the wall and for the first few months of my life, I slept in a drawer in that dresser. My mother would open one of the drawers, take out the clothes, and line it with a blanket and pillow. My dad's sister, Francis; her husband Benny; my dad's brother Pat and his wife Nettie were the only ones to come and see my mom and me. Lillian and Benny became my godparents.

The day I was christened, my mother decided to take me up to my grandmother. My mother had not seen her mother-in-law since the day she came to Lucy's mother's apartment. With the help of Carmella, my grandmother Louise's sister, she started towards her. They presented me to my grandmother, and Carmella said, in Italian, "Look, Louise! Liberty is back." From that day on, my mother and grandmother were very close. In fact, my mother became my grandmother's favorite daughter-in-law.

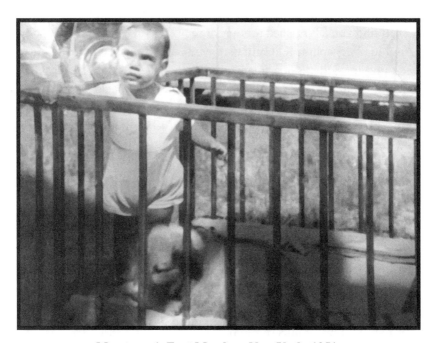

**Me at age 1, East Meadow, New York, 1951.**

# 4

# Brooklyn to Long Island

We were living in our one-room apartment, and still my father was returning to his mother's house every night. My mother had had enough of it, but my grandmother said, "My son deserves better than a furnished room, so he is to still come home every night. He has to get a home before he can leave."

So he did.

On a trip home from Jones Beach, my mother and father decided to stop and look at houses that were being built in Levittown. My Uncle Freddie had moved out to Valley Stream, Long Island, and he raved about it out there. The call of the '50s was, "the city is no place to raise a family, move to Long Island." Even though plenty of people believed that someday the Long Island Sound, the ocean, and the waters to the north and south would meet, and the Island would be eaten away by massive flooding, they still went. My parents loved the small houses they saw; they were perfect for a small family. A real estate man came up to my father and asked, "Do you like these houses?" My dad answered, "Yeah, but I can't afford anything like this." The agent asked him, "Are you a veteran?" "Yeah, I am," dad responded. "How much money do you have?" asked the man. "I've got three bucks in my pocket," my father answered him. Not only was that what he had in his pocket, it's pretty much *all* he had.

The man said, "Give me the three bucks, and you own a house."

My father handed over the three bucks, and in return was handed a receipt from Trylon Realty. My parents were now the owners of a Randal home. The house was built in East Meadow, and in November of 1950, the three of us moved into our new home on Putnam Drive, strapped with a mortgage of $48.00 a month. Of course, Aunt Lil came with us, but moved out in three months, after she married Uncle Tony.

Now that dad made his home on Long Island, he also had his work there. He worked for Fairchild Jet Engine in Farmingdale. Fairchild was famous for making the Hellcat Fighter plane during World War II. But since there was no more war to fight, it was only a matter of time until Fairchild would fold. While my father was working at Fairchild, he was also attending school, and in 1953 (at mom's suggestion) he passed the test to become a New York City policeman.

Dad's career as a cop started in 1953 as a patrolman at the 77th Precinct in Brooklyn, where he stayed for ten years. He suffered a lower back injury in a radio car accident in 1959, and because of this he was taken off the streets and moved to the criminal courts at 120 Schemerhorn Place in downtown Brooklyn. After five years at the courts, he traded his blue uniform for a shirt and tie and was moved to the N.Y.C. Property Clerk Office at 400 Broome Street in Manhattan. From there, after serving as a cop for nineteen years and ten months, he retired right before Christmas, 1972, with three-quarters pay for the rest of his life from the NYPD.

At work, dad saw it all, and was deeply affected by what he witnessed and experienced. He tried to bring a child back to life that had starved to death. He'd be called to domestic disputes and find women beaten beyond recognition. Encounters with crazies were common. One guy went after him swinging a Christmas tree around his head. Another time, a guy kicked in a glass door and went after my dad and his partners with a big chunk of the glass. Dad had guns pulled on him numerous times. He saw mothers crying because their sons were being taken to jail for drugs, gambling, drunkenness, assault, and even murder. He was once handcuffed to Mafia don Joey Gallo.

My father would try his hardest not to bring his job home, but it was hard for him. He'd yell at us when we didn't like what Mom made for dinner, because he had seen children starving. He'd call us idiots if my brothers and I talked tough. When I grew my hair long as a teenager, he would beat me up just because I looked like some of the guys he locked up. My sister Louise did something to piss him off once, so he held her by her ankles out the kitchen window, about twelve feet from the ground. My sister was so defiant she kept yelling, "Go ahead, I dare you to drop me." If it wasn't for her friend catching her and breaking her fall, she probably would have split her head open on the concrete below.

I had a love-hate relationship with my father in my adolescent and teenage years. He made me feel insecure by calling me names like "stupid" and "idiot," which is something I would never wish on any child. I threw a snowball at him once, and he came after me. When he grabbed me, he tried to suffocate me by burying my face in the snow. He would hit me, and sometimes I would run behind my mother, because he wouldn't dare hit her—but then he'd throw punches around her to get to me. As my face was buried in her waist, she'd say to him, "Not the head, don't hit him in the head." Sometimes when I cowered behind her, she'd tell him, "You'll have to get through me first." My dad would walk away all pissed off, saying, "You protect your sons too much; they'd be fags if it wasn't for me." Although I hated when he brought the job home, and there's no excuse for violence, I now realize the stress and strain he was under.

Later, when I was playing with the Rogues in high school, I needed a new kit but couldn't afford one. My father liked to "spar" with me, which I hated.

On one of the hottest days of the year, he came home from work and started, and I swung back at him. My finger caught on his pocket, and it ripped. It was one of his favorite shirts. He got really, really pissed and started to hit me harder than usual. I ran away from him, down the stairs into the laundry room, where my mom was. I ran into a closet, and he came after me and slammed the closet door on my leg a few times. Maybe it was the heat that made him lose control of his temper. My mother was screaming, "Jimmy, you're gonna break his leg! Stop!" The next day, I had a big bruise, and he felt so horrible he took me to Frank Wolfe's Drum Shop on 48th Street in Manhattan, and bought me a brand new four-piece set of Slingerlands.

I didn't understand my father then. There were plenty of times I just couldn't wrap my head around his reactions. I get it now; I realize that he was a Brooklyn cop and he couldn't leave his job at work all the time. When he tried to—and I'm sure he did try—he came home to a house full of kids that looked just like the kids he'd been arresting all day. He moved us to Long Island for a "better life," but I guess it turned out that kids were the same all over.

I think my father loved me, but I'm not sure he ever liked me. He was a tough guy, but I would have to guess that when my mother got pregnant, he was scared and confused. He had a beautiful woman on his arm; he used to say my mother was his Sophia Loren. To be honest, my mom married my father not just because she was pregnant but she needed someone to take care of her. Later in life she told me she didn't love him in the beginning, but as time went on she learned to love him. When I came along, my mom was totally engrossed in me; I became her whole world. She said I, in a way, filled the emptiness that came with her losing custody of her first two children, Frankie and Anita, to her first husband.

My father would never admit it, but I'm sure, in his way, he was jealous of the relationship I had with Mom. I was never able to stand up to the tough-guy persona that he had—and wanted me to have. He would grab my hand and tell me my nails were too long. He'd say, "How are you going to make a fist with nails that long? They'll dig into your hand when you punch someone." Then again, I was growing up in a totally different world than he did. He fought in the streets; in the '60s we played music on the beach. He fought World War II; we protested Vietnam. He was a cop; I wanted to be a drummer.

Dad became proud of me when I became successful. When I had children, I saw him as a better grandfather than a father. In the end, he would tell me he loved me and I would see him tear up when I would tell him I loved him and he was my hero. I miss my father and think about him every day. Violence begets violence. My dad hit me to show control—that he was in charge. Unfortunately, being his son, his way of doing things was passed on to me. It took some serious mistakes and my life coach—an angel sent from God named Ali Berlin—to guide me past the violence that I inherited.

I once asked my father what he would have done if he didn't become a policeman. He said he wanted to be a career criminal. He was a badass when he was young, a badass in the army, and he was a badass when he came out. He said, "Growing up was like what you see in movies like *A Bronx Tale* and *Donnie Brasco*. One day dad got a call from his "gangster friends." They wanted to meet with him and talk about a job they wanted to pull. The job was on his beat. My father was nervous to meet them, telling my mother they might kill him if he refused to go along with their plan. My mother told him, "Take the baby; they won't touch you if you have him." The baby was me, I was nine months old at the time. So dad and I went to meet his old crew. They told him they wanted to rob a store while he looked the other way during his foot patrol. My father said, "Look, I have a family now. I can't do that." Agitated, the guys threatened to kill him, but they couldn't because he was holding me in his arms. The next day, they pulled the job—and got caught.

In East Meadow, my mother gave birth to my sister, Louise, and my brother, Vincent. The house was getting too small for our family, so in January of 1957 my dad bought a house in Seaford, Long Island. I was in the first grade and had to leave my friends. The one I would miss the most was Elenore Shultz. She lived with her family in the house right behind us and we were always together. We got in trouble for breaking a case of soda bottles with a golf club. In our neighborhood, the trash cans were underground. You had to lift the lockable entry door to put the trash in to be picked up. One day, Elenore locked me in the can. She remembered later in the day, and came back to let me out. My mother got curious when I kept staring out the window saying "I almost never saw the birds again." We were four years old and already a girl thought of me as trash.

# My Drum-Part 2

I have never been much into drum solos. I always thought of them as self-serving, like masturbation; the drummer gets his rocks off while the rest of the band leaves the stage for a cigarette. Plus, girls hate them. These days, when some rock drummers do a solo in concert, it comes with a lot of gimmicks that might include fire, smoke, and pyrotechnics. Tommy Lee of Mötley Crüe rose up in to the air and was turned upside down during his solo. He once fell and knocked himself unconscious when his head hit the floor. Bobby Blotzer from Ratt would end his solo when a six pack of beer would descend from the ceiling on a rope and he would pop open one of the tabs and guzzle a cool one.

Two of the greatest drum solos I have ever seen were on TV. One had no drums at all, and the other incorporated the drums into a dance routine. They were performed by Buddy Rich on "The Muppet Show" and Fred Astaire in the movie *Damsel in Distress*. Buddy walked around a room playing on pots, pans, tables, walls, and anything else he felt like hitting with the drumsticks. He never once played a drum. Fred did a tap dance. He played tom toms, a snare, and cymbals with sticks. As he tapped to the rhythm on the floor, he kicked two bass drums with his feet as accents. Astaire was famous for his dancing and was never considered to be a drummer.

It doesn't matter what the person is playing on, it's all about what he's playing and how it feels when it translates to the listener. The beat should move the feet. New York City has made the "paint bucket" drummer so famous that it has spawned Broadway shows like *Stomp* and *Bring in 'da Noise, Bring in 'da Funk*.

There's a saying, "It's not the arrow; it's the archer." In the drumming world it's not the drum set, it's the drummer that makes you move. Sitting behind my drum set in a live situation makes me feel like the most powerful person in the room. I will keep the members of the band together and we will travel as one musical unit through the night. I will also relay a passion and an emotion that will force people to stand up and cheer. I will cover many different kinds of emotions in one night from song to song.

Merrick Road in Seaford, Long Island, New York.

Captain Eddie's, Seaford.

Pete's Pet Shop, Seaford
(where I bought my first 45s).

# 5

# Seaford

Whe people ask me where I grew up, I tell them "3834 Niami Street in Seaford, Long Island, New York." In Seaford, my youngest brother, Sal, was born, and most of the character I am today was developed. The first time I fell in love, I lived in this house; the first time I saw the Beatles on TV, I was in this house. I lived in this house when I experimented with drugs, when I started drinking, when bands broke up and new ones started, and when relationships were over and I thought I would never live to see another day. I always returned to this house.

Seaford in the late '50s and early '60s was a great place to grow up. We lived south of Merrick Road, which was considered Seaford Harbor. North of Merrick Road was called Seaford Manor, which consisted of middle-class and upper-middle-class homes and families. (There were no rich people in Seaford.) All the churches and schools were in Seaford Manor, while Seaford Harbor was more of a fishing village where lower and middle income families lived in converted summer cottages. There was a lot of property in Seaford Harbor to be developed. Niami Street was one of those blocks. The ten homes built on Niami St were known as Heller homes, named after the architect. My dad bought the model. It was a split-level, which allowed for a cathedral ceiling in the living room and dining room.

Christmas presents remained unwrapped because my mom said "Santa never wrapped gifts," but they sat under the tallest of tall Christmas trees. My parents threw some great parties in that house. I used to look over the balcony that led into the upstairs bedrooms, watching my mom and dad and their friends drinking Seagram's 7, Canadian Club, and cheap scotch. They'd smoke Kent, Lucky Strike, or Pall Mall cigarettes while dancing to cha-cha, mambo, and swing records. Chubby Checker changed their dance steps when he came out with the remake of Hank Ballard and the Moonlighters' "The Twist" in 1960. My mother bought a twist dress. It had rows of fringes that would sway in the opposite direction than her body was twisting. She had one dress in black and one in white, which she accented with my black high-top Converse sneakers and argyle socks. During these times I felt like I was a spectator in an arena watching the power of music. This became a release to bring out people's hidden personalities. I didn't realize until I got older that B.B. King makes you want to get drunk, the Stones make you want to fight and Al Green makes you want to make love.

Seaford was bordered by Wantagh to the west, Massapequa to the east, and North Massapequa to the north. Head south and you'd come to the meadows, marshlands, Zack's Bay, the barrier beaches (Jones Beach), and the

Atlantic Ocean. You could walk a few blocks from my house to the cattails and marshlands; men would walk down the streets with hip boots and camouflage jackets with brightly-colored hunting licenses pinned to their backs. You knew it was duck season when men with unloaded shotguns, the barrels broken over their shoulders, walked south past the house. I wasn't allowed in the meadows during that time; I was told it was too dangerous. A little kid could be mistaken for a duck. The hunters also used duck boats to get out to the bay. The duck boat was low to the water, painted green, and covered in cattails and marsh grass. It usually carried two hunters and was propelled by a small Johnson or Evinrude engine. Speed was not a necessity; Seaford Harbor had a series of canals that ran from Merrick Road all the way to Zack's Bay. At four miles per hour, this ride took almost forty-five minutes from the most inland point.

The canals would freeze over in the winter and were great for ice skating. The Niami Street Canal froze solid every winter. Everyone had a boat. In the summer, besides your bike, this is how you got to your friends' houses. In the summer we would swim in the canals. The best place to go would be Captain Eddie's. It was the town dock where anyone could rent a boat from Eddie or just fish off the dock. A lot of people from Brooklyn would come to Captain Eddie's to do just that.

My friends and I would walk to Captain Eddie's down Sands Lane, which was only big enough for one car to go down at a time. It was covered in volcanic stone, which killed your feet. When we got to the dock, we would swim on the opposite side of where the public was fishing; it was the side where they'd park the police boat. There was a sign that said "no swimming," but when the boat was gone, it became the perfect place to swim. It had been dredged and made deeper so the boat wouldn't hit the bottom at low tide, so we didn't have to wait for high tide to swim. The dock poles were about ten feet from the water, which made them great to jump from.

After a day in the water, we would go to the bait shop at Eddie's. He always had a giant metal cooler filled with soda bottles floating in ice water. I still remember lifting the top of the cooler and seeing the bottle caps: Grape Nehi, Orange Crush, Hire's Root Beer, and Coca-Cola. My favorite was Grape Nehi. The sweet of the soda washed away the salt from the water, and with a big burp I was ready to head home. If we had no money for soda, we would stop across the street from Larry Marone's house—he lived on Sands Lane—and drink from a pipe under the dock that was continuously running artisan well water. It was cold and delicious.

Everyone knew each other in Seaford. My friends and I would hang out at George's Candy Store on Merrick Road. The owners, George and Helen Wissner, had two sons. One of them, Scott, was in my school. On Sunday mornings we would go in to George's and buy a chocolate donut and a chocolate egg cream with the money our parents gave us to put in the basket at Saint William the Abbott Catholic Church. Each year just before Valentine's Day George would display an assortment of candy boxes in the shape of hearts. George used to let me pick one out and pay for it a little at a time with the money I would make from shoveling snow; he knew it was for my mom.

Every summer the carnival would come to Seaford. It would be set up at the Seaford railroad station. At night my friends and I would go to meet the girls from school. I hated the rides, but I would get talked into going on them. I have a fear of heights, but Larry Marone would insist on me going on the ferris wheel with him. When we got to the top of the wheel, he would rock the seat. I would be holding on to the bar so tight that my knuckles would turn white, and I'd have to close my eyes and beg him to stop. There was also this stupid rocket that went around in a circle and flipped you upside down. Why I went on it, I'll never know. The worst, however, was the Octopus. This ride had eight arms that went up and down with a car on each that spun around; one night it made me puke. I ran behind a truck so no one could see, but the truck pulled out as soon as I started to throw up. That was it for me: girls or no girls, I went home.

On cooler days we would play "guns" in the woods. The "woods" were a corner lot that had yet to be developed. The weapon of choice was a toy Fanner 50 model like the ones the lawmen used on "Texas Rangers," or a Rifleman-style Winchester that was an exact replica of the one Chuck Connors used on "The Rifleman." There was only one rule: No gun could shoot through the bushes. When Larry Marone's older brother Frank was in the military, he would bring home dummy hand grenades. The military used them for combat training. We used them in the woods. I always wanted to be on Larry's side, because with the hand grenades he had a better chance of winning. The grenades were made of cast iron, so it could really hurt if you got a direct hit.

Sometimes a dirt bomb fight would break out. A dirt bomb was a moist clump of dirt almost the consistency of clay. The best place to find dirt bombs was at a new construction site. When the tractor dug the hole in the ground for the foundation or cesspool of a house, the dirt would be piled up. Good dirt bombs would be found at the bottom of the pile of dirt. They were perfect for throwing at your friend. When they sat in the sun for a few days the dirt would dry out a little, and when you hit someone with a bomb the dry dirt would give the illusion of smoke. If the pile of dirt was high enough, a dirt bomb fight could evolve into a game of "King of the Hill." One of our gang would claim the top of the hill and the others would climb the hill and try to throw him off.

Once we found a porn magazine and took it into the woods for a look. It was in black and white, but really graphic—men and women doing things that our parents hoped they could keep us boys from ever seeing at the tender age of nine. When I got home later that day, my father asked, "What were you guys doing in the woods today?" I said, "Nothing." He said, "You weren't looking at some kind of magazine?" I said, "No." Then he pulled the porn magazine out from behind his back and said, "You guys weren't looking at *this*?"

There it was, our magazine! How did he get it? How did he know what we had done that day? He told me to look out the kitchen window. Our kitchen was on the second floor of the house, and from the window I could look into the woods—and see the exact spot where my friends and I had been gawking at the pictures of naked men and women having sex. He rolled up the magazine, hit me in the head with it, and said, "I don't ever want to catch you or your friends looking at something like this again." But I heard him laughing as he walked away. When I turned back from the window, he was looking through the magazine himself!

When I was eleven, it was by boat that I met Danny and Mike Brock and Jerry Tufano. Jerry's sister, Suzanne, eventually became Russell Javors' wife. Danny and Mike had an older stepbrother, Richie, who loved music. He would play "I Wonder Why" by Dion and the Belmonts and show us the vocal parts. Jerry, Danny, Mike, and I would try to imitate the singers on the record. We would each pick a vocal part, and I always took the bass, since my voice was already cracking. We would imagine what it was like to be Dion and the Belmonts. I would watch Richie get into the song. "It was for his generation," I thought to myself. "This is rock 'n' roll. If Dion is cool and Richie feels what Dion feels, then Richie must be cool, too." Soon I realized that everyone who liked Dion and the Belmonts was cool. I wanted to be just like Dion; he could be both the broken-hearted, misunderstood teenager in "Runaround Sue" and the overconfident, more than-able guy who could accomplish and handle anything in "The Wanderer."

My cousin Tina Zarconie married Bob Carillo. Bob was a singer in a vocal group and knew my appreciation for music. One day while my family was visiting, Bob handed me an album and said, "These guys are really big in England. I don't hear it. You can have this." The album he handed me was *Introducing... The Beatles*. I had only just heard of these guys. From the first time I played that album, I knew this band had a pulse in their music that I had never heard before. Their energy was through the roof. I recognized some of the songs: "Twist and Shout," "Boys," and "Chains" had been done by American artists, but there was one song that stuck out and had so much energy it killed me. "I Saw Her Standing There" was the greatest thing I'd ever heard. I had to know more about this band and their music. The album didn't list their names or who played what instruments, but on "Boys" the singer yells, "All right, George!" so at least there was one clue.

This album came out in the United Kingdom on March 22, 1963, and was called *Please Please Me*. In the U.S., Capitol refused to release it, so it was released by the Vee Jay Record label as *Introducing... The Beatles*, but omitting two songs: "Ask Me Why" and the title song, "Please Please Me." The album never placed on the charts—but I had it. It wasn't until January 20, 1964, with the release of *Meet the Beatles!*, that I would finally find out who the rest of the band was, and that they sang and played their own instruments. The single "I Want to Hold Your Hand" came out on January 13, 1964, with a picture of the band on the cover.

I was in the eighth grade when the Beatles were on their way to America—actually for their second time; they had come before, but with almost no fanfare. My classmate Terry Fogarty's father worked for the airlines at Idlewild Airport (which later became JFK). Terry came into school with a poster of the Beatles his father received at the airport in anticipation of their arrival. Terry asked me if I wanted it. I said, "Are you kidding?" The Beatles were on the wall in my room as fast as I could get them there.

Mike's Barber Shop was where we got our haircuts. Mike was Italian and spoke with a broken English accent. When the Beatles became popular, Mike Cody, Jerry Tufano, and I went to Mike's and got squareback haircuts. When our hair grew in, this cut would let it grow over our collars. When Mr. Cody saw us, he flipped out and drove us right back to Mike's and told him to "get that shit off their necks." Mike would only give us regular haircuts from then on, so we eventually went down the street to Ernie's Barber Shop. Ernie was more like an older brother to us. He looked like Moe from the Three Stooges. He knew boy's hormones were raging at fifteen and sixteen years old, so he would set us up in a room in the back of his shop and let us watch black-and-white porn films on a projector.

Nat's Shoe Repair was right next door to Ernie's. Standing about five feet, four inches tall and in his mid-forties, Nat's real name was Ignacio Calcasola. He was built like a rock and had an infectious laugh. When I got a little older, my friends and I would spend time at Nat's; he loved music and hanging out with us young musicians. There were three of us that Nat took seriously enough to let us hang around his store: me, Charlie Raymond (a drummer), and Bob Cadway (a guitarist). We'd walk into his shop about noon, and ask him if he had eaten lunch yet. Always being swamped with work, he'd say no. I'd walk up to the machine he was working on and turn it off while Charlie or Bob would turn the sign in the window from "open" to "closed," and we'd take Nat out to a restaurant.

At lunch, Nat would talk about life and music for hours, then he would get pissed at us for keeping him out so long. Now he would have to work after hours to get all his work done. We set up a stereo in the back room of Nat's store and listened to his recordings of jazz pianist Oscar Peterson and trumpeter Miles Davis. One time Charlie and I set up drums in the back room, and to our surprise this attracted different merchants from around the block who were into music. Jack from the department store liked Elvis, while Lou Paoli from the dry cleaners loved singers like Perry Como and Dean Martin—we found out that Lou was quite a good singer. This was when I also met fellow drummer Dom Famularo, who was Lou's cousin.

Later, when I was around twenty-one and a full time musician, Nat would sometimes come out and hear me play. I think he was a frustrated musician. He didn't play anything, but loved music so much that he always wished he did, and he always told us to follow our dreams. The shoe repair business was something he didn't mind, he said, and he loved the rain, he said, "Because if a pair of shoes is gonna go, they're gonna go when it rains."

Nat wanted a simple life. He loved his wife and son, but hated the responsibility of owning a house. He didn't like to work all week and then have to do things around the house on the weekends. "Libby," he said, "Get an apartment. Everything is taken care of for you." You would never know by how big it was, but Nat had a bad heart. For years he was on high blood pressure pills, and eventually he started seeing a doctor. We all got a big kick out of that, because the doctor was Asian and his name was Doctor Shu. After giving him a physical, the doctor thought Nat was in fine shape and he could stop taking the blood pressure pills.

I stopped in to see how Nat was feeling. He looked fine and said he felt good. I don't know why, but as I was leaving I asked Nat if he believed in God. "Yes," he said, but he didn't go to church. "But you believe in Jesus and all that stuff, right?" I asked. He assured me that he did. That night Nat had a heart attack, and he died the next day. I loved Nat, and my mother told me that she believed he loved me. I believe in angels and that people guide you not only in this life, but also from the next. I feel that Nat played a big part in my success, and I think of him every time I put on my shoes.

Recently I visited a shoemaker here in Brooklyn, where I now live. The shop was just like Nat's, and it made me feel close to him again. The shoemaker, Rosario Capa, is an Italian immigrant in his seventies. As we began talking, in his Italian accent he asked me what I did for a living. When I told him I was a musician, his eyes lit up. He loved music, especially the opera. As a boy back in Italy, he used to play the drum in the village band, practicing on a wine barrel in the basement. Later, in Brooklyn, he followed his passion and tried singing professionally, but turned to shoe repair to support his new family. He told me how lucky I was to be able to make a living at what I love to do. He now sings at the Italian mass every Sunday in church.

Rosario, like Nat, imparted wisdom to me. "To be good," he said, "you must have passion for the music. You may not understand the words because of the different language, but you can feel the passion that the singer has for the music. Some people who are considered great musicians can read the notes for the music, but they do not have the passion. I do not know notes but I know passion. This is very important."

# My Drum-Part 3

When I sit behind my drums in the studio, it is time to create. I am like a writer sitting behind a desk. The heads on the drums are the blank paper on which I will create something new. My sticks are my pencils. They will translate my thoughts to the drumheads. You can hear the emotion of what I'm thinking and feeling as I strike the stick to the head, which makes the head and wood shell of the drum resonate with sound— in the same way you know what the writer is thinking and feeling when they craft the words across the paper for you to read. Whether it moves you or not depends on how it is translated between the drummer and their drum, or the writer and their paper.

I never thought of my drum as a simple membranophone—a skin stretched over a round wooden shell that I struck with a stick to make sound. I had a relationship with the drums and together we built our own history. As a street musician, I took from the rhythms of everyday life. I saw the drum set as a giver of life; a way of expression; a channel for my energy. The drums gave me a title. I became the drummer, a reason to be. The drums gave me a want and a desire to be good at something. They made me popular. I found out that to know them is to love them. When I had my first real set at twelve years old, I would sleep on the floor in my room underneath my drums. They became a part of me. They are always there, like a best friend, celebrating my greatest achievements and catching me when I fall. Without me they are just a silent combination of wood, plastic, chrome, and brass, held together by glue, lugs, and wing nuts; they have no voice. They wait for me to sit behind them and bring them to life.

# 6
# Why the Drums?

Even before I knew what I was doing, I always loved to bang on things. I started out banging on my mother's pots and pans with her wooden spoons. I'd sit on the floor, empty out the kitchen cabinets, and wail away. It drove my parents crazy. By the age of 1½ they had bought me my first drum for Christmas. When I went to school I'd get in trouble for banging on the desk. My parents would have to come to school to "discuss the matter" with the teachers.

School was not one of my favorite places to be. I didn't mind going to school and I didn't mind coming home. It was the part in the middle that I had a tough time with. I hated getting up early, I hated snow and cold weather, and I hated school. In the winter, I would have to get up early just to stand at the bus stop in the snow and cold weather, just to go to the place I hated the most. The only thing I knew was that I loved music. In fourth grade, the teacher taught us a drinking song that wouldn't be allowed to be taught in schools today. The lyrics were:

> *Drunk last night*
> *Drunk the night before*
> *Gonna get drunk tonight*
> *Like I've never been drunk before*
> *'Cause when I'm drunk I'm as happy as can be*
> *'Cause I am a member of the Dutch family*
> *Oh the Dutch family*
> *Is the best family*
> *That ever came over from old Germany*
> *There's the Amsterdam Dutch*
> *And the Rotterdam Dutch…*

And on and on the song went.

Schools were different then. We would hide under our desks in an air raid drill in case there was a real nuclear attack—as if the desk would protect us from a hydrogen bomb. I can remember our music teacher coming into the fourth grade class in 1960 and telling us she had just heard a song she thought was "a disgrace to music." The song went "Uh, ah, uh, ah." That was the only part she remembered, and she hated it. Turns out it was "Chain Gang" by Sam Cooke. I thought to myself, "I like that song." Was this my first experience with "a square"? Events in my life started to coincide with the music I was so into.

In sixth grade I had a crush on Denise Bacugres. That year Randy and the Rainbows had a hit with their song "Denise." I think I kissed her once. After Denise, and still in sixth grade, I had a crush on Sheryl Rapuanno. This was 1962, and the Four Seasons released "Sherry." I would sing along to the 45s and make believe I was singing to the girls in my school. I was romancing vicariously through the songs.

In Seaford, the only place that sold records was Pete's Pet Shop. Pete Pecoraro was Alice Pecoraro's dad. I went to school with Alice and we graduated together in the class of '68. I would mow the neighborhood's lawns, collect my money, and ride my bike to Pete's. His shop was located on Jackson Avenue between Merrick Road and Verity Plaza, a three-minute bike ride from my house. Although the shop was mainly full of snakes, mice, and goldfish, there was a little oasis of music to be found: a rack of Top-20 singles, and a few albums.

The first single I ever bought with my lawn-mowing money was "The Book of Love" by the Monotones. The year was 1958, and when I brought it home it still had that pet shop smell. When Stereophonic records came out, we asked Pete what that meant and why it made records cost more—after all, the cover looked exactly the same. Pete said he didn't think it was much of a big deal, he said, "If you have a special record player, you get some stuff that comes out of here," pointing to the right, "and some stuff that comes outta here," pointing to the left. As far as he was concerned, it wasn't worth spending the extra money. I loved going to Pete's.

I often dreamed of what it would be like to be one of the Beatles; what it would be like to play in a band that was the most popular band in the world. I would wonder what it would feel like to be an equal part of that band, then make records and hear my band on the radio, and then tour the world and be so popular that I became irresistible to women. To do what I loved and get paid for it must be the most gratifying way to travel through life.

I decided to go after my dream. The drum was my instrument of choice to take me on my journey. I became part of a phenomenon that took me into the life that I had dreamed. It started out just as I had imagined it would, but in the end, it was nothing like I thought it would be. There were four things I needed to do to get started: practice, be dedicated to my instrument, play differently from anyone else and come up with my own style, and put myself in the right place at the right time.

I knew I needed to be as good as the drummers I admired, so my first priority was to practice. Records were my books. I would set my drums up next to the record player, put on a record, and play to it. I would turn the record player up loud so I could play hard and feel like I was actually in the band. I became the drummer on that record. The downside of this was I never learned to read music, but at the time, I didn't care. After all, the Beatles didn't read music. Plus, rock and roll was based on the feel of the music; it wasn't something you could read off a chart. It was a teenage revolution that was born in the heart, not on paper.

I tried to take lessons with a drum teacher in a local music store. He sat me down with a practice pad and a set of sticks and started to teach me rudiments. I asked him, "When are you going to teach me how to play like Ringo?" He said, "Why do you want to learn how to play like Ringo? He stinks." I said, "Well, I saw him on TV last night and all these girls were screaming for him and I don't see any girls knocking on your door." That was the end of my lessons. I had to teach myself.

I wanted to know what it was like to be in a rock band. I didn't want to learn rudiments. If I wanted to learn how to play a paradiddle, I would have gone to the drum shop and asked the guy behind the counter—who was probably a drummer—how to do a paradiddle. I'm sure he would have been glad to show me while he sold me a pair of sticks. I would have gone home and locked myself in a room and practiced that paradiddle for a year. I probably would have come out of that room as the best paradiddlist in my town. But that wasn't what I wanted. I wanted to find the heartbeat of rock 'n' roll. This led to a lot of obstacles I needed to get around and hurdles I needed to get over. I decided to flow with the drums rather than fight them. I found out years later that I wasn't alone. Buddy Rich and many others did the same thing. I developed a natural "Moeller grip." Although I was playing hard, I was unknowingly developing a technique that would keep me from hurting myself.

I couldn't read music, so for me to learn a song, my routine was to learn the lyrics and sing along in my head to follow the arrangement to the song. As I was learning the drum parts and singing along with the song, I began to notice the drummer did his drum fills when the singer stopped singing or when a transition was coming in the song. His fills would accent or take the listener to another place in the song. He would set up different movements in the song. This was how Ringo Starr played in the Beatles— you can always sing the melodies while playing his drum parts. I realized that if I couldn't sing the song and play the drums at the same time, then I was playing too many notes or fills. Less was more. I learned to never lose focus of the song and to remove everything that I knew didn't fit, in the way a sculptor looks at a piece of rock and sees the statue and chips away any stone or material that isn't part of the statue.

I need to know the lyrics to a song because they set the emotional pace of the music. I like to get emotionally involved in the song. I need to know what the song's about. There's a story being told. A drummer's purpose is to enhance the story with the drum part without stepping all over the song. In a conversation between two or more people, emotions will go from one level to another depending upon intensity and topic. A song is a melodic conversation with emotional ups and downs that eventually gets to a level that drives a point across. The drummer needs to know where those levels change lyrically so the drums can change with them. When creating a drum part for an instrumental, my first approach would be sparked by the title. I'm going to play a song called, "Gonna Love You Like an Angel" a little differently than a song called "Gonna Smash My Car into Your House." Mind you, if you put the word "baby" at the end, it moves them closer together in a metaphorical sense. (Just kidding.)

My very first set of drums was a kiddie set. It was made from corrugated cardboard for the shells and paper for the heads. It was a three-piece: snare, tom-tom, and bass drum. The bass drum had a painting of a circus clown on the front. It had a little ride cymbal, a wood block, and a small cowbell. The bass drum pedal had a red wooden ball as a beater. My brothers, Vinny and Sal, saw a show on TV one day with a guy jumping on a trampoline. They decided to use the bass drum as their trampoline and jumped from the bed to the drum. On the first jump, Vinny went through one side. Sal was next and finished off the other side.

Some days I would come home from school to find there was nobody home. My dad was working and my mom had gone out for some reason. I would get so upset that I would turn all the porch furniture upside down and throw it off the porch onto the front lawn. My mom always tried to be at the house before I got there, but sometimes I would beat her, and she'd actually see me throwing the furniture off the porch as she was driving towards the house. My parents knew I needed something to channel my frustrations. They thought they'd give the drums another shot.

It was now 1961. My mother's friend Lucy was moving to Las Vegas. Her son Jimmy had just bought a brand new red sparkle Ludwig drum kit. He was a very good drummer then, and was moving to Vegas to try to make it big. Now that he had a new kit, he was selling his old one. It was a mother-of-pearl Leedy set: four-piece with a 26″ bass drum, from the 1930s. The bass drum had a beautiful painting on the front of a rowboat going down a river with mountains in the background.

Back at school, I had joined the band. I had to bring my own sticks to school, so now I had advanced from drumming on the desks with my hands to drumming on the desks with my sticks. The sticks were taken from me many, many times. Because I started playing later than most kids, I was a sixth-grader in a fifth-grade band. The band teacher didn't like me much; I wasn't very good at a double-stroke roll. I felt like "The Star Spangled Banner" went on forever. The teacher put me on the bass drum. That was very boring. The teacher didn't think I had what it took, and he told me, "Put down the sticks, you'll never do anything with them." I still can't do a very good double-stroke roll. Meanwhile, Gene Chandler was singing "Duke of Earl," Sam Cooke was "Twistin' the Night Away," the Orlons had "The Wah-Watusi," and Dion (my favorite) was killin' it with "The Wanderer."

In 1962 my old drum stands started to break. The only place I could get them repaired was located in the Bar Harbor Shopping Center in Massapequa, the town next to Seaford. There was a serious rivalry between the Seaford High School and Massapequa High School football teams. In addition, the local Massapequa tough guys didn't like guys from other towns going into theirs. I was scared to go, but I decided to walk there anyway. I had to get my stands fixed. As soon as I crossed the line over into Massapequa, they came at me. I was thrown to the ground and punched over and over, and when they were done, I looked up just high enough to see the Massapequa tough guys walking away and laughing. I pulled myself up, took my broken stands and went home. When I got there, I told my mom what had happened and that I was nervous to go back and get the stands fixed. My mom, who grew up on the Lower East Side, told me, "Next time, before they touch you, give them a good kick in the balls and run as fast as you can!" I went back, and it worked.

That Christmas, my parents bought me a new set of drums. I needed to stay current; no one was playing the drums that I had. Under the tree was a set of silver sparkle Tempo drums. Kent and Tempo drums were very popular beginner sets. The set had a snare, one tom, bass drum, hi-hat, and ride cymbal, but no floor tom. (I eventually got one, but not that Christmas.) They were purchased at Time Square Stores or TSS in Levittown. Compared to my old set, this one was really beautiful. It looked great next to the Christmas tree; that year the tree was actually silver as well, with red, green, and gold balls. There was a light that we set up that would shine on the tree. It had a rotating three-color gel disk that changed the color of the light from red to green to blue. As the disk rotated, the gel changed the color of the tree. I would turn the light away from the tree, and point it straight at my silver drums: Now I had color! That was my first light show.

My dad would leave the house every time I'd start practicing. He'd go to the movies most of the time. I thought about it differently then, but I guess he was very supportive of my drumming. I practiced to records constantly; my mother loved it because she always knew where I was, but it drove my father nuts. In 1963 "Easier Said Than Done" by the Essex was one of my favorites songs to play. One time my parents brought over a drummer friend of theirs to see if he could "teach me a few things." After he heard me, he said I had a great feel, but he couldn't teach me anything since I was too far gone with rock 'n' roll, and I knew so much more about it than he did.

# My Drum-Part 4

I get a rush of happiness when I see my drums like I get when I see the woman I love. Things are not always perfect in my relationship with the woman I love, but all is forgotten when I hold her close. It's the same with my drums. I feel them in my heart; they affect my breathing. I have put so much energy into playing my drums and I have taken them to such a level that I have been called a musical athlete. During my heavy drinking days, there was nothing like a good sweat behind the drums to cure a hangover, but now I find that my youthful heart and mind will sometimes push my aging body to its limit. There is a difference between "I want to play them" and "I have to play them."

There is nothing like playing when the temperature is just right. I like my muscles to be warm. I like it when I start to sweat about three minutes into the first song. It feels like all the impurities are coming out of my body as I rip through the music. The more my body warms up, the easier it seems to get to the level where I am most comfortable. It is so much more satisfying than going to a health club. Eventually, I break into a runner's high and I don't feel aches anymore. Even my head is clear of any bad thoughts from the day. Now I am the drum. I'm bathed in sweat and I am drumming like it is the last time I am going to do this, and this is how people will remember me when I die. I have decided that if I die while I'm playing my drum, that's okay. I just don't want it to happen in front of too many people. I feel like that would be embarrassing.

**Me with Ringo's kit at Beatle Fest, 2018.**

# 7

# Liberty Meets Destiny

Ⓘn school everyone loved the sports stars, the thrill of competition with other schools, and the celebration of a team victory. A school football game played on a crisp fall day on the school field, with the school band playing songs by John Philip Sousa—what could be better?

I hated it.

From the first bonfire and pep rally, when I got shot in the ass with a paper clip while I stared at the fire, it was a total waste of time to me— other than seeing the girls in their cheerleading outfits. Except all the girls liked the sports guys, and I hated sports. I played little league baseball when I was in elementary school, and eventually made it onto a team called Jerry's Lunch Bombers. I found out I needed glasses when I couldn't see the ball coming at me.

Back in the 1960s, the only glasses available were the kind that Buddy Holly wore: black rims with lenses that resembled the bottom of Coke bottles. Contact sports gave me the creeps. Wrestling was the worst; I don't want to be in an embracing hold with another sweaty body unless I'm dating them. I failed gym in eleventh grade because I wouldn't wear a gym suit. I hated the idea of the locker room. Being stripped down to my "tighty whities" with a bunch of guys was not my idea of having fun. It was bad enough that at the beginning of every school year I had to drop my pants so a doctor could grab my balls and have me cough. So sports were out, and when I told someone I wanted to be a musician, their reaction was like I told them I was going to be the first man on the moon. The concept was so far out there, so unattainable, no one could conceive that I could be successful at it. They thought it was foolish and pointless. I toured with Mitch Ryder in 1968 and have never stopped working since then. Neil Armstrong walked on the moon in 1969. We showed them!

In seventh grade there was nothing for me to relate to. There were singers and instrumentalists. Elvis belonged to the generation before me. Girls had no interest in some guy who rebelled against school, took shop classes, wore glasses, hated sports, and was obsessed with music. At the time, there were kids that played the fluteophone, but as far as anyone else who loved music like I did, I knew of no one.

There were two very different and separate groups of kids in Seaford schools: the Collegiate and the Gees. The Collegiate boys had a look similar to that of the Beach Boys or Jan and Dean. They wore madras shirts with beige Lee or Wrangler slacks, moccasins or penny loafers, and white socks or no socks at all. They also wore Letterman jackets. The Collegiate girls wore pleated skirts to the knee—the rule was they had to get on their knees and the skirt had to touch the floor—plain white blouses with button-down collars, penny loafers with knee-high socks or colored tights, and navy blue or beige wool coats with barrel buttons which came to their thigh. The guys either had flat-top haircuts or wore their hair parted to the side; the girls' hair was cut short to the neck, and they hardly wore any makeup. The Collegiate knew they were headed to college.

The Gee boys had the James Dean look: black pants, solid color shirts (purple was way cool), leather or suede black shoes with taps on the heels (which were better for sliding down the halls), black socks or socks that were the same color as your shirt, and a long black trench coat, at all times open. Gee guys would wear their hair combed back on the sides with a pompadour in the front, and a square back or d.a. (duck's ass) in the back. The Gee girls wore black skirts as short as they could get away with, ruffled blouses, black shoes with nylons or black tights. Their hair was teased high and spayed with tons of Aqua Net, and a pound of pancake makeup was always on their faces: blue eye shadow, mascara, and thick black eye pencil. All the Gees wanted was to get out of high school. Their look was similar to Bernardo in *West Side Story* or the members of the Ronettes.

I was a Gee. I had been taken under the wing of a seasoned Gee, Mike Lackous. My mom and dad were friends with Mike's parents; they lived down the block from us. I knew Mike from school. He was a tough guy. Once a guy was after Mike's girlfriend, so at a school dance, Mike and a couple of his friends, the Fagan brothers, took this guy into the bathroom to kick his ass. Before he went in, Mike told me to stand at the door and make sure no teachers came in. He said if they did, he would kick the shit out of me. Great! I was in seventh grade, skinny as a rail, maybe 5′10″ and weighed about 110 pounds, and I had to tell the teachers to take a hike, or I'd get my ass kicked by Mike. I stood there listening to this guy get beat up in the bathroom and all I could do was pray that no teachers would come by. Another time, Mike and I were serving detention with a bunch of other clowns, and Mike was chewing gum. The teacher said, "Lackous, spit that gum out." Well, Lackous spit out the gum right onto the floor. That was just the kind of guy he was. By me watching the door that night, I was guaranteed protection from anyone by Mike and his buddies.

Mike played a Fender Jaguar guitar and had an instrumental band. The drummer in the band was Ronnie Levine, who I also knew from school. My mom brought me to Mike's house to hear the band play. Ronnie let me sit in for a song. After I played they said, "This kid is pretty good." Not too long after that, Mike's band had a gig to play a party in the basement of the Fagans' house. Ronnie couldn't make it, so Mike told me I was playing. During the party, one of the Fagans sang "You Can't Sit Down." It was so bad that we returned to instrumentals for the rest of the night. We played "Walk Don't Run" by the Ventures, "Rumble" by Link Ray, and a song I had never heard again called "Jibber Jabber." Of course, before the night was over, a fight broke out. For me, it was the coolest: I was hanging out with older, cool kids—not to mention the older, cool girls who thought I was "cute" because I was younger and played drums. I had a smile plastered on my face all night long.

Sometimes the Gees and Collegiate would clash. If a Collegiate would step on a Gee's suede shoes, he'd get his ass kicked. If a Gee liked a Collegiate girlfriend, the whole football team would be after him. The Gees hung out at Bob's Hamburgers on Merrick Road in Seaford Harbor. The Collegiates hung out at Hubie's Hamburgers on Sunrise Highway in Seaford Manor. (Bob's was later knocked down to build the Seaford- Oyster Bay Expressway, and Hubie's became a Burger King.) One night, two guys from nowhere came into Bob's with guitars and sang Ray Charles' "What'd I Say," but they changed the lyrics to dirty words. They sang, "See the girl all dressed in pink, she's the one who made my finger stink…" They went on and on, and to the bunch of teenage boys that were there, these two guys were the greatest.

I was never one to date my own kind. My crowd was tough, mostly Italian; I had dark skin but I liked very conservative girls with light skin— the lighter the better. So, as a Gee, I had a problem: I liked Collegiate girls. They thought I was a nice guy, but wanted nothing to do with me. I wasn't their type, because I hated school and sports. I once had a fight in a Bohack's parking lot with a Collegiate guy because he found out I liked his girlfriend. A Collegiate girl invited me to a party in Wantagh once, so I went. When the football team found out, they chased me all the way back to Seaford. I was constantly getting my ass kicked.

By the end of 1963, I had nothing going for me. President Kennedy had just been assassinated, and the country was upside down. Musically, Elvis was just putting out greatest hits albums and making mediocre movies. The Top 20 didn't thrill me, and the Top 10 was killing me. Music was just not inspiring me the way it had before. I still had no girlfriend and still hated school. I had my drums, though, so I could at least practice "Wipeout." However, I had just been given the album I discussed earlier, by a group I was determined to find out more about.

At this time, in eighth grade, the question I pondered was, "What will I do when I grow up?" My answer came on February 4, 1964. My family, like every other American family that night, had the TV tuned to "The Ed Sullivan Show." There they were in black and white: The Beatles. I watched as the camera panned the audience in the theater, and stared at all the girls who were screaming for these "not-that-good-looking" guys. Then I panned my living room and saw my sister and her friends screaming for them. That's when it hit me. I found my way to meet girls. I pointed at the screen and said, "Fuck the buzz roll, *that's* what I want to do."

From that day on I got very serious about playing my drums, and I knew I had to be in a band. Overnight, everything had changed. They were here for our generation. Elvis was out, madras was out, leather jackets were out, Gees and Collegiate were out, all the hairstyles we knew were out. Everything we knew was no more; everything was different now. It was now cool to be a musician. I played drums "like Ringo Starr." Ringo was cool, so I was cool. Like Richie, Danny's brother with Dion and the Belmonts, I was cool. All girls were up for grabs; we became one generation. Finally, I found a direction. I will follow the Beatles.

After the Beatles came the British Invasion: the Dave Clark Five, the Rolling Stones, the Kinks, the Zombies, Billy J Kramer, and more. It seemed as if the music gods woke up and said, "Enough of this shit!" and blessed us with our own classic era of music that still stands today. By the end of the year, the Beatles owned the charts:

#1. "Can't Buy Me Love"

#2. "Twist and Shout"

#3. "She Loves You"

#4. "I Want to Hold Your Hand"

#5. "Please Please Me"

# My Drum-Part 5

There are times when I think I hate my drum. Just like when I think I'm mad at the woman I love, it's not her that I'm really mad at; I'm mad at what's happening around us. Once our emotions are in tune, we have to be physically warm to each other to achieve the passion that we can create between us. The gig might be outdoors; it's cold and I can't get warm. I look at my drum and I just see a block of stone. When I strike them with my sticks it will feel like I am striking an anvil with a hammer. The shock waves will travel into the bones in my arms. I know that we will never be warm enough to achieve the passion that we are capable of.

Sometimes it might be a shitty gig; the other players aren't that compatible, and I am constantly fighting a tempo battle with one of the members. It feels like I'm paddling upstream with one paddle. I can't wait for that gig to be over. But when the groove is locked and in the pocket, it's like riding down a river on a rubber tube in the summer with a cool drink in your hand. The funny thing is that I can, and do, share my love/hate relationship for my drum with the woman I love—but it doesn't work the other way around. If I am upset at something that concerns her, I cannot bring that emotion on stage when I'm with my drum. My head must be clear. My drum demands full attention.

I hate going to see another band if I haven't been playing for a while. I get jealous of the drummer, as if with every beat he is hanging over the woman I love—the woman that was mine not too long ago. Sometimes the rhythm is in my head to the point of insanity.

**The Rogues at Roosevelt Raceway, New York, 1964.**

# 8

# The Rogues

**M**y very first band was called the Rogues: Mike Cody on bass, Jerry Tufano on rhythm guitar, Mel Wach on lead guitar, and me on drums. Mike, Jerry, and I went to Seaford High School. Jerry was a year older than Mike and me. Jerry and I had been friends for a while, and when he got a Kent guitar for Christmas, we started playing together. We had a friend, Eddie, who knew Mike. I can remember the first time I met Mike. He walked into Eddie's backyard, skinny as a rail, tall, wearing black suede shoes, black socks, black turtleneck (which the Beatles wore on the cover of *Meet the Beatles!*) black trench coat (open), and his black hair was parted to the side like Paul McCartney's. He resembled Paul in stature. We talked about starting a band. Mike wanted in right away, but at the time Mike didn't play anything. He had no instrument, but knew that being in a band would impress the girls, so he went out and got himself an Epiphone guitar that came with lessons.

Mike and his family lived in a beautiful house north of Merrick Road. His dad was the vice president of the Teamsters union—he eventually became president. We would rehearse in Mike's basement. His guitar player friend, Mel, would sleep over on the weekends when we rehearsed. Mel was great, he could really play. We were an all-instrumental band because no one could sing. Our song list was "She's Not There" by the Zombies, "Wipeout" by the Surfaris, "Needles and Pins" by the Searchers, "Louie Louie" by the Kingsmen, "House of the Rising Sun" by the Animals, "I Like It Like That" by Chris Kenner, "Night Train" by Jimmy Forrest, "Guitar Boogie Shuffle" by Duane Eddie, "Greensleeves," and a whole bunch of Ventures tunes.

Mike's father thought we were great. Mike kept getting new guitars, and finally got a Mosrite Ventures model bass guitar. One beautiful summer's day we came out of the basement with our equipment and played in the backyard. All the kids in the neighborhood came into the yard. We had about thirty kids back there. It was our first live performance in front of people, and it was great. The cops came because someone complained, but Mr. Cody took care of it. Later on in my career, Mr. Cody came to see a Billy show at Madison Square Garden in New York. The marquee outside read "BILLY JOEL TONIGHT." Mr. Cody asked me if I'd like to have it changed to read "LIBERTY DeVITTO with BILLY JOEL TONIGHT." He said if I wanted, he could make it happen.

Mr. Cody got us most of our gigs. We played Teamsters parties, and you might say we had a captive audience. Our best gig was the 1964 World's Fair. We played the New York pavilion, along with another band from Seaford, the Spectrum, who had a girl drummer and singers. My father said we were so nervous he thought we were gonna shit in our pants, but we were cool. We worked the whole Beatles vibe: four guys, same outfits—black suede shoes, black socks, black pants, light green striped shirts with tab collars, and dark green sweaters. Mr. Cody purchased the outfits for us.

We still had no singer. One day in school, my neighbor, Christine Parisi, who was on the student council, asked me if the Rogues would like to play at a school dance. Most of the time only seniors got those gigs. I said okay, and then she asked if we would get a singer. We got Charlie Kowanatez, who was a senior and Jerry's friend. He said he'd do us a favor, but he didn't like the idea of hanging out with underclassmen, no matter how good we were. We did the gig, and he sang all the words to our usual instrumental set plus a load of Beatles tunes. The gig went really well, and we realized we needed a permanent singer, so we recruited Vic Tarabrelli. He was a good-looking kid with blonde hair, the same age as us.

We played the Battle of the Bands in the high school gym and won, which led us to playing more and more dances, and getting a lot more popular around Seaford. Once Mike spray-painted "the Rogues" on a wall across from Bob's Hamburgers. A friend asked me if I had seen it. I said, "Yeah." He asked, "Lately?" The next time I saw it, it said "the Rogues SUCK."— no doubt the maliciousness of a rival band.

Armed with the new Slingerland kit my dad had bought me, the band played the Battle of the Bands in Wantagh. Wantagh was the rival town next to Seaford. The Rogues needed to win. Back then your band and all its followers was your gang. It wasn't a gang that fought with knives and chains, but with music, and the spoils of the battle went to the winning band. When I say spoils, I mean *girls*. The Rogues played hard—hard like an army of Scottish freedom fighters there only to win. We chose our best tune, and on my count, "1,2,3,4, *BOOM!*," launched into "I Ain't Gonna Eat Out My Heart Anymore" by the Young Rascals. It came on with such a fury, everybody ran to the back of the room. I think our volume kept us from winning that one. We went back to Seaford with only the girls from home.

Mike and I went to a Battle of the Bands in Freeport one night, just to check it out, thinking if it was cool, maybe we could get the Rogues to play their next one. Freeport was predominantly black, but we never thought a thing of it. After the Battle was over, we walked down the block to get on the train. A group of black guys came at us. We stood out there and didn't belong. One guy pulled out a straight razor, looked me right in the eyes and said, "Motherfucker, I'm gonna cut you up." I thought I was dead, my life was over. Then his face changed, he said, "I know you from somewhere. Aren't you Randy's friend?" It turned out he was friends with Randy Hart who, a week earlier, had introduced me to this now knife-wielding guy at George's Candy

Store when I went by to use the payphone. Randy and this guy had spent some time together in jail. When he realized who I was, he started hugging me, saying, "How you doin', man?" He introduced me to the rest of his friends and told me, "You should be careful around here; it could be dangerous. Say hello to Randy when you see him."

In 1966 the *New York Times* ran a story called "Black and White on Long Island: Like Oil and Water." Neighborhoods were often divided by one road. North of the road would be white and south would be black. North of the road had better schools, and the houses sold for more money. The people were white and privileged. South of the road was poor, harassed, and black. Guys would get sent to jail for things that would get a white kid a slap on the wrist. Freeport was like that. Mike and I got on the next train to Seaford. I didn't return to Freeport until my draft physical in 1969.

When the Rogues played in bars, only Jerry and Charlie Kowanatez— who sang with us now, since the audience was more his age—were of legal age. Mike, Mel, and I were under 18 and not allowed to be in bars. In the '60s you could buy proof from a guy who was being drafted. The army was giving him new I.D. anyway, so he'd sell you his draft card and registration card. In the bars I was known as Vic Zito. We sounded good in the bars, so we were hooked up with an agent who said he'd get us gigs at the Long Beach clubs. Long Beach was the place to be in the '60s. Right on the Atlantic Ocean on the south shore of Long Island, it had rows of beach houses that college kids rented for the summer. They partied like the privileged frat boys and girls that they were.

The agent got us an audition at a bar called the Irish House on Long Beach Road. They loved us and took us on for more and more gigs. One night when we were playing, the Irish House got raided by the vice squad. The Rogues ran to the roof; the cops followed. They asked for our I.D.'s and proof of age. I was so nervous that when they asked when I was born, I gave the wrong year (which only made me 17). Mike did the same thing. As we were taken away, I could see the look on the face of the owner of the Irish House, showing how disappointed he was that we had lied to him. Because of us, he got in trouble too. The agent said he never knew we were underage—but of course he did.

We were taken to police headquarters in Mineola. My father and Mr. Cody came to get us. Mr. Cody was so furious that he was screaming at the cops, "What the hell are you doin'? These kids were just out tryin' to make a buck." My father was afraid that he and Mr. Cody were going to get arrested. After that night, the Rogues changed our name and became the Poor Boys. We continued to play bars.

One of the greatest experiences I had with the guys in the Rogues was when the Young Rascals played at Wantagh High School (one town away from Seaford). With Felix Cavaliere on organ and vocals, Eddie Brigati on vocals and tambourine, Gene Cornish on vocals and guitar, and Dino Danelli on drums, the Young Rascals were from Garfield, New Jersey, and played rock, pop, and blue-eyed soul from 1965 to 1972. I loved the Rascals (which later became their permanent name). This was the second time I was going to see them, having seen them open for the Byrds sometime before.

We got to Wantagh High School really early to get up front, since it was general admission. A big gangster-looking guy in a dark suit came up to us and asked if we knew anyone who had a bass guitar. The Vagrants, who were the opening act, seemed to have forgotten the bass player's bass. The Vagrants were an American, Long Island-based, rock and blue-eyed soul group from the 1960s. The group was composed of Peter Sabatino on vocals, harmonica, and tambourine; Leslie West on vocals and guitar; Larry West on vocals and bass guitar; Jerry Storch— AKA Jay Storch—on organ; and Roger Mansour on drums.

Mike's Mosrite bass was at my house, so we said yes. The gangster-looking guy said, "Take the limo and go get it, and when you get back, I'll take you backstage to meet the Vagrants." It was the first time Mike, Jerry, or I had ever ridden in a limousine. When we pulled up in front of my parents' house, my father thought we had stolen it. Once we returned to the school with the bass, the guy did as he promised, and took us backstage to meet the Vagrants. While we were backstage, I looked across the hall, and could not believe my eyes. Sitting right there, right across the hall from me, were the Rascals. You need to understand when I was a kid I only knew of one road that took you to the Hamptons on the South Fork of the east end of Long Island. The Rascals played a club called the Barge out there—it was literally a floating barge on the water.

At fifteen years old, my world was pretty small. I knew nothing about the Long Island Expressway or the parkways that lead east. I only knew of one road: Merrick Road. Known as Merrick Boulevard inside New York City, Merrick Road travels along an old right-of-way that was one of the original paths across southern Long Island, stretching from Queens to Montauk Point. It is an east–west urban arterial in Queens, Nassau, and Suffolk Counties, running east from the Queens neighborhood of Jamaica, through Merrick, past the county line between Nassau and Suffolk, and becomes Montauk Highway at the Amityville-Copiague village line. The easternmost portion of Merrick Road, from Carman Mill Road to its eastern terminus, is signed as part of New York State Route 27A (NY 27A).

Merrick Road ran right through Seaford. I hung out at Bob's Hamburgers and George's Candy Store, got my hair cut at Ernie's Barber Shop, my family got our clothes cleaned at Paoli's Cleaners, I bought Keds and Converse sneakers at Jack's Shoe Store, and shopped for school clothes at Mid Island

Department Store—all located on Merrick Road in Seaford. I was so into the Rascals that sometimes I would get crazy thinking they had to drive right past where I was standing to get to the Hamptons. I would close my eyes and imagine a big black car driving past me with the four Rascals inside. Little did I know, they probably took the Long Island Expressway.

As we were visiting the Vagrants, the big security guy saw me staring and said, "Would you like to meet them, too?" I tried to be cool and said, "Yeah, sure." Inside I was exploding. What luck! Meeting the Rascals was my next major step toward success. I had never met any stars before, let alone any of my idols. They always seemed so out of reach—they existed to me on TV, radio, and records. When I walked into the room, the first thing that surprised me was that they were a whole lot smaller than they looked on TV, but the thing that impressed me the most was how friendly they were. I felt like they were my cousins and I was at a family reunion. Dino Danelli showed me how to twirl the drumsticks and explained a lot about drumming to me. They were all smiles and knew how excited I was to be in their presence.

At that time, my girlfriend Regina had just broken up with me (again) and I knew she was going to be there for the show. I asked Felix Cavaliere if they could dedicate Mustang Sally to me. He said yes. I thanked them, got all their autographs, and went out to watch the show with the other thousand kids. With the front rows now taken, we watched the show from the side of the stage, but I didn't care one bit, I was in Rascal Heaven. They played all their hits, and in the middle of their set Felix called Eddie back to the organ. He whispered something to him and Eddie ran to the microphone. He said, "This is for Lib" and they played "Mustang Sally."

The next day my ex-girlfriend told me she never even heard them say it. She said she had gone to the bathroom during that song. It was still one of the greatest nights of my life. Yes, I loved the Beatles, but it was hard to emulate four guys from Liverpool with straight hair in a bowl cut, English accents, with names like McCartney, Lennon, Harrison, and Starr (Starkey). I was an Italian kid from Long Island, U.S.A., with wavy hair, a "Luong Ilind" accent, and a vowel at the end of my name. When the Rascals hit the scene, I was *in*. Three of them were Italian. Dino Danelli immediately knocked Ringo off the number-one drum stool for me. Dino was my new drum god, and the Rascals ruled my musical kingdom.

Oh, and yes, the Vagrants were great, too!

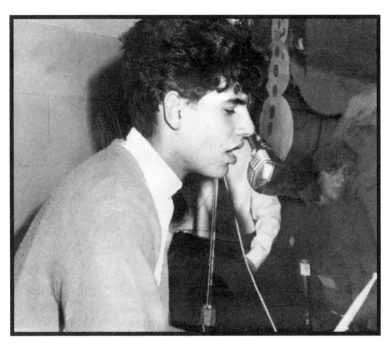

**Performing at Seaford High School, late 1965.**

# 9

# The Crystal Circus

After our vice squad bust and our name change to the Poor Boys, the Rogues were never the same. Jerry was contemplating college, Mike was seriously in love with his high school sweetheart Valerie, and Mel was tired of schlepping to Seaford every weekend. I was getting bored with the band, too. The last gig the Poor Boys played was at the Pink Room. The Pink Room only contained the necessities: a bar, jukebox, toilet, and a stage. Armed with new phony I.D., I stopped in one night. The band was all about up-tempo gospel R&B music, with the sweet sound of "Isn't She Pretty" by the Temptations. They were taking it all the way to church. They had three singers upfront and their harmonies were terrific, pushed by a Hammond organ, lead guitar, and drums.

The end was in sight for me with the Rogues. The organ player, Terry Anderson—who also had a girlfriend named Terri—had seen me play with the Rogues. At the end of the set, Terry came up to me and told me the band was splitting into two bands. One of the singers, Roy, was taking the drummer and the guitar player and forming his own group, while Terry and the other two singers were putting their own band together. He said they had a guitarist already, and they'd like me to come down and play with them.

A few days later I was banging my drums in Terry's garage with Billy Hennessey on vocals, Tony Presto on vocals, and Don—who's surname has left me—on guitar. Terry played bass on the Hammond organ foot pedals just like Felix in the Rascals. Billy, Tony, and Don were from the two towns that surrounded Seaford: Wantagh and Massapequa. They asked me to join the band, and I immediately said yes. One thing that excited me was that I had gone from the Rogues, with no vocals, to a band with three-part harmonies.

They told me they wanted to call the band the Bells of Grapefruit. After a few rehearsals we found out the other singer from the original band was already booked in the Pink Room and had also taken the name Bells of Grapefruit, so we came up with the name Crystal Circus. Crystal meth was very popular then, even though none of us did drugs of any kind. This band was exactly what I wanted. It was the Rascals with one more front man. We became the house band at Club Anthony in Wantagh. This was a giant step up from the Pink Room, as Club Anthony was also an Italian restaurant.

This time I was the only one underage. The owner, Anthony, made the best pepper and egg sandwiches on toasted Italian bread I'd ever had. He always helped me out with problems I was having with my girlfriend— Regina and I were back together again—and I always remember Anthony as a real stand-up guy. One night the Rascals were playing at Nassau Coliseum, which was not far from Anthony's. For the first set, we did all Rascals tunes. At the end of the set a guy came up to me and said, "I was watching you, and you play great. When you were nearing the end of 'What is the Reason,' I thought you'd never do it, but you played it perfectly." I told the guy that Dino Danelli was my mentor, and said "Thanks, I'll take that compliment." It's funny how a total stranger's words like that can give you confidence in your playing and make you feel good about yourself. Even though you're still far from the summit, this kind of thing brings you to a new level and encourages you to keep climbing.

We would play parties up at SUNY Oneonta from time to time. Meeting at Club Anthony, we'd load the trailer that Tony would pull with his car. Terry's Hammond was a C3 with a Leslie tone cabinet, and it weighed a ton. The Hammond organ is an electric organ, first manufactured in 1935. Various models have been produced, most of which use sliding drawbars to specify a variety of sounds. Until 1975, Hammond organs generated sound by creating an electric current from rotating a metal Tone Wheel™ near an electromagnetic pickup, and then strengthening the signal with an amplifier so it could drive a speaker cabinet. The organ is commonly used (and associated) with the Leslie speaker cabinet. With a bench and pedalboard, the Hammond C3 weighs 425 pounds.

I would ride with Tony and Billy, who would teach me harmony parts during the four-hour ride to upstate New York. We would do "NBC" harmonies, which is the three notes of the classic NBC jingle (or "pnemonic"). Interestingly, the notes G, E, and C were chosen because the company was owned by General Electric (G.E.C.). Each guy took a note and we would sing:

*Skeeters are a hummin'*
*On a honeysuckle vine,*
*Ol' Kentucky home*
*Hmmmmmmmmmm....*

I really learned to appreciate harmony during those rides. From time to time we would invite people to come down to see the band at Anthony's. Maybe they'd be interested in booking us for more gigs or see if we were good enough for a record deal. They always passed. Only one guy was straight with us. Tony had been late for this meeting, so the guy decided to break the bad news to us and explain. "Everyone loves Tony," he said. "He's one of the greatest guys anyone has ever met. He has a fantastic voice, as big as Johnny Maestro's. Why do you guys think, with a voice like that, Tony never made it?" After he put it to us that way, we knew what the problem was. Tony was born with a deformed arm. It was smaller than normal and non-functional. Managers and agents were too concerned with the look of the band to look past Tony's arm and concentrate on his talent.

The guy told us, "Get rid of Tony, and you'll get somewhere with Billy as your singer." Tony also wore a wig—not just a hairpiece, a full-on wig, even though he wasn't bald. It was pitch black and shoulder length, and was more funny than anything else. Terry would take that wig and stick it out of the shirt buttons on his chest or have it hanging out of the zipper on his pants. Everyone else in the band had long hair, except Tony. Tony's day job was conservative, and kept him from growing his hair long. The band stuck it out with Tony, and we never got signed.

We broke up in 1966 when Billy Hennessey got drafted into the Army and was off to Vietnam. Our last gig was at Club Anthony the night before Billy was leaving. It was horribly sad, his friends were all crying and saying goodbye. From the time he took his physical to the time he left, he couldn't believe how fast it went by. He was being taken out of the only environment he ever knew. I wrote to Billy and sent him drumsticks in Vietnam; after a while I didn't hear from him anymore. I still don't know what happened to him.

# My Drum-Part 6

You can start to imagine a drummer's personality even before he takes the stage. Just the sight of his drum set tells you if he will be conservative, radical, or somewhere in between. There are no rules for a drum set. I have seen sets as small as a bass drum and snare drum to as big as four bass drums, eight toms, and three snare drums. I have seen sets with just a hihat, sets with fifteen cymbals hanging off them, and a full-on drum set with no cymbals at all. I have seen drummers using vintage drum sets and guys who use total modern, electronic sets.

You can tell the style of music a drummer will be playing before he plays by the sizes of his drums. If a set has an 18" bass drum, 13" piccolo snare, and small toms, the drummer is most likely a jazz or funk drummer. If they have a 26" bass drum with deep snare and toms, stand back, they intend to rock the house. There is no limit to the drummer's expression for color and design of the drum set. I have seen sets on the traditional side, with a natural wood grain finish, to the more radical: flames, pinup girls, skulls, and even drum sets finished in the flag of the drummer's home country. There are no rules; anything goes. Some drummers even decorate their set with stickers that express their world views.

One look and you will know if the drummer who sits behind the kit is conservative, radical, political, sexual, religious, or just plain crazy and out to have a good time. If they're not like that off the kit, they will become that when they get behind the drums. The drum set is the place they express their alter-ego. The drums are not like any other instrument; they are Carnival and Mardi Gras. They do not conform, and they have no rules. Their only limit is the drummer's imagination. They are played loud, soft, or muffled; with heads wound tight or loosened to the point of flappiness. Even a broken cymbal is used as an "effect" in the set. Different sounds have been achieved by removing the bottom heads from the toms or removing the front head of the bass drum.

How the drums are tuned is all up to how the drummer hears them. A certain sound can be achieved by using a piece of duct tape or placing a towel over the head of the drum. Often the drummer's wallet was used to change the sound of the snare drum in the studio. At one time, a sanitary napkin was used to slow down the wear of the bass drum head when struck by the beater of the pedal. Today there are specific products for the drummer's every need.

Promotional postcard for New Rock Workshop gig, 1967.

Performing with New Rock Workshop.

# The New Workshop

The New Rock Workshop was the house band at a club called My House in Plainview Shopping Center on Old Country Road, in Plainview, Long Island. It was an underage club; they had no liquor license. I had not been in a band since the Crystal Circus broke up about six months earlier. I did still have Regina as my girlfriend, but by this time I could tell I was losing her to my mistress, Music. I was deep into this new group, Cream. They had a jam-psychedelic style and their drummer, Ginger Baker, was playing differently than any other drummer had ever played. He would become my next mentor.

It was 1967 and music was changing very fast. I needed to keep up. My friend from school, Mike Baricelli, went to see the New Rock Workshop, and the next day at school he raved about them. Ronnie Levine (from the Mike Lackus days in Seaford) was now the singer and front man for the band; he no longer played drums. My old friend Mel Wach from the Rogues was playing guitar, Harry Barber was playing organ, and Richie Patrucco was playing bass (Harry and Richie were Seaford High School alumni). Mike Baricelli talked about this band in a way that made me really jealous, telling me how good they were, how popular they were becoming, how their audience was growing and growing, and that I should be in a band like this.

That night, my girlfriend Regina, Mike, and I went to see the New Rock Workshop. We were standing in line waiting to get in when Ronnie walked out. My girlfriend was surprised when he grabbed me and pulled me away. When I got back in line, they asked me what Ronnie was talking to me about. I said, "He told me his drummer is leaving and he wants me in the band." Larry, the drummer, was getting drafted. Mike's jaw dropped, I think it was the first time he realized how good I was. Now I had a new band. It probably cost me my girlfriend, but looking back, it was worth it.

As we walked through the door of My House, I knew I was walking into my new world. There was a foyer with offices on the right and another opening straight ahead with swinging saloon doors that led into the club. There were two bars that just served soda, one on the left wall, and one across the back. The stage was straight ahead. When Mel came out of the dressing room to say hi to me, I noticed he was wearing some of the hippest clothes I had ever seen, and his hair was long. This was no longer the Mel I knew from the Rogues; he looked great. When the band took the stage, they commanded attention. They had smoke machines, strobe lights, light poles with four different colors, and the sound was full and loud. Mel was playing through a Marshall amp and the sound was great. He now moved all over the stage (whereas he had stood perfectly still in the Rogues), and sounded just like the guitar player in Cream, Eric Clapton. Harry and Richie were also tight. I even thought that the drummer was great, but I never doubted for a second that I could fill his shoes. Ronnie's transition from drummer to front man was terrific. He swung around a pole that was the stage ceiling support. This was all really different for me. The excitement was uncontainable; I had never seen anything like this before. The New Rock Workshop's arrangements for songs had psychedelic breakdowns, changes in tempos, and long jams. They were similar to the Vagrants when I saw them with the Rascals.

I was so excited about the music it was easy for me to learn the songs and become part of the band. Ronnie took me to Paul Sergeant's on West 4th Street in Greenwich Village in Manhattan to shop for clothes. The New Rock's song list contained "Wake Me Shake Me" by the Blues Project, "How Could I Be Such a Fool?" and "You Didn't Try to Call Me" by the Mothers of Invention, and "Said I Wasn't Gonna Tell Nobody" and "You Got Me Hummin'" by Sam & Dave. There was another band that played My House that also did Sam and Dave's, "You Got Me Hummin'." They were called the Hassles. They had the same instrumentation as we did and a front man that also swung around that pole in the middle of the stage. Their organ player also sang; I would always say hello to him when we passed each other in the club. Even though we were in rival bands, we were still cordial. He called himself Billy Joe but his real name was Billy Joel.

The Hassles watched us and we watched them. Billy sang a song called "Colored Rain" that I loved. I thought he wrote it until someone gave me a 45 RPM promo copy called "Here We Go Round the Mulberry Bush." The flip side was "Colored Rain." It was Steve Winwood's latest single with his new band, Traffic (and I became an instant fan of that band). It was around this time that I became friendly with two other musicians who always came up to talk to me after I played: Doug Stegmeyer and Russell Javors.

The New Rock Workshop opened for a lot of acts at My House: the Critters, who had hits with "We've Got a Marrying Kind of Love," "Mr. Dieingly Sad," and "Younger Girl"; Jackie Wilson, who had hits with "Baby Work Out" and "Lonely Teardrops"; and the Soul Survivors, who did "Expressway to Your Heart." These pros all had a tremendous influence on me as I watched them perform, but the band I remember the most was a band that scared me to death the first time I saw them: the Vanilla Fudge. I had heard of the Fudge but I had never seen them. FM radio was very new at the time, and WNEW was launching their brand new, first-in-New York station. They didn't have any disc jockeys yet; they just played music. They played songs from albums that were too long for AM radio—songs that were longer than three minutes and five seconds. (The Beatles were the only ones to have a longer song played on AM radio: "Hey Jude.")

The night before the Fudge were set to play My House with the New Rock Workshop opening the show, I went to the Action House with some friends to check them out. The managers of both bands were friends and the Fudge management company ran the Action House, so I got in, even though I wasn't eighteen years old yet. When the Fudge came on, I could not believe my eyes. These guys were incredible. I was shocked. Their sound, their show, and their arrangements were all unbelievable. Their drummer, Carmine Appice, played harder and had a bigger set of drums than any drummer I had ever seen. He used a 28" bass drum. When I saw it, I knew I had to have one. (Carmine was the guy who convinced John Bonham to use a bigger bass drum when Led Zeppelin was the Fudge's opening act.) I could not believe we had to play before these guys on the following night. I didn't sleep all night.

After our show, which went really well, I stood right in front of Carmine's drums and watched everything he did. It was even more incredible than the night before, now that I could see him up close. Not too much later, I had a Ludwig burgundy sparkle set with a 24" bass drum. Not as big as Carmine's, but a big leap from a 20". Carmine influenced my playing then and still does to this day.

Danny Mazur and Irwin Mazur were brothers. Danny managed the Hassles and Irwin managed the New Rock Workshop. Irwin owned My House and had an assistant named Marvin, whose nose twitched whenever he'd lie. Marvin would tell us about the bookings he was taking care of, all the gigs we'd get, and all the money that was on the way to fill our pockets, nose twitching all the while. He was a bad liar and Ronnie and he were always fighting.

One day in school during my senior year, I got a call to go to the office. When I arrived there I saw Mel and Marvin with Mr. Peterson, the principal. They had convinced the principal to let me out of school to let me go record in the studio. By now all my teachers knew I wanted to be a musician and school was just in the way. So they let me out, with Marvin's nose twitching all the way to the car. We were on our way to Ultrasonic Studios at 149 North Franklin Street in Hempstead. Shadow Morton had produced the Vanilla Fudge albums and had recently had a falling out with the band. Shadow had produced The Shangri-la's tune "Remember (Walking in the Sand)" on which a young Billy Joel played piano. He was looking for a new project and had heard about us.

The first thing he did was play the Fudge's arrangement of "Ticket to Ride" in our headphones at volume level ten. After the entire five-minute, 40-second version, Shadow said through the talkback, "That's what you guys will sound like." We recorded the music tracks for "You Got Me Hummin'," but then Shadow reconciled with the Fudge and we never got to do the vocals or finish the song. Soon after that, the Hassles released their version of "You Got Me Hummin'" on United Artists, and it became a regional hit.

The Hassles were going strong and the New Rock Workshop just couldn't keep up. The New Rock Workshop disbanded due to the constant fights between Ronnie and management. Richie Patruco, the bass player, had a longtime heroin habit and would sometimes be so laid back he'd play a song half a bar behind the band, or he'd just fall asleep during the set. Harry had been replaced on the Hammond by a friend of Mel's because Harry was considered to "not have a good look about him." Even though Harry played great, management said we needed to replace him. Andy Bycoff came in; he couldn't play, but in management's eyes he looked better. All of this caused too much tension in the band because most of us were Harry fans.

On August 23, 1968 my friend Richie Caruso and I went to see Jimi Hendrix and the Experience at the Singer Bowl in Flushing Meadow Park, Queens. The Soft Machine, Janis Joplin with Big Brother and the Holding Company and the Chambers Brothers were also on the bill. Richie and I took dexedrine (uppers) before the show. There was a guy sitting behind us with a gravity knife that he kept flicking open. In between each act he would yell, "Bring on the electric nigger, bring on the electric nigger." Richie and I couldn't take it anymore so we decided to take a walk to the stage to check out Hendrix's equipment.

As I was looking at Mitch Mitchell's drums, I saw the Hassles' drummer John Small and Billy Joel sitting on road cases on the stage. I said, "How the hell did you get up there?" They told me, "Everyone thinks we're roadies! When the American guys ask us who we're with, we speak with English accents and they think we're with Hendrix and when the English guys ask us who we're with, we speak with our American accents and they think we're with the other bands." I said, "Nice!" Richie and I were sent back to our seats. Thank God Hendrix came out right away; the guy behind us kept yelling and flicking his knife but he changed his vocabulary. That night, between the excitement and the pills, I didn't sleep at all.

Soon after that, Harry Weber approached me. Before Billy was with the Hassles, Harry was the band's organ player. He had a drug problem and was fired from the Hassles, but wanted to start a new band. (He knew me from My House.) Because of Harry's problem, we only played once together, in my parents' basement, when we auditioned a guitar player named Russell Javors. Russell's father dropped him off in front of my parents' house with his amp and guitar. He was fifteen years old, and said he had seen me play at My House, and since that time he wanted to be in a band with me. Unfortunately, this new band Russell was auditioning for would never happen. Harry passed from this world too young, too soon.

**Playing in the summer of 1968.**

# The Detroit Wheels

In the summer of 1968, I got a call from the front office of Breakout Management. Breakout was run by Phil Baseal, who also owned the Action House and managed the Vanilla Fudge. I was asked if I would like to jam at a Breakout rehearsal studio in Oceanside with a few guys. When I showed up at the studio, there was a bass player there named Ivan Elias and the guitarist from the Vanilla Fudge, Vince Martel. This was a big deal for me; I was jamming with an actual member of the Vanilla Fudge. I was thrilled; my name and reputation were starting to take me places.

This was to be the first of many jam sessions. We riffed on blues licks and rock guitar lines. Vince was great, he just wanted to play. He had a lot of ideas and knew that more the more you play, the better you get. I, especially, was getting better. I was learning how to improvise on the drums, and go from one feel to another in the same tune. For example, we'd go from a straight feel to a shuffle, and then into a double-time shuffle, and so on. These were great lessons from a seasoned pro. The longer these jams went on, the more Ivan and I became friends. We were playing tight together—bass and drums, the foundation. I was loving this new musical road I was traveling down. I am thankful to Vince for this giant step in my musical career and what it eventually led to.

During the time I was jamming with Vince, I got a call from Rusty Day of the Detroit Wheels. The Wheels, who had risen to fame as Mitch Ryder's backup band, were touring and were now in New York. Their drummer, Johnny B. (Bananjek), was going back to Detroit to play with another band. Rusty said they had gone to Phil Baseal's office and asked if they knew of any good drummers. The person they spoke to said, "There's a kid who jams with Vince in the back room, he's pretty good." Rusty got my number and gave me a call.

I had just turned eighteen and was living at my parents' house. I didn't drive, so I told them to come to me and we'd play in my parents' basement. I didn't tell my parents until they were on the way over; I figured that way they couldn't say no. I told my mom and dad who they were, and that I had all their records. My mom liked the songs, so with my parents' blessing I was good to go. The band pulled up in a black stretch limo, pulling an orange and silver U-Haul trailer containing all their equipment. Johnny B. was still traveling with them. He got out of the car and said, "Hi, bye, and good luck" to me, and then he was off to the airport.

The band was Rusty Day on vocals and harmonica, Terry Kelly on guitar, and Jimmy McAllister on bass. Jimmy was the only original member of the Detroit Wheels. He didn't play on the records with Mitch, but somehow he owned the name Detroit Wheels. They brought their equipment into the basement and we started to play. To my surprise they were a total blues band. We did the Jimmy Reed songs "I Ain't Got You," "Ain't That Lovin' You Baby," and "Hush Hush." The band was great. They wound up staying at my house for a week and a half, sleeping in the basement and on the floor in my room. My mother cooked meals for them and we practiced every day. At night we would drive to All American Hamburgers and Carvel in Massapequa where all my friends hung out. We'd pull up in the black limo with "The Detroit Wheels" written on the front fenders.

The one thing my father questioned was when Terry Kelly went into the bathroom; he'd be in there for an hour. My father would say, "What the hell's with this guy? He's in the bathroom forever." It turned out that Terry was a junkie and he was shooting dope in my parents' bathroom. We got out of the house just before my dad caught on. We headed towards Hershey, Pennsylvania, where we had our first—and last—gig. It was four nights in a shitty club. We did all the blues numbers and the owner would come up to the stage and say, "If you don't play the hits, I'm gonna bounce you out on your ass." So we did a shitty version of "Jenny Takes a Ride." While we were there, we toured the Hershey factory, where they make all that yummy chocolate, and Rusty dropped his pants and mooned the women who were making the Hershey's kisses.

After the four nights, we drove straight to Detroit. I had never been off Long Island, so I was thrilled. They ditched the trailer in the back of somebody's house, because they'd had it for eight months and never paid for it, so they couldn't bring it back to U-Haul. Then the band broke up. I stayed at Rusty's parents' house for a few days and visited the Rouge plant, where Rusty's father worked. I had learned of the Rouge while taking auto mechanics in high school. The Rouge was an amazing place. They would start on one end of the complex with iron ore, and after many steps a brand new car would be completed at the other end. The place was huge.

Soon, however, I knew it was time to get on a plane and get home. This was the first time I had ever flown. A few months later, Rusty was back on Long Island with a new group. He teamed up with Jim McCarty (the original guitarist with the Wheels), Carmine Appice, and Tim Bogart from the Vanilla Fudge to form the group Cactus. Rusty came to visit me and my folks for dinner and told me he was going to look for a gig for me. He told me, "You better always practice and be ready." He would get me a gig and didn't want me to let him down, saying, "Don't embarrass me." A few years later, Rusty and his son were killed during a drug deal gone bad.

**Me (left) and Mitch Ryder, fall 1968.**

# Mitch Ryder

## (AKA William S. Levise, Jr.)

I n November of 1968 I was back in Seaford Long Island, still living at home. The phone rang and the voice on the other end said, "Hi I'm Ron Giordano—that's G-I-O-R-D-A-N-O—and I got your number from Rusty Day. I'm Mitch Ryder's tour manager. We're on tour and our drummer, John Siomos, has gotten sick. We need someone to fill in for him. Rusty said you were pretty good." All I kept thinking while this guy was talking was 'Rusty, you came through.' I asked Ron when he needed me. His reply was, "Tonight." I told him I didn't have a driver's license and would need to get a ride from my Dad. "Could I come in tomorrow?" I asked. He said, "That would be great."

The next day, my father dropped me and my drum kit off in front of the Mayfair Hotel on Seventh Avenue in Manhattan, where my gear was then loaded onto a bus. The bus was nothing like today's touring buses. This bus was rented from the Domenico Bus Company in New Jersey. No bunks, no front or back lounge, no bathroom, just seats like a regular city bus. When I slept, I slept across the seats with my Navy pea coat as my pillow. There was no luxury at all. As we drove to somewhere in Connecticut—they played college theaters at that time—the entire band introduced themselves to me. They were called the Spirit Feel. I felt really comfortable.

The band was big: seven-piece with rhythm section and horns. Mitch's security guard, John Romeo, and Mitch's brother Mark also rode the bus, and Paulie was the driver. Mitch was not on the first ride, he went up in a car. Jimmy Lumus, the sax player and musical director, asked me if I knew Mitch's songs, to which I replied I was a huge fan and knew them all. He told me to watch him for the stops and endings, and the band would help me along. When we got to the gig, I set up my gear and played Ginger Baker's drum beat from Cream's version of "Born Under a Bad Sign." One of the horn players came over and told me that after he heard me play that groove, he knew everything was going to be all right. We went over a few things and then it was showtime.

The show ran about two and a half hours, with John Romeo, Mitch's bodyguard, going on first. He sang a few R&B tunes that I was familiar with, and was followed by Mitch's brother Mark. These guys did cover songs by Sam & Dave and Otis Redding. The first time I saw Mitch was when he walked on stage. The show was a blur, but it went great. After it was over, I packed up my stuff, showered, and climbed back on the bus, still not having met Mitch. The band told me how good I was and that they were very pleased with the show. I couldn't believe I was playing with a guy who had hits in the Top 10. (Mitch's hits, which we played that night, included "Jenny Take a

Ride," #10 in 1965; "Devil with a Blue Dress," #4 in 1966; and "Sock it to Me Baby," #6 in 1967.) I was not only excited to just meet Mitch, but I couldn't wait to hear what he thought of the show.

With my bell-bottom jeans, green paisley Nehru shirt with long belled sleeves, and hair down to my shoulders, I was looking good and felt like I was on top of the world. As I sat staring out the window, Mitch finally jumped on the bus, full of energy, and plopped down in the seat next to me.

Mitch looked and me and said, "Did you have a good time tonight?"

I said, "Yes."

"Do you like doing this?"

"Yes."

"Would you like to do this forever?"

"Yes!" I was so excited.

He said, "Blow me!," got up from the seat, and ran to the back of the bus.

I was crushed and speechless. I had just been assaulted by a Detroit hitter! I figured that was it, I'd never play with Mitch Ryder again. No one had ever said anything like that to me before. I'd have to get myself home, and then what would I tell everyone? That Mitch hated me? I sucked? I had started feeling like the guy who always got the gig, with everyone telling me how good I was, and now I'd be going home a failure. How would I face my friends?

Overhearing the exchange, the rest of the band laughed and assured me that was just Mitch's sense of humor. I didn't believe them. As we started back to New York City, Mitch called me to the back of the bus. I figured this was it—I went back and stood in front of him. He was very calm, and while drinking a Coke, he said, "You're a good little drummer, thanks for helping out." As I turned around to go back to my seat, a smile broke across my face. I'd never forget the way I felt that night. My dreams were coming true.

I stayed on tour with Mitch for six weeks. We went up and down the East Coast, playing colleges and theaters from Vermont to Florida. When we were playing close to New York City, we headquartered ourselves at the Mayflower Hotel, and we'd get back from our gigs with plenty of time to go out to the clubs. There was a place called The Scene, owned by Steve Paul. I don't remember much about the music there, but I do remember this girl who was following me around one night. She would be right behind me every time I turned around, no matter where I went in the club. This was my first experience with a girl I didn't know. At the time, the band members were sharing hotel rooms, and I was rooming with trombonist J.D. Craine, an old road dog from Texas. I was in the room with "Miss Whatever-Her-Name-Was" when J.D. walked in. I looked up in horror, and J.D just went, "Oops," and slowly backed out the door, allowing me my first on-the-road experience. It was fantastic.

Some of the people we shared the bill with while on tour were Wilson Pickett, Rufus Thomas, and Carla Thomas. At Big Daddy's in Florida I went to see Wayne Cochran, another blue-eyed soul man. It was quite an experience for this young kid from Seaford, Long Island. To kill time on some of our longer trips, the band played cards. That's when I found out I was a bad gambler. I always lost money. Mark Ryder would always encourage me to play, telling me he would teach me. Right, he taught me how to lose my money to him! He was good at spotting a sucker. John Romeo had a portable record player and a stack of the best 45s. This was the first time I heard "Nobody's Fault but Mine" by Otis Redding. John kept saying Otis was *funky*. I asked him what he meant by that, and he said, "You know when you slip into an old pair of broken-in shoes, they're so comfortable you feel good wearing them, even though they're kinda beat up? They're funky." Comfortable, no anxiety— just *funky*: that was my life at the end of 1968.

I bought that record player from John Romeo—no doubt I paid too much for it—and used it to learn all about funk. Hanging with these guys took me into a whole new world: rhythm & blues, black music. Mitch was blue-eyed soul, but he learned from the masters. At the end of the tour I asked the guys in the band what records I should buy to learn the funk. They told me about the Meters. The time I spent on that bus shaped my drumming style and taught me about music that came from and touched the soul, thanks to Mitch Ryder.

In recent years I played with Mitch again at a Rock 'n' Roll Hall of Fame event. I was at rehearsal while my wife, Anna, was coming over in the bus from the hotel. Mitch was also on that bus. Anna noticed him and introduced herself. She said, "Hi Mitch, I'm Anna, Liberty's wife." Mitch replied, "He's famous because of everything he learned from me."

# My Drum-Part 7

For many, the drum has been a safe place to hide from the routine of daily life. I have friends in the New York Police Department that play drums; they are part of the NYPD drum corps. We have played together numerous times, including at one of my clinics. I went on a drive-along with them one day. This is when they take a civilian with them in a patrol car for their full shift. They took me and two members of my family, we put on bulletproof vests, and went into some of the neighborhoods that were part of their patrol. Seeing the conditions the people live in gave me a clearer picture of the message from rap music. I came from a white privileged world and had been sheltered from this kind of living. What the real rappers are telling us is what it's like to be a person of color in America.

Much of modern music was born in the ghetto or on the streets. Musical styles were created by a sax-playing junkie in a smoke-filled club in Harlem; a hillbilly country boy from Tupelo, Mississippi; a group of singers under a lamp post in the Bronx, New York, with no instruments at all; four guys from a shipping town called Liverpool, England; a house converted into a studio in the ghetto of Detroit, Michigan; or a place like where we were standing in our bulletproof vests: the projects of Bedford Stuyvesant, Brooklyn, New York.

We went to the roof in an elevator that stank of urine. When we got there, they told us this was where gang members took target practice, did drugs, and sometimes brought nonconsenting women. The cops said that a few of their co-workers had been killed when they responded to a call and were hit with everything from bowling balls to refrigerators that were thrown from rooftops. We visited Central Booking, in downtown Brooklyn, where arrested suspects are taken before they are arraigned. It's so depressing that even the cops hate being there. At the end, I asked them how they deal with all this stress on a daily basis. They told me that they think about their drum; how they can't wait to get to play again. The thought of their drum waiting for them gets them through the toughest of days; all of the ugliness is washed away when they are concentrating on the rhythm.

**Living in Baltimore, 1969.**

# 13

# Baltimore

A few weeks after I left Mitch, his tour ended, and so did his band, the Spirit Feel. I got a call from J.D. Crane and Jimmy Lumis, the two horn players from Mitch's band. They told me they were starting a new band. They had a manager, Dave Hutchinson, who owned a club called Hollywood Park just outside of Baltimore. They asked me if I was interested in joining the band, and said that there was a place for me to live right above the club; J.D. was living there already. I agreed. I packed my drums in my dad's Chevy station wagon, and, because I still had no driver's license, I got my friend, Linda "Lulu" Docherman to drive. Richie Caruso, my best friend at the time, also came along for the ride.

When we arrived at the club, we thought we had to have been in the wrong place. It was a dump. Built in 1910, it looked like it hadn't had any work done since then. There was a junkyard next door that sat on a polluted river. As I walked in., the club part of the building wasn't bad; it was on the main floor. The bar was in the front of the place and it was the first thing you saw. It was horseshoe shaped, so you could sit on three sides and watch the action. On the far side of the bar was the dance floor, with tables lining the left and right of it. The stage was straight ahead. Upstairs were the living quarters, with four bedrooms. One was J.D.'s, which had a sign on the door that read, "Man does not live by bread alone. He must have marmalade." Only one of the other bedrooms actually had a bed in it. There was a bathroom at the end of the hall that was pretty gross.

The entire building was sagging in the middle. If you put a ball at either end of the floor it would roll and settle in the middle of the building. When I arrived, J.D. was there, and I met Dave. Richie, Linda, and I got something to eat at the greasy spoon down the block before they left. When they drove away, I looked at my drums in their cases and, quoting Oliver Hardy, said, "Here's another fine mess you've gotten me into."

The gigs weren't bad. The band was good and we quickly learned enough songs to play three sets. We played every Wednesday, Thursday, Friday, Saturday, and Sunday night. During the day we worked on new material. The interesting thing about playing the club was that there were always two bands. When it was time for one band to be done with their set, and time for the other to start, a fire siren would blast. I'm talkin' a real siren, one that would be mounted on a fire truck. This notified the band that was on the stage that it was time to play the last song of their set, and it was time for the next band to get to the stage. The next band would start with whatever song the previous band had been playing.

Sometimes the drummer from the other band would jump off the drums, lay on the dance floor, and light his farts on fire. I got so sick one night I kept throwing up off the side of the stage. Time off was spent getting high. Mike, our singer, had a farm out in the country, and we'd go out there to get high and just groove on the setting. Other times at night we'd get high in one of the rooms upstairs from the club. After we smoked, we'd take a plastic dry-cleaning bag and tie it in knots, hook it to a hanger, and hang it from the ceiling. Then we'd place a bucket of water underneath it. We'd light the bag on fire from the bottom and sit and watch the melting plastic fall off in clumps and drop into the bucket. The flames fell at different sizes and in different time increments. It would make a "whoosh" sound when it was falling; the higher it fell from, the longer and louder the "whoosh" would be. It would fizzle out and make a 'psssssssshut' sound when it hit the water. It would hold our attention for hours, as the knots in the bag would slow down the melting process .

One day I got a phone call from my mother. She told me my grandmother (my dad's mom) had slipped into a coma. Everyone in the family had gone to see her and my father wanted me to come home to see her before she passed away. I had to work, but I said I'd be there as soon as I could. I was able to get home six days later. My grandmother had shown no movement or reaction to anything since she had gone into the coma. When I walked in, she reached up and touched my hair and said, "Liberty's home." At the time, I had long hair and a mustache, but she saw me with short hair and clean shaven; she said she was happy that I shaved. She stroked my face and told me how happy she was to see me, then she slipped back into the coma. Everyone there that day was sobbing, it was unbelievable. The next day she died. I loved my grandmother; she was one of the greatest women I have ever known. She always held me close to her when I was young and would tell me in her broken English, "Watch out for the girls; they'll get you in trouble!" I was the last one she saw, and everyone felt she waited until I came home to die. A few days later, I returned to Baltimore. I believe my grandmother is my guardian angel.

One night, Skip, our guitar player, had a party at his apartment. The party was me, Skip, J.D., Jimmy, and his girlfriend. Skip had some Grateful Dead acid, which had a peace sign on it. We all did half a tab each. I had done LSD before with Richie and Linda, and we'd drive to the TWA Terminal at JFK Airport because of the long tunnel in the terminal. Everyone went there when they were tripping. The acid made everything beautiful: the lights, the colors; it felt futuristic. But this trip would be different. After we dropped the acid we smoked some pot. I was really high from the pot when I felt a sensation come over me. It was a high that shot right past the pot. I grabbed on to Skip and said, "I'm getting too high." He started laughing. I said, "You don't understand, I'm getting too high." I was having a hard time handling it. I was freaking out.

Jimmy gave me some thorazine, which is given to mental patients to calm them down. I went into a bedroom and laid down, and that's where the colors started. Everything was beautiful. I put my head under the covers and it was like a long white tunnel; my hand turned into a chicken's foot. When Jimmy's girlfriend came in to check on me, her blonde hair was turning red, blue, purple, and gold. Her face looked like the sun; she looked like the pictures of the Beatles that were in *Life* magazine. I finally fell asleep. When I woke up the next day, the colors were gone but I was still high. I was high for a week; I was getting really scared. I flew home and my dad picked me up from the airport. He could tell something was wrong with me. He kept asking me if I was alright. I kept telling him I was okay.

When we got back to Seaford we passed St. William the Abbott Church, where my family were members. My dad asked if I wanted to go in and pray. I said okay. We sat in the church where I attended catechism, made my first holy Communion, my Confirmation, and where my girlfriend Regina and I were thrown out of mass one Sunday because I was doing my Felix Cavaliere imitation on the bench in front of me to the sounds of the organ for Sunday morning worship. My father and I sat silent for about ten minutes. He asked if I felt better and if I was ready to go. I said yes. When we got outside, he asked, "Is there something you want to tell me?" I said, "Yes, but let's go back inside." We sat down in a pew and I told him that I had done LSD, that I had been high for a week, and I was scared. I couldn't believe I was telling him this because he said that if I ever did drugs he would kill me. I looked at him and said, "Are you going to kill me now?" He started to cry. "I just lost my mother," he said. "I don't want to lose my son, too." He held me while he cried. I said, "I always thought you'd kill me if I took any drugs." He said, "I knew it would eventually happen, because of the business you are getting into."

After a few days home, I felt whole again. I returned to Baltimore only to tell the band that I was quitting. My dad drove down to get me. In the months that I was in Baltimore I had twisted my right ankle in a pothole and had to play the bass drum with my left foot, got the flu so badly that I threw up off the side of the stage after every song, got drunk, got high, and got to use the rubber my father had put in my wallet before I left home. But I did learn another lesson on how to play. Walter Bailey, the bass player, taught me how to lay back. He advised me to hold the sticks behind center and grip them loosely.

A few months later I went back to Baltimore to play with another band, the Legend. We all lived in a band house with our gear set up in the garage. I guess I didn't learn my lesson, because I had another bad trip. This one was a "thought and anxiety" trip. What if I get drafted? What if my girlfriend breaks up with me? That kind of insecure shit. I leveled the trip out by crushing and ingesting Contact cold capsules and finally passing out. I stayed a month, but the whole time I was thinking, "This sucks. Why am I here?" I did discover a few new things, like baked bologna with maple syrup and American cheese melted on top of apple pie.

One of the guys in the band was in the Army reserves and had to report to Fort Hamilton in Brooklyn every two weeks. I packed up my drums and hopped a ride with him one week. He dropped me off at my parents' house and I never went back.

# My Drum-Part 8

My drum has enabled me to escape emotionally from a world of hurt. I can sit behind them with a set of headphones on and play to a tune and be transported to another time and place. When a relationship broke up in my life, I could sit behind my drum set and say, "No matter how bad you broke my heart, you cannot stop me from playing my drum." Music allows a person self-expression. Everything from dancing a few steps to someone yelling, "Turn that shit off!" is an expression of how someone is feeling the music. Music is a gift. If someone were to take away that gift, it would be the same as stealing a soul's very expression. It has been said, "If you want to know the situation in a country, don't ask the politicians; ask the poets and the musicians." Music is one of the truest forms of freedom.

**Performing with Richie Supa, 1969.**

# 14

# Supa's Jamboree

I became friends with Joe Stetz, who was a frequent patron at My House. In 1969 Joe opened a clothing store called Imagination Plus in Massapequa. I needed money, so I worked there a few hours a week. One day a guy came in with a bunch of albums under his arm. He asked me if I would like to buy one for two dollars. The cover was plain white except for the words *Get Back to Toronto*. I took a shot and bought it, and when I got it home and opened it, it had titles that I had never seen before. Typed on the label of the record was I.P.F. Records presents *Get Back to Toronto*.

Side One
1. Peace Message/Get Back
2. Teddy Boy
3. On Our Way Back Home
4. All I Want is You

Side Two
1. I Got a Feeling
2. Let It Be
3. Don't Let Me Down
4. Sweet and Lovely Girl
5. Get Back
6. When You Walk
7. Christmas Message

This was a few months before the May release of the Beatles' *Let It Be* in the states. I put it on my record player and what I heard changed my life. Sure enough it was the Beatles rehearsing new material—and it sucked. They sounded like shit. Songs were just being worked up. Up until this point I thought groups went in the studio and just recorded greatness—especially the Beatles—but here they were playing unenthusiastically, George was singing flat, and they played "Teddy Boy" so much that John started to sing, "Swing your partner dosey-doe." For the first time in my life I thought, "I can do that! I'm already that bad; actually I'm a little better than that!"

This album showed me that it takes work—hard work—to make great music. I wanted that. I quit my job at the store—I was never a very good salesman anyway—and just listened to music. What made a song so great? Why did the drummer play something seemingly simple when I thought he could play something flashier, more technical, or "better?" I had a lot to learn, but careful listening taught me great lessons. I discovered that the drummer, whether it was Ringo or any other drummer in a band I liked, played to complement the song. Some of the drummers on my favorite records were studio drummers, like Hal Blaine, who was a master at playing for the song in different styles. He played on so many hits that later in life, I was crushed when I found out that Hal Blaine was actually six of my favorite drummers. Bobby Graham was another one. Bobby was the English version of Hal. In fact, studio drummer Andy White replaced Ringo on "Love Me Do" and "P. S. I Love You." Luckily, Ringo proved himself in the end. Gary Chester was another, playing on hundreds of songs for bands such as the Coasters, the Monkees, and the Lovin' Spoonful, to name a few. I learned from these masters, and others, teaching incognito.

One day I stopped by the store to see Joe, and he mentioned that he had a friend who was putting together a band. Richard Goodman, AKA "Super Jew," AKA "Supa" was the singer/guitarist in the Rich Kids. The Rich Kids were one of those legendary Long Island bands, up there with the Fudge, the Illusion, and the Vagrants. I had seen the Rich Kids play once and I was blown away by their theatrics on stage. Their set closer was a version of "Hey Joe." Psychedelic lights would swirl around while powerful guitar riffs got louder and louder, and then Supa would get shot by an unseen gun and fall off the stage (into a roadie's arms, of course). Joe said Supa was done with the Rich Kids and was looking to start a new band. Music had changed from the psychedelic sound to the more natural country-rock being played by Credence Clearwater Revival and The Band.

Joe said Supa was still looking for a drummer and asked if I was interested. When I said I was, Joe called Supa on the spot, and put me on the phone with him. Supa asked me a bunch of questions: "How old are you?" "Where do you live?" and then, "Who have you played with?" I told him about new New Rock Workshop, to which he disinterestedly replied, "Yeah." I told him I had jammed with Vince Martel from the Fudge. He gave the same unenthused "yeah." Finally I told him I had just gotten off the road with Mitch Ryder. This got his attention. "You were on the road with Mitch Ryder?" he responded. I realized that Mitch was my key to opening the doors I couldn't even knock on before. I had a serious resume. Supa asked me to meet him in a rehearsal space he had and to bring a bass player, if I knew one. I called Ivan Elias from the jams with Vince Martel. We met Supa in the basement of a store in a strip mall in Massapequa on Merrick Road, and jammed for hours.

Supa already had a guitar player, Howie Emerson, and we recruited John Hipps on piano through an ad Supa had placed in *The Village Voice* newspaper. We practiced every day. Supa was turning out lots of material, as he had landed a deal with Paramount Records. One day, Supa told us that as a goof he was going to try out for the Broadway show *Hair*. He went, auditioned, and he got the part. Supa was in *Hair* for a few months, and we all couldn't believe he let it all hang out in front of a live audience. His character, Burger, had a nude scene. He continued to practice with us (with his clothes on) and write songs. Things were going really well, and then Supa got his draft notice. Vowing that nothing would stop him from making music, he went through the tests that were required, failed his psychological exam, and was rejected from military service. It was the summer of 1969, and we hadn't started to record yet.

On the day before my nineteenth birthday in August, my draft notice arrived. My father was at Jones Beach with my family. Walking up to him with my crumpled draft papers in hand, I said, "You said you fought the war to end all wars and now they want me!" I threw the papers at him and stood there, more scared than angry, as if he could do something about it. Picking the papers up off the ground, he handed them back to me and said, "Go take the physical; they probably won't even want you."

My dad dropped me off in Freeport and a bus took me to Fort Hamilton in Brooklyn for my physical. I kept telling myself that I would try as hard as I could to beat this, but if I did get drafted I would not fight the system and would do my best as a soldier. Supa had told my father, "He's gotta get out! He's gonna be big, this will ruin everything."—but my father couldn't care less what Supa had to say. I took the physical and I failed. I was classified 4F, medically and mentally unfit for service. Women and children would go before I did; I was that low on the list. This was the highest rejection possible, but as far as I was concerned I couldn't have done any better. That day changed my life; I became a man. In Vietnam that same month, 510 young guys about my age were killed in action.

My dad had been right. Both my parents cried tears of joy when I told them the Army didn't want me. Vietnam and the draft made me realize that there was something out there that was much bigger than me, and that reality was a lot different than my limited definition up until that time. Coming face to face with the fact that there was a force out there that could, at a moment's notice, pull you out of everything you knew, changed my sense of security. In fact, I realized that there really isn't any such thing as total security. When I saw the guys that were chosen to go crying and shaking and in total disbelief, I realized that life isn't something you take for granted—and I would never take it for granted again.

I realize now that in the encounter at Jones Beach with my father, I was telling a man who jumped into Normandy on D-Day and fought in the Battle of the Bulge that he wasted his time. Speaking from the little world that I thought revolved around me, I was telling him that his war had apparently been a failure, and that he was a failure. What he told me in his one-sentence response was, in essence, "Be a man, go do your duty like me and my brothers." When he said that they wouldn't want me, he was almost saying, "You don't know how good you have it, you ungrateful, disrespectful punk." I was so self-involved that I didn't realize that the mere fact that I was standing there, with my long hair and bellbottoms, at the age of 19, living a life whose most disastrous moments were bad acid trips or a broken heart, was proof enough that not only was his war a success, but that my father was a hero.

I was so far out there that his desire for me not to go was even greater than my own. I couldn't understand that if I had to go, my father would be fighting a war every day at home, and would die of a broken heart if I were killed, just like all the other parents whose children went—and just like my neighbors and friends that I never saw again, or the ones who did come back wearing necklaces draped with war souvenirs or dog tags from their buddies who died in their arms.

Back in Long Island, we were playing a lot. We played clubs like Leones, Zeros, and one night even the Barge in the Hamptons, where the Rascals played. I was thrilled. After our gig at the Barge, we were up on the top deck smoking hashish. When it came to my turn to suck on the pipe, I accidently flipped it over and a hot piece of hash fell off the deck onto a blanket. Looking down, we could see that the blanket was now smoldering. Racing downstairs, we found the blanket in flames, and threw water on the fire just in time. When I think about it, we should have let the Barge burn. Imagine the press we would have gotten! "Supa's Jamboree Burns Down the Barge." Now that's overnight success.

Supa was shopping for producers and was meeting with Buddy Buie, who worked out of Studio 1 in Atlanta, Georgia. Buddy made all the Classics IV hits, including "Spooky" and "Stormy." He came to New York to meet the rest of the band, and we had lunch at a Chinese restaurant in Manhattan. Buddy had a deep Southern drawl and defined "good ol' boy." When we got our menus, he wanted to know what a pu pu platter was. Well, the only time we Long Island boys had eaten Chinese was when our moms would order takeout if there was a blackout and they couldn't cook, so none of us knew what a pu pu platter was either. Buddy ordered it anyway. When it came to the table it looked delicious, but we were puzzled by the blue flame burning in the middle. We thought there was something wrong with it, like they forgot to put the fire out before they brought it to the table. So Buddy decided to put it out with his cloth napkin. As he was fanning the flame, of course the napkin went ablaze. He kept waving it over his head, making the flames worse and scaring all the suits that were in there for their power lunches. The Chinese waiters came running at Buddy, yelling in Chinese, while, in his deepest Southern drawl

Buddy was saying, "Now wait just a minute, hold yer horses,"—to which the waiters were yelling, "Hoses? We have no hoses!" They told us, "You go now." That was the end of our power lunch, but Buddy had a great time and agreed to produce the record.

The album, *Supa's Jamboree*, was recorded in Buddy's Studio One in Doraville, Georgia. Supa had flown down to Georgia a week early, while the rest of us drove. We took turns driving, with each guy taking shifts of a hundred miles. The plan was for Supa to cut two tracks with studio musicians. These musicians had just finished recording an album under the name the Atlanta Rhythm Section: J.R. Cobb, Barry Bailey, Paul Goddard, Robert Nix, Dean "Ox" Daughtry, and Rodney Justo. Their album was engineered by Rodney Mills, who would also engineer Supa's album, and were also previously known as part of the Classics IV. They toured with Roy Orbison as the Candymen and kept the name when they recorded albums on their own. Buddy had worked and written songs with these guys before, and felt confident with them. On Supa's album they recorded "Burned" and "Unwritten Words." Buddy felt these two songs were really important and wanted these guys to play on them.

Buddy wasn't familiar with us yet; he had never worked with us before. The band and I cut the rest of the tracks on the album. Barry Bailey and JR Cobb of the Atlanta Rhythm Section played guitar with us on some of the tracks. For two weeks we were all cooped up in two rooms at a local Holiday Inn, eating breakfast every morning at the Waffle House. We worked late hours and I often fell asleep in the studio's offices, which were upstairs. The drugs of choice were hashish and alcohol. One night, Buddy was mixing a track and we all got so stoned that Buddy had to stop the session. He kept sticking his fingers in his ears and violently moving them around over and over again until he got so frustrated that he yelled, "That's it! We gotta stop, I can't hear anymore." When he was stoned, Buddy couldn't hear anything, but he'd often say "This shit is so good it ought to be illegal." The bass player with Atlanta Rhythm Section, Paul Gaddard, was a real good ol' boy. He would come to the studio to record, plug his bass directly into the console, open a Styrofoam cooler filled with ice, take out a bottle of vodka and a bottle of tonic water, mix himself a drink, put on his bass, sit in a chair and say, "Okay, I'm ready." He'd sit and play all night.

After the Supa's Jamboree album was finished, the band drove back to New York, while Supa stayed to mix the album with Buddy. When I got home, I was told that my mother's son from her first marriage, Frankie, who was in the Navy and stationed in Seattle, had been hit by a car and killed. My mother was not able to go to the wake, she didn't find out about his death until two weeks after it had happened. At the time of his accident, she was in the hospital having surgery. Frankie left a wife and a daughter, Tracy. My mother, to this day, has never met Tracy. Frankie's father, my mother's first husband, said that if Tracy ever sought out her grandmother, she'd be taken out of his will. The man was still haunting my mom.

Supa flew to New York a week later and we went right into tour rehearsals. The Supa's Jamboree tour was done in one Dodge van for equipment and a Volvo station wagon for passengers and luggage. That Volvo was packed tight; at least five guys with luggage. One guy would drive from gig to gig while the rest of the guys in the car would pass a bottle around. I drank too much Jack Daniels one night and puked all over the side of the car while it was in motion. It never stopped. Basically, we had a rolling barroom. When we did stay in hotels, which was hardly ever, we stayed in cheap ones. We played college field houses or anyplace they'd put us; we played one gig in a cafeteria. We also got to open for Grand Funk Railroad and the James Gang.

After a Grand Funk gig in Cleveland in November of 1971, the van and Volvo were headed back to Long Island for a break. We had been out for two or three weeks, and I was looking forward to getting home. It was snowing really badly when we left, so Howie, who was very paranoid, opted to stay in a hotel and fly home the next day, which turned out to be a very wise decision. I drove the van with Flip, who was one of the roadies, in the passenger seat. Supa and the rest of the band were in the Volvo. The snow was getting worse but we headed out on Route 80 anyway. Flip and I were singing songs—mostly the oldies we grew up on—when I hit a patch of black ice and the van went out of control. I tried to keep it on the road but I couldn't. As I went off the road the van hit a mile marker, went airborne and dove nose first into the side of a ditch. It flipped three times up the incline and three times back down; settling in the ditch. As we tumbled, I thought that this was death and I would just tumble through eternity. That's when I remember screaming; I was terrified. When the van stopped, I was on the floor between the front bucket seats covered in glass, snow, and dirt. I felt warm fluid all over my face. Flip saw it coming and had put his hands flat on the roof and his feet on the dashboard. He was able to roll with the van. The equipment had flown out the back and was lying in the snow.

The Volvo pulled up behind us and the guys came out and saw the van and ran down to it. They sat me upright in the driver's seat with the door open. Supa put me on his back with my arms wrapped around his neck and carried me up the embankment. He helped me into the passenger's seat of the Volvo. A tractor trailer truck had stopped ahead of us and, through a blur, I could see his trailer lights blinking. The driver came to the car and said that there was a cop car at the next exit. I could hear him tell Supa that he would radio ahead on his CB, tell them what happened, and they'd wait for us so we could follow them to a hospital. My vision was so blurred I couldn't see the truck driver; I could only hear his voice. Supa put me in the Volvo and followed the cops to Bashline Hospital in Grove City, Pennsylvania. On the way I asked Supa if I had been cut anywhere. He said my face was starting to swell up.

When I got to the hospital, I was able to walk, but threw up on the way in from swallowing so much blood. When I got into the emergency room, they cut off my shirt and my sweater because they couldn't fit it over my head. It turned out that I hit the steering wheel with my face, but the impact was so fast that no skin was broken, it was all internal. I had what was called "a facial blowout." My nose was broken, my top jaw was broken away from my skull, and my left eye had fallen into my sinus pocket because the bone that held it up was smashed. I was bleeding from my eyes, nose, mouth, and ears. They had to wait three days to operate because my head was so swollen. The resident doctor couldn't handle the complicated fractures, so they called in a specialist. Dr. Jack Fassenger, a thirty-five-year-old oral surgeon, came in. While he looked in my eyes with his light he asked if I had any insurance. I said no. He said, "Bummer." The hospital not being exactly state of the art, he had to bring equipment from his office. The operation on my face took four and a half hours. Because I had no insurance, the doctor felt bad and only charged me $800.00. I was told that if I was brought to a New York City hospital, I would have needed several specialists to do what this one man did alone.

Supa and the band stayed overnight on the night of the crash and then came to see me before they set off for home. Meanwhile, the doctors had called my parents and informed them that I had been in an accident and had a few bruises on my face, but I was alright. They were on their way to pick me up. My mother, father, and sister arrived later that day. When my mother and father walked into my hospital room, my mother immediately fainted. My sister was in shock and, in her surprise, jerked her mouth open so fast that she altered her jaw alignment. My father just couldn't believe it. At this point, I hadn't seen myself since before the accident.

I stayed in the hospital about seven days. About three days after my surgery, my mother walked me into the bathroom in my room. I looked in the mirror. All I could think of was that I would have to go live in a bell tower like Quasimodo. I was hideously ugly and I thought I would never look normal again. My time had run out in the hospital; I had to leave because my dad was paying out of pocket. I flew home with my mother while my father and sister drove. My jaw was wired shut, with wires coming out of my head to hold my face onto my skull, and six feet of gauze was stuffed into my left nasal sinus to hold up a plastic implant that was to replace the bone that held up my eye. There was tape attached to the wires coming out of my head and a safety pin hooked on to the gauze so they wouldn't slide into my face. All this would eventually have to be taken out.

People couldn't look at me without making a face. I was turned over to the top oral surgeon in New York. My mother and I were sitting in a doctor's office about two weeks after the operation and a woman in the waiting room kept looking at me and taking deep breaths; as she exhaled she turned her head away and said, "Oh my God." My mother finally had enough and looked at the woman and said, "You should have seen him two weeks ago. He looks good now!" People who knew me could not imagine how I was ever going to look like myself again. My aunt would come to me and put holy water on my face. Probably worst of all, for the first time in my life, I doubted that I would ever play drums again.

Supa's Jamboree broke up after the accident. We never toured again, and the record died because Paramount Records went out of business. Supa did his next album solo. He was becoming known more as a songwriter than a performer. Other artists were beginning to cover Supa's songs. "Stone County Wanted Man," which was on the *Jamboree* album, was covered by Johnny Winters, and "City Sunday Morning" was covered by B.J. Thomas. Later, Supa wrote and performed with Aerosmith; he wrote "Chip Away the Stone" and "Amazing," and co-wrote "Pink" with Steven Tyler.

Supa now heads a detox center in Florida called Recovery Unplugged, which is based around recovery through music. We are still very close. I love him and call him brother.

# My Drum-Part 9

I believe the center of a human being is the heart. If music comes from the heart, then it must be at the center of your life. You will never achieve greatness if you are unwilling to accept that. My love for drumming starts in my heart. I can't help it; I must drum. I feel in my soul what my heart has created, and I express it and bring it to life with my body. My body is a vessel that carries the rhythm. I've got rhythm like others have the mind to create stories, or the patience and passion to teach. It has always been there, and it will always be there. It's mine, given to me by a higher power. I am so powerful in music that when musicians gather as a group to play with me, they are only as good as I am. When I am aligned with the music and myself, I am the rhythm, the center of all music—and yet I never feel completely aligned until I am playing with other great musicians. I believe a band is only as good as its drummer, because I believe the music starts there.

# 15

# Wedding Bands

Aband is playing a wedding. There's a saxophonist, a guitarist, a bassist, a keyboardist, a singer, and a drummer. The singer has to go to the bathroom. He's gone so long that the sax player tells the guitar player to go look for him. The guitar player doesn't come back, so the sax player tells the bass player to go look for the guitar player and the singer. The bass player doesn't come back, either, so the sax player then sends the keyboard player to find the bass player, guitar player, and singer. He doesn't return, so the sax player decides to go look for them all himself— leaving the drummer alone. One of the guests walks up to the drummer and asks, "Can you play Misty?" The drummer answers, "I am."

A band is only as good as its drummer, but a drummer alone can't get out of his basement. A drummer is dependent on other people for his entire career.

After my accident, I was through with the drums. I wanted nothing to do with music anymore—and I especially did not want to tour. Russell Javors and Ivan Elias would always come over to my house and encourage me to play. "No way," I told them. "I'm done." I was back to looking like myself again; actually, I think I looked better than I did before the accident. Now engaged to my new girlfriend, I started looking for a "real job." I tried to get work as an electrician, because I took electrical shop in high school. I wanted a union job, but it was impossible to get unless you were grandfathered in. Lawn maintenance was where I ended up, which wreaked havoc on my newly healed sinuses. So I quit.

I then tried to work for a company that made yarn cutters for automatic loom machines. The guy I worked with had what you'd call a "Napoleon complex"; he was about four feet, ten inches tall and always wanted to fight. I quit. Then I started working for my cousin building kitchen cabinets. While I was attaching hinges to the cabinets with an electric drill, the chuck suddenly caught my hair, which had grown past my shoulders at the time, and rolled it up to my head. The drill had to be cut out and I lost a clump of hair. I quit. Next I found a job working with Ivan in a place called Falla Mail Man. They put together those annoying envelopes of junk mail that you still receive every now and then, the ones you throw out without even opening. I found the same thing always happened with all these jobs. When I drove to work, I had the radio on and the music would be calling me back. So once again, I quit.

Bob Rey, a friend from high school, played drums with the Gus Colletti Orchestra at a catering hall, the Naragansett Inn in Lindenhurst, Long Island.

The term "orchestra" was used loosely; it was just your usual wedding band. Gus was an Italian favorite and everyone who ran the place had an Italian last name. I think they may all have been connected to the social order of the "broken nose." Bob had asked me to sit in for him a few times, but I told him I was done drumming. Still, he kept trying to get me to play. After rejecting him about half a dozen times, he came to me one day and just told me, "I booked you on a date. You have to play." I thought to myself, "Have I just been made an offer I couldn't refuse?"

The gig was with the Sunny D Orchestra, another house band, that was looking for a new drummer. I'm guessing the old drummer was so old he died. Anyway, Bob lent me a tux, shirt, and bowtie. With my hair in a ponytail, I set off to play "someone's wedding." On the way to the hall I was thinking, "What am I doing? I played with Mitch Ryder. People heard me on the radio just a few months ago when the local Long Island station, WLIR, played Supa's Jamboree! This is the worst career move I have ever made." The thought of simply not showing up crossed my mind, but I kept thinking how I'd be letting Bob down. I figured what the hell, and continued on to the hall, where I met the band.

The average age of the band members seemed to be about 102 years old. They consisted of a chain-smoking, scotch-drinking plumber on sax, a trumpet player who probably couldn't blow a bubble if he was chewing a mouthful of Bazooka, and an accordion player who could barely pick up the accordion (but claimed to have played on "Tennessee Waltz" by Patty Paige). Sunny D was one of the managers of the Naragansett Inn, so he would come in and out of the room to sing while showing rooms and hosting potential clients, and he'd wear an array of different colored tuxedos with frilly shirts. My favorite was his powder blue tux; the sight of it had me thinking, "If I'm not dreaming, please shoot me." The whole thing seemed ridiculous; I couldn't believe I was involved with these guys.

When we got to the bandstand, the trumpet player turned to me and said, "The bride wants us to start with a merengue." I thought to myself, "A merengue? What the hell is a merengue?" Up until that point I thought merengue came in a pie and was served for dessert. This was the beginning of my education. I learned merengues, bossa novas, and all kinds of ethnic music. I played Sinatra, Louie Prima, and Glenn Miller. The "old timers" in the band turned out to be some of the greatest guys and the greatest music teachers I had ever met. The wedding band was filling a hole: my true desire to play. I learned a ton on the job and stayed at the Naragansett Inn for two and a half years.

Eventually, the band wanted to add a bass player, so I got Ivan the gig, but he soon left to play with a group called Scandal, so I recruited the guy who had been dating my sister, Doug Stegmeyer, to replace him. I broke my engagement off with my girlfriend because I realized I wasn't ready to get married. I spent every weekend at the Inn, started to date the waitresses, and found out how big the back seat in my new '57 Chevy really was. I even got a weekday gig working with the plumber from the band. I actually spent more time with him than his wife; I was with him seven days a week.

On the weekends we would make money playing weddings, and during the week I was plumbing. I learned more about music in those two and a half years than ever before. Other things I learned included lots of facts about plumbing, payday is on Friday, shit flows downhill, and it's bad to bite your fingernails. I also joined the Musicians Union Local 802. I was happy: I was making money—even though it was only about $35 a gig— and I was back into drumming. There is truth in the words spoken by my friend and fellow drummer Kenny Aronoff: "Never turn down a gig. You never know who you might meet and what you will get out of it." I got an education that I took with me and continue to use today.

Oh, and I met some pretty crazy ladies.

**Afternoon lunch, Topper style, with Russell (standing) and Doug.**

# 16

# Topper

Russell Javors: Guitar and Vocals
Howard Emerson: Lead Guitar, Slide Guitar, Dobro
Doug Stegmyer: Bass and Vocals
Liberty DeVitto: Drums and Vocals
David Brown: Guitar
Dean Kraus: Keyboards

Right after my car accident, Russell was persistent. He would constantly call me and talk about music for hours, having not taken the hint that I was done with music. He'd leave handwritten notes in my room when I wasn't home, saying things like, "Our hands are our tools; without our tools we are nothing." From the first time he saw me play at My House in Plainview, he said, he knew he had to be in a band with me. The other "hands" Russell was referring to were Doug Stegmeyer and Howard Emerson. Little did I know at the time that Russell would be the biggest influence in getting me back to playing the drums, and I will always be indebted to him for that.

It had been about six months since my accident. Recuperating beautifully, I was feeling human again—but I still hadn't played the drums. (This was still before I started playing in the wedding band.) Russell invited me to his birthday party, saying a bunch of his friends were going to jam in his parents' backyard. "Okay," I thought, "Maybe if I go see him play he'll leave me alone." At the party, what I saw was pure rock 'n' roll. There were no strobe lights or smoke machines, just pure Rolling Stones, Small Faces rock 'n' roll. Russell did a version of "Blackbird" in which he sang and his friend Kenny Romanowski played a ripping guitar solo after every vocal line. The other guy playing guitar equally as good, if not better, than Kenny, was Howard Emerson. Howard also played slide. Doug Stegmeyer was playing bass, and Dean Kraus was on keyboards.

Russell was also a songwriter, and his style was black comedy. His lyrics were funny but had a depressing overtone. He knew the guys he needed to play those songs and bring them to life, and his dream band was him, me, Doug, and Howard. Although I was very impressed at what I heard that day, I was still not ready to give in to the music. Russell would constantly drop over to see me and would play songs he had written; bizarre songs like "Ugly Lady," about an ugly couple that fall in love and have an ugly child.

*Ugly lady, let me take you home*
*Make a poor man your friend*
*It's a cold but ugly smile that paints your face*
*Turn away, turn away, turn away*

*You're not lookin' good.*

*Western Union, send a telegram*
*I'm in love with you, stop.*
*It's a cold but ugly smile that paints your face*
*Turn away, turn away, turn away*
*You're not looking good.*

*She closed the light, she hit the switch with her good hand*
*She's lookin' at me, she got the smile on her face*
*Her back hit the sheets, she couldn't sleep*
*Lookin' at me*

*Ugly baby, you've got mommy's eyes*
*Thank the Lord she can see*
*It's a cold but ugly smile that paints your face*
*Turn away, turn away, turn away*
*You're not looking good*

*She closed the light; she hit the switch with her good hand*
*She's lookin' at me, she got the smile on her face*
*Her back hit the sheets, she couldn't sleep*
*Lookin' at me*

Then there was "One Arm Man," the story of a guy who is going to get his arm amputated, telling his girlfriend that it will be okay.

*I went down, down to the station*
*You know the time had come for an examination*
*My left arm was green and cold and crooked*
*I waved goodbye, got on the train,*
*I knew I'd never wave goodbye again*

*I'll just have to try and overlook it.*
*Susan my darling, do not cry,*
*I'm gonna be your one arm man.*
*Susan my darling, dry your eyes,*
*The other one's good*

*I went down, down to the doctor*
*The doctor pulled my arm out of its socket*
*It hurt so bad I don't believe it*
*Closed my eyes, I felt the pain*
*I knew I'd never see that arm again*

*I'll just have to try and overlook it*
*Susan my darling, do not cry*
*I'm gonna be your one arm man*
*Susan my darling, dry your eyes*
*The other one's good*

These songs were pure theater; tragedy and comedy. Russell had a vision, and he wanted me to be a part of that vision. Sometimes he would come into my bedroom while I was asleep and play a record at full blast to wake me up. One morning I woke up to Dave Edmonds' remake of Fats Domino's "I Hear You Knockin'" at full volume while Russell freaked out about how great the record was. The sound, the arrangement, the musicianship, and the vocal were pure rock 'n' roll. He felt renewed faith that rock was not dead and that, with the players he had in mind, we could do it just as well, if not better.

By now music had me drunk, undressed, and she was ready to make love to me again. I couldn't hold out any longer. Russell's vision was about to become reality—but only to a point. Someone else would eventually dictate a drastic change in its direction.

We had our first rehearsal in Russell's parents' basement. As we learned Russell's original songs, we began to develop our own sound. We called it the Topper sound: a rhythm section foundation made up of drums, bass, and acoustic guitar with a slide guitar or another acoustic guitar playing lines around the vocal. The band would do stops that weren't just cold stops. We would all grab the last note and choke it. We fell upon this by accident. One day, Russell was leading us through an arrangement and said, "Stop." We all heard him at the last second and weren't sure of what he said, so we all kind of muffled our instruments to hear him better. Eventually we started to call these breaks "Topper stops."

Doug had a brother named Al who was an engineer in a local studio. When the studio wasn't being used, Al would sneak us in to record for free. When we'd listen back, we felt we really had something going. Al got busted sneaking us in and got fired from that studio, and then proceeded to get fired from two more studios for sneaking us in. We never paid to record. At one rehearsal, we got really stoned on pot and in the middle of one of the songs we were playing, we all just stopped. A vibe had come into the room and we realized we had just crossed into the next level of musicianship—or the next level of pothead! Either way, we were getting really good.

The early '70s were a tough time to have an original rock band. *Billboard's* Top 40 chart was different than it is now; the number one album in no way represented the number one single. Led Zeppelin could hold the number one spot on the album chart, but Helen Reddy would have the number one spot on the singles chart with "I Am Woman." The vibe in the clubs then was a new dance craze called disco. Artists like Barry White and songs like "TSOP (The Sounds of Philadelphia)" were heading the craze. It was growing in popularity and it was the sound that filled all the clubs on Long Island. People wanted to dress up in their polyester disco suits and dance the night away to a straight four-beat bass drum pulse that stayed the same for every song. It was mindless, and it reeked of drugs and sex. People didn't want to spend the night listening to original material played by four guys that looked homeless.

Topper would play small bars "for the door." We would charge people a few bucks to get in to the club and that was the money we would split. The bar would make its money from the sale of alcohol. At the end of the night, we would sometimes end up with $8.00 each. Actually, that was a good night; usually we would end the night owing the bar money from our alcohol consumption. We all needed money; it was time to rethink Topper. The recordings we made were getting some interest, but the popularity of disco was keeping us from going anywhere. I was playing weddings on the weekends—gigs were scarce after New Year's Eve and didn't get going strong again until April or May—and rehearsing with Topper during the week. I was twenty-two years old, broke, living in my parents' house, and driving a beat up '57 Chevy. I needed to make some money. I'd been approached by two top-40 cover bands from Seaford: the ST4 (Silver Tone 4) and a three-piece group called Blue Hare.

The ST4 had been around playing clubs as long as I could remember. They were a group of upper classmen and were the most popular band in Seaford High School. Johnny DeSantis, their guitarist and leader, had become a very smart businessman and the band was making a lot of money; Charlie Brucia was the drummer for a while (and eventually became my accountant); and Richie Patruco, who played with me in the New Rock Workshop, was the bass player/singer. The ST4 were the house band at a huge club in Farmingdale, Long Island, called the Cloud Nine. Bobby stopped by the house one day and asked me to join the band. Knowing that they stayed very current when it came to the music they played and that they would be in their disco transition, I flat-out turned them down.

When I was sixteen years old I would sit on the curb outside a club called the Locker Room on Merrick Road in Seaford and listen to three guys from my high school play music. They called themselves Blue Hare: Charlie Fararra on guitar and vocals, Tony Anzalone on bass guitar and vocals, and Ronnie Levine on drums and vocals. Ronnie and I would work together years later in the New Rock Workshop. Blue Hare would play "I'm Your Puppet" by James and Bobby Purified, and whatever else was in the top 40 then. I'd listen and think about how great it would be to do what they were doing; I couldn't wait to turn eighteen. Blue Hare broke up when Charlie and Tony got drafted into the Army and were shipped off to Vietnam. Ronnie went to art school, and when they got back from Vietnam, Charlie and Tony put the band back together, this time with drummer Charlie Raimond (also a Seaford High School graduate). They played six nights a week, and Charlie would tell me about his drawer full of hundred dollar bills: the band was always paid in cash, and because they were playing so much, they had no time to spend the money. After about two years of banging around the local clubs, Charlie was offered a gig in Las Vegas in a house band at one of the hotels. This was the point at which Tony asked me if I wanted to replace Charlie in Blue Hare. Again, I knew they were headed towards the disco craze.

My sister Louise had just married Bill Apostiliedes. Bill and his buddies were heavy drinkers and deep in to blues music. I had been into the blues—the '60s group style—but after meeting Bill, I realized I had only scratched the surface. Bill and his friends introduced me to Charlie Mussellwhite, Lil' Junior Parker, and Buddy Guy. These were the people that came before the R&B music that I loved so much already: Otis Redding, Aretha Franklin, and Wilson Pickett. For Bill and his buddies, the blues wasn't just a kind of music, it was a way of life. Maybe not the poor, sittin' 'round the shack part—they were all construction workers—but definitely the drinkin' and fightin' part. The music had me hooked. It was so laid back, with the drummers so far behind the beat that they were almost in the previous measure. And how those drummers could shuffle! There was no way I was going to play top-40 disco. I turned Blue Hare down again; I was now only going to play music I believed in—music that had heart. I wanted to feel the pain or joy, and live the life of this real music. I would continue to play the weddings and rehearse with Topper while listening and drinking to the blues.

Out of the bad comes good. For about a year I was dating a waitress from the catering hall where I was playing weddings. She decided to stop seeing me, which broke my heart—but that wasn't the only thing that was broke. So was my wallet! I took the breakup as a sign that it was time to move on, and went back to see the boys in Blue Hare. Luckily they weren't happy with their new drummer, but they made me beg because they knew I was broke; Tony saw it immediately when I pulled up in front of his house in my dilapidated '57 Chevy. It had become my blues car. They told me they were about to take a vacation—February was a slow month in the clubs, so they took two weeks off—and gave me a list of songs to learn. When they got back, I started playing with them five nights and one afternoon per week. This soon progressed to six nights and one afternoon, and suddenly I was making more money than I had ever made before. I had no time to spend it; I would play at night and sleep all day. If I wanted to see a girl it had to be on my one night off or after the gig.

Another thing I had no time for was Topper. I had to quit. When I did, Russell's wife Suzanne told me I could never set foot in her house again, and that I would be nothing without Russell. (When Howard quit, they nailed his guitar to Russell's wall.) Russell understood that we all needed money and talked to Suzanne. It was a hard decision to leave Topper. I had known Suzanne since I was banging my drumsticks on the back of her seat on the school bus when she was eight years old and I was twelve. Knowing I loved the song "Just like Romeo and Juliet," sung by the Reflections (written by Freddie Gorman and Bob Hamilton), Russell wrote a song for me with a similar melody, laying out his feelings about making it big. He called it "Overnight."

*I know I need my music*
*I don't believe I could leave my music*
*Cause I need my music*
*I throw my head in my hands, it's a weakness*
*I'm feelin' better and I know it's gonna work out right*
*It's a crazy feeling*
*Round and around, around my head is spinnin'*
*Sometimes you look like you're done but you're incomplete*
*I don't care if I have to work my fingers to the bone.*
*Overnight, you got your name in lights*
*One day you'll wake up you don't have to try*
*Play it right, you got a limousine*
*One day you'll wake up and go for a ride*
*As long as you know that it's only a matter of time*

In the end, I was finding it really hard to leave Topper. Because I had one night to myself during the week, I thought maybe I could play with Topper on that night. Instead of rehearsing, maybe we could play in one of the clubs that Blue Hare was playing. I knew the owners of the clubs, so I figured I could get us some gigs. I got us into the Tabard Ale House in Wantagh, Long Island. The owner, Charlie Laverty, said he'd have an "all the beer you can drink" night, and Topper would play. The one thing Topper needed to do was to learn some cover songs. We had about a day to rehearse, so we learned some songs we were familiar with.

The Topper guys and I had been getting into reggae music from Jamaica. Russell had discovered a Jimmy Cliff album called *The Harder They Come*, which was the soundtrack to the movie of the same name. Johnny Nash had a hit with "I Can See Clearly Now," and Eric Clapton had "I Shot the Sheriff" out as a single. Someone had told me that the Clapton song was written by a reggae musician named Bob Marley and was originally done by his group called the Wailers. One night while I was driving home from a gig with Blue

Hare, I was tuned in to the local black station, WBLS. It was about four o'clock in the morning, and a song came on that compelled me to pull my car over to the side of the road and just listen. I could not believe what I was hearing; the groove was fat and the singer was superb. It had an attitude that I had never heard before; it was as honest as the blues. Listening to the lyrics, I could tell this must be the original "I Shot the Sheriff" by the Wailers. The next day I went directly to the record store and bought the Wailers' albums *Burnin'* and *Catch a Fire.*

Topper's set list was about ten of Russell's originals plus Jamaican reggae songs like "The Harder They Come," "Stir It Up," and "I Shot the Sheriff," and (of course) blues songs like "Boom, Boom, Out Go the Lights" by Bacon Fat, "Hideaway" by John Mayall and the Blues Breakers (featuring Eric Clapton), and "Sweet Home Chicago" by Junior Parker. On the nights when we played an all-blues set, we called ourselves Smoky Robust and the Flags.

Free beer night at the Tabard Ale House was a smash. My brother-in-law brought all his blues friends, and my brother Vinny brought all his rock 'n' roll friends. Topper was introducing reggae to Long Island. The owner of the Tabard said he hated our sound and we were the worst band that ever played there, but he had to admit he had never sold as much beer in one night as he did when we played.

I had gone from contemplating giving up music to now playing seven nights and one afternoon a week. After getting stoned one night before a Topper gig, I was exhausted but happy. Resting one hand on my floor tom and the other on my snare drum, I leaned against the back wall of the stage and thought, "Well, I guess this is what I'm doing for the rest of my life."

**In New Orleans, 1976, as the crazy Billy Joel ride is about to begin.
L to R: Me, Billy, Brian Ruggles, Richie Cannata.**

# 17

# Rock 'n' Roll 'n' Billy Joel

Following Billy's popular breakthrough with the release of *The Stranger*, "Piano Man" would become one of his most well-known songs, but in 1973 it was only a minor hit. The song peaked at #25 on the Billboard Hot 100 chart in April of 1974. Still, Billy had developed a cult following. His 1974 follow-up to the *Piano Man* album, *Streetlife Serenade*, didn't do as well. It peaked at #35 on the charts, but it did not enjoy the relative success of its predecessor and marked the beginning of Billy's frosty relationship with critics and the music industry in general. Streetlife Serenade only had one single, "The Entertainer," which made it to #34 on the charts. The fact that it wasn't a hit didn't bother Billy as much as it bothered the record company. Billy always thought of himself as a songwriter first, then a piano player, then a singer, saying "singing is just yelling in key." Of course, he knew that if wanted his songs heard, he'd have to record and perform them.

When Billy needed to replace his bass player, he asked Brian Ruggles for advice, and Brian suggested his fellow Syosset, Long Island native Doug Stegmeyer for the job. Brian was, and still is, Billy's right hand man. Friends with Billy from their days on Long Island, Brian moved out to California to work for Billy during the *Piano Man* tour. Brian wore many hats: tour manager, roadie, monitor engineer, and front of house mixer. He was also a consultant on the *Turnstiles* album. When Billy moved back to New York, so did Brian.

After I got the gig with Billy, Brian and I would become close, and we liked to have fun. We partied hard. In fact, an Australian promoter gave us shirts that read "Filthy" and "Dirty." I forget which one I was; it really didn't matter anyway, we could swap shirts at any time. When Brian later got married, I was asked to be an usher. As the wedding date drew near, a dinner for the wedding party was planned. I got a call from Joe D'Ambrosio at Phil Ramone's office, asking if I was able to do a session, but it was the same night as the date of Brian's dinner. Feeling loyalty to my friend, I said I couldn't do the session. Joe became insistent, and told me to cancel the dinner; I *had* to be there for this session. "I can't," I told him, "I'm in the bridal party. Anyway, who is the artist?" Joe said he couldn't tell me. "That's ridiculous," I said, "Who is it?" "Phil doesn't want me to tell anyone," Joe responded. "Well, if I am going to cancel going to this dinner, I need to know who I'm going to be recording with!" Joe finally broke. "Paul McCartney," he said. "Holy shit! Are you kidding?" "No," said Joe. I told him to give me an hour to think it over.

This was a tough situation. On one hand, I had promised Brian I'd be at his rehearsal dinner, but on the other, it was Paul McCartney! *A fucking Beatle!* As I did so often when in a tough spot, I asked my mom for advice. "Mom," I said, "I have Brian Ruggles' rehearsal dinner on the same day Phil Ramone wants me in the studio. What should I do?" "Lib," she responded, "You made a commitment to your friend and you need to be there." Pausing, she asked, "Who is the session with?" "Paul McCartney," I said. Looking me right in the eye, she said "Frig Brian Ruggles" (Mom wouldn't use the work "fuck"). I called Joe back and told him I was in. (Joe said he'd already told Phil I'd be there.) I did the session and as luck would have it, I never had to tell Brian, because the dinner was moved to a different date. I don't think Brian ever knew.

After being recommended to Billy by Brian, Doug got the call from Billy and was soon bound for California. Topper did one last gig to celebrate Doug's success. All I can remember is Russell's father walking towards the stage with a tray full of shots for the band. Howard didn't drink much, so it was up to Doug, Russell, and me to empty the tray. I can still see Doug leaning up against the wall trying to play his bass. We were going to miss him.

One night during the tour supporting *Streetlife Serenade*, Billy was walking down the hall in his hotel and happened to overhear familiar voices as he passed by a room. Pausing, he recognized the voices of his band members, and they were putting him down to some friends of theirs, saying they were bored, unhappy with Billy, and didn't like playing with him anymore. They added that they felt he wasn't that much of a talent. Billy noticed that Doug's was not among the voices he heard.

Already growing tired of Los Angeles, to Billy this was the last straw. The time was perfect for him to clean house and move back to New York. In L.A., he was using studio musicians to make his records and a totally different band to play live. Billy had grown tired of that arrangement. Keeping only Doug on bass and Brian doing sound, Billy decided it was time to move back to New York, and once he did, he resolved to use the same band for both recording and touring, to have a consistent sound and feel to his music. The first thing he wanted was an aggressive New York-style drummer.

Doug had been calling me from the road, telling me that Billy was unhappy with his band. Now that the time was right, Doug told Billy he knew the perfect drummer. From my perspective, other than "Piano Man," I wasn't very familiar with Billy's music. Doug kept telling me about the "Billy mania" he was experiencing on the road. In 1974, I went to Staten Island College to see Billy perform. Doug introduced me to Billy as "the guy I've been telling you about." Billy said, "I remember you," and we reminisced a little about the My House days. As I watched the show, I was blown away. Billy and his band were great, and as soon as Billy hit the first few notes of "Piano Man," I saw what Doug meant by "Billy mania." The crowd went nuts. I was hooked. I really wanted the gig.

My audition was held at Columbia Studios in Manhattan. Billy was on the piano, Doug was on bass, and Brian was in the control room. I had already met Brian through Doug; we got along great and had a lot in common, primarily our love of alcohol. We'd get drunk in the bars together and talk about music. Brian would say, "Man, you'd be great on the road. We gotta get you in this band." Billy's plan was to play a few songs with me and then look to Brian in the control room for either a thumbs up or down, determining whether I was in or out. Brian already knew which way his thumbs would be pointing, but he had to play it cool. Billy decided he wanted to do some new songs for my audition, wanting to see what I could come up with without knowing the material. He was pretty amazed at how fast I came up with parts. Brian waited about fifteen minutes and then gave Billy the thumbs up.

I was in.

For twenty-five years, Billy was unaware that Doug had given me a tape of all Billy's new material the night I went to go see them at the Staten Island gig. I had done my homework. After offering me the gig, Billy asked if I needed anything. Looking down at my old half-burgundy, half-silver sparkle drum set, I said, "How about a new set of drums?" "Let's go," he responded. At Frank's Drum Shop on 48th Street, I picked out a seven-piece set of Pearl Drums in black with fiberglass shells and no bottom heads. Billy put them on his American Express card. I think they cost around $1500.00.

To celebrate, we went to Mikell's, which was uptown near the brownstone duplex Billy was renting on 96th Street. The house band there, Stuff, included legendary New York studio musicians Steve Gadd, Chris Parker, Richard Tee, and Cornell Dupree. When we arrived, Billy's wife and manager Elizabeth Weber was there. Billy and Elizabeth had met while Billy was playing with the Hassles, and in L.A., Elizabeth had also worked as a waitress at the Executive Lounge, the bar which inspired "Piano Man." Going by the name Bill Martin at the time (Martin is Billy's middle name), Billy was playing there and writing songs while waiting out a bad record deal.

At Mikell's, Billy introduced me to Elizabeth as "his new drummer." Shaking my hand firmly, Elizabeth looked me straight in the eyes and said, "Congratulations, you'll still have to prove yourself to me." On a subsequent evening, after way too many drinks, I got into my '74 Ford Bronco, Elizabeth got into her Aston Martin sports car, and we raced from J.P.'s on 72nd Street to the Joels' apartment on 96th Street. Running red lights and driving on sidewalks, and with Doug as my co-pilot, I beat her to the apartment. I think that was when I proved myself, and by the grace of God, thankfully I did it without killing myself or anyone else.

My first gig with Billy was in November, 1974, at the CBS Records convention at the New York Hilton in Midtown Manhattan. I was really nervous. In addition to Billy, Doug, and me, the band included Michael Brecker on sax and Ira Newborn on guitar, and we had a full orchestra as well. We performed "Piano Man," "Streetlife Serenader," "You're My Home," and two new songs, "New York State of Mind" and "I've Loved These Days." CBS thought we did a great job; they were thrilled with the new songs and couldn't wait for the next album. It was a perfect show, the first of many to come.

# My Drum-Part 10

If I could play alone I would rule the world, but because my gift is to be shared, the higher power only gave me one note. I live in a world that only feels, like someone that only hears or only sees. I wish I could become two different people, one playing the drums and one that stands in the crowd and listens, but I can't, so I will be the only one who will never hear what it sounds like when I play live. I will live by feel. My greatest hope for you is to have you feel what I feel and for you to take that feeling with you for the rest of your life. The places I've lived, the people I've met, and things I have experienced—both negative and positive—along with my passion, have given me the desire to take the road less traveled.

**On tour with Billy Joel, 1976.**

# 18

# *Turnstiles*

Now as full-time members of his band, Billy wanted Doug and me to work on his new album with him, but Columbia had a different idea, and they had their choice for producer. They wanted Jim Guercio, the producer of all the Chicago albums and the owner of Caribou Recording Studios in Boulder, Colorado, where Elton John had recently recorded. Ironically, Elton had just fired his drummer, Nigel Olsson, and bass player, Dee Murray. Guercio recruited them to play on Billy's new album and, of course, the record company backed this. Plans were made and Billy went into Columbia Studios in New York to record with this lineup. Doug and I spoke to Billy every day to find out what was going on. He told us one day flowers came to the studio for Nigel and Dee. The card read, "I heard you're playing with another piano player. Love, Elton." As the recording progressed, Billy hated what he heard at these sessions, so he fired Guercio, which also ousted Nigel and Dee, and left Columbia Studios.

Billy returned to Long Island and booked himself into the Howard Johnson hotel in Westbury. Along with me, Doug, and engineer John Bradley, he recorded *Turnstiles* at Ultra Sonic Studios in Hempstead, Long Island. When we started to record, we'd listen back to takes of songs, and Billy started to comment about places in the songs where he wanted guitar. "We know guitar players," Doug and I responded, and that's how Russell Javors and Howard Emerson got on the record and Topper became the Billy Joel Band.

Jim Smith played acoustic guitar on "Angry Young Man." The budget for the album was so tight I had to bring in my Guild D35 acoustic for Jim to play; nothing was rented. When we recorded "New York State of Mind," Billy wanted a sax solo. Doug's brother Al had just used a sax player in the studio named Richie Cannata. Al said he was really good, so Doug and I went to a club in Farmingdale called the Cloud Nine to see him play. He was great and fit the bill perfectly, so we invited Richie to the studio. When he arrived, we were working on "Angry Young Man." Richie got nervous, thinking, "What the hell would I do with my sax?" and trying to figure out how he would fit. On a break, Billy played him the basic track to "New York State of Mind." Richie's feet were then planted. All his sax parts were done during overdubs at Caribou Studios in Boulder. One other detail about the record is that I don't remember getting paid to record it.

Billy's manager at the time was John Troy, and Billy knew it was time to move on. (John is referenced in the line "Johnny's taking care of things for a while and his style is so right for Troubadors" in the song "Say Goodbye to Hollywood.") Elizabeth, now Billy's wife, told Billy that she thought she could do a better job at managing him. Billy said, "Go ahead," and in the dining room of their apartment on 96th Street, Manhattan, Elizabeth started Home Run Management. She hired Dennis Arfa to do the bookings.

During the *Turnstiles* tour, we were playing clubs or doing opening slots—most without any billing—for the Beach Boys. Near the start of the tour in Chicago, the house lights went out and the crowd went nuts, only to find when the lights came up that it was Billy Joel onstage. You could feel the disappointment in the crowd. It went from cheering to a big sigh of disappointment, like the air was being sucked out of the room. Billy said into the mic, "If there are any reviewers out there who are going to compare me to Elton John," he paused, and then proceeded to flip them his middle finger. That night, we played *Turnstiles* in its entirety. When we opened for Hall and Oates, we got better reviews than they did. In fact, one night their crew and ours came to blows over a review that mentioned we were better than them!

We opened for ZZ Top when they decided to go above and beyond for their Worldwide Texas Tour in 1976. To showcase their pride in their home state, they took a 35-ton, Texas-shaped stage on the road. The stage was adorned with native Texas plants like agave and cactus, but what made this tour memorable was the fact that there were live animals as well! Bison, vultures, steer, and rattlesnakes all found their way onto ZZ Top's stage, and they brought along a full time animal expert to ensure the animals' health and safety. They found a place for us to set up somewhere behind a picket fence! No animals were present when we played, however.

Dennis had the idea of us playing small theaters to build an audience, with the hope that we'd work our way up to arenas. The plan worked, and as the *Turnstiles* tour progressed, we got our first taste of true insanity. Having had heard that comedian Rodney Dangerfield would go out into the audience between shows in a terry cloth robe and shake hands with the fans, Russell thought it would be a great idea for us, the band, to have robes when we met our fans. He picked out blue robes with white trim for us, complete with each person's "road name" embroidered on the chest. Russ was "Otis Boring" (since he liked to say, "Oh this boring ride," etc.), I was "Bertha D. Blues," Doug was "The Eel," and Richie was "Rico." One day I went to the mall and had a new addition stitched onto my robe. That night, as I turned around in the meet-and-greet room, jaws dropped and people started cracking up when they read:

*Who the fuck is Billy Joel?*

Billy loved it!

The fun continued. There was a time when our lighting designer's mother was backstage at a gig. We all loved her, and she had the best sense of humor.

I came out of the dressing room in a cooking apron and gave her a huge hug. We talked for a minute and when I turned to go back to the dressing room, everyone could see I was totally bare-assed! Like I said, she had a great sense of humor.

We all had cassette recorders and headphones to listen to music while on the road. One day we were on a flight somewhere in Texas. I was deep into some music, eyes closed while tapping time on the empty cassette box, when I felt a tap on my shoulder. Opening my eyes, I saw the man next to me trying to get my attention. He looked about fifty, and his brown suit, pot belly, and ten gallon hat gave him away as a Texan. Motioning for me to take off my headphones, he stuck out his hand to shake mine and said, "My name is Bubba, what's yours?" As we shook hands, I said, "My name is Liberty." "Liberty nice to meet you," he responded, "I think we're going to get along just fine if you'd stop banging that fucking box on your leg." Call me a wimp, but when he released my hand, this New Yorker did what any tough guy would do: I got up and changed my seat.

We were on tour for a while and were headed to Salt Lake City with a long layover in Denver, so we called the girls from Caribou Ranch and told them to meet us at the airport in Denver. (In 1975 there were no security checks; a passenger could leave the airport and come back to make a connecting flight.) The girls ended up taking us to a Chinese restaurant where we proceeded to get hammered. We ordered everything on the menu, and what we didn't eat, we threw at each other. The girls were all over us, and we were all over them. The management finally had enough when they caught Doug and one young lady having sex in a stall in the restroom. The manager came over to us yelling, "Get out, get out! I've never seen such animals! Get out, don't pay, just *get out*!" The last thing I remember about this meal was me and Billy rolling down the steps in front of the restaurant.

We still had time to kill when the girls dropped us off back at the airport, so we decided to grab a few wheelchairs and have a race to the gate. By the time the flight started boarding, I was so fucked up that I fell, with half my body on the ramp and the other half in the plane. The pilot had to step over me to get on board. One of the boys helped me up and took me to my seat. We were still at the gate when the flight attendant passed my seat with the refreshment cart, and I got caught stealing a few of the little bottles of booze. The next thing I knew, there was air security sitting next to me for the flight. I fell asleep and woke up in Salt Lake City. The next night we were in a restaurant and a gentleman walked over to our table and introduced himself. "Hi, I'm Bill Athas," he said. "I'm the liquor distributer in Salt Lake." A friendship was forged right there on the spot.

After a gig in Athens, Ohio, I was at the wheel driving back to the hotel with Doug, Richie, and Russell. We passed a small club that looked like it was jumping with college girls. One of the boys said, "Let's stop." I didn't want to. They all said, "Come on, it'll be fun." "OK," I replied. "One beer and we're out of there." Have you ever seen the movie *Old School*, where Will Farrell promised his wife he wouldn't drink and then ended up running down the road naked? Well, I didn't get naked, but I did end up having more than one beer. A lot more. When I drove to our hotel, which wasn't that far, we had one more passenger. Doug had managed to find a friend for the night.

Back in the *Turnstiles* days, we toured in two rental cars. We adopted a road trick passed down from one of our truck drivers where you would drive the car forward at about forty miles per hour, then step hard on the brake and at the same time, throw it into reverse and put the gas pedal to the floor. This would have the car still going forward while the traction wheels were going backwards, which led to a lot of smoke from the tires, the smell of burnt rubber, and skid marks (with the transmission falling out of some cars). When we got back to our hotel, I thought I'd perform a few of these maneuvers in the hotel parking lot. All was going great until my last run; I forgot to put the transmission in reverse when I stepped on the gas. I was headed right towards the hotel, and I couldn't stop in time. The car went over the cement parking block, through some bushes and a gate, and stopped right in front of the room of an old woman who was just finishing her nighttime walk with her dog. She had a priceless look on her face of sheer terror.

With the car skidded to a stop at a precarious angle and the front wheels still spinning, I glanced through the window next to the old woman's room, and there was our truck driver, Boom Boom McNeil, giving me the thumbs up. When Richie, Doug, and Doug's new best friend got out of the car, I tossed the keys to Richie and said, "Park this for me, will you?" and went to bed. The next morning, I could hear a knock on a door down the hall. An annoyed voice that I recognized as Billy's said loudly, "What?" Another voice replied, "Athens police." "You want room seven," said Billy, "Shit, that's my room," I said to myself. "Bastard! He threw me under the bus!"

A knock came on my door. Slowly opening it, I said, "Yes?" The police pointed at the rental car black tire tracks and said "Are you responsible for this?" I couldn't lie. "Yes." They put me in the police car, strangely, in the front seat right next to a mounted shotgun. I thought, "Okay, officers, you'll get no trouble from me," as they took me down to the station. Our tour manager at the time was Jeff Shock. Over six feet tall with a high-pitched voice, Jeff suddenly appeared. "What's going on here?" he asked. The cops explained the situation and Jeff said, "I'll follow you." When we got to the police station, one officer was asking questions. He wanted to know how the black tire tracks got onto the pavement in the parking lot. I told him the brakes were sticking. Then he asked how the car got into the hotel. I told him the brakes had failed. The other officer was checking to see if I had any prior record. I knew I was in deep shit now because I had recently been arrested for assaulting a police officer back in Nassau County on Long Island. It showed up in my record, even though that charge was reduced to a speeding ticket. But they knew I was a bit of a troublemaker. I was busted and would have to go in front of a judge.

Unfortunately, this all went down on a Saturday. One of the officers told me the judge was on a fishing trip and wouldn't be back until Monday. "He can't stay here," Jeff exclaimed. "We have a show tonight!" The officer responded, "Well, you could bail him out, and then he could skip bail." Jeff said, "Great, where do I pay?" With that, the officer turned to me and warned, "Make sure you don't get stopped in Ohio for the next seven years, or you'll go straight to jail for not showing up for sentencing for this arrest." From that day on, whenever we played in Ohio, I was never Liberty DeVitto on the room list again. Some of my aliases were Bertha D. Blues, Pastor Pasta, and Ytrebil O'ttived (my name spelled backwards).

The best way to cure a hangover on the road was stopping for a Quarter Pounder with cheese, large fries, and a chocolate shake from McDonald's. This meal was eaten on the run, because the next gig was in a college fieldhouse about three hundred miles away. On the way, we would have milkshake wars. This was when one car would ride just ahead of the other and bombard the other car with whatever milkshakes were left. A chocolate shake making contact with the windshield was the best; it totally cut out the driver's vision. The sight of windshield wipers slopping shake off the windshield was a vision of victory.

The *Turnstiles* tour took us to England for the first time. I went out to dinner with the promoter. Dinners always included a lot of wine and booze. I'd recently discovered lager and lime, a drink consisting of beer and Rose's lime juice. I loved it and drank a lot of it. One time in the States, after dinner, we returned to the hotel ready for a good time. This particular hotel happened to have an indoor pool, and that night there was a high school prom happening around the pool. Alcohol will affect your memory, so I don't know how it happened, but I ended up throwing the prom queen in the pool in her gown. My memory being a blur, I think we all jumped in after her. The same thing happened in England. Me and the promoter, the great Alex Leslie—his company was titled ALE for Alex Leslie Entertainment—used to get together every day off around noon for cheese sandwiches and pints in the local pub. Lager and lime was so refreshing that I could drink a hundred of them, and at times I came damn close. We were out one afternoon and one of Alex's buddies picked us up and took us pub hopping until we were somewhere with a girl, a gown, and a pool. This young lady and I had a bit of an argument, which ended with (you guessed it) her going for a late swim in her party dress. Alex ushered me into a cab back to the hotel.

The next morning, I asked Alex how his friend got home. He said his buddy was so drunk that while driving home he'd hit a telephone pole and ended up in the back seat of the car. When the cops found him, he was passed out. They started to interrogate him, but he said he didn't remember what had happened. He'd gotten into the car and fallen asleep, and his driver must have run off after he hit the pole and just left him there. A little quick English thinking and the cops didn't charge him with anything—and gave him a ride home to boot!

### "SAY GOODBYE TO HOLLYWOOD"

One of Billy's favorite groups was Ronnie Spector and the Ronettes, and they were his inspiration for "Say Goodbye to Hollywood." This song was done in the Phil Spector format all the way, from the vibrato in the voice to the tambourine and castanets that I overdubbed. I think we nailed the "Spector" arrangement without all the echo of the famous "wall of sound." I also overdubbed a snare drum in the bridge because my hi-hat was recorded too loud on the basic track. The snare needed to be doubled so it could be brought up in the mix. All the overdubs, including Richie's sax solo, were done at Caribou Studios in Boulder, Colorado.

The song is the story of Billy leaving L.A. It's about the people he left behind and the way you always lose friends when you move on. At the end of the song, on the fade, I was getting up to walk out of the studio while Billy was fixing some vocals and you hear him say, "Hey DeVitto, where ya goin?" He said he kept it in because it sounded real New York; he was glad to be back in the greatest city in the world.

I eventually got to play with Ronnie Spector for a few years after I parted ways with Billy. She actually recorded "Hollywood" with Bruce Springsteen's E Street Band. Still a wonderful artist with that signature voice, I love her dearly and have the deepest respect for her talent.

### "SUMMER HIGHLAND FALLS"

When Billy played this song for Doug and me, he only had part of it finished. Doug and I thought it was great and strongly suggested that he finish it. The drum lick going into the song is the same as the drum lick going into "Help Me" by Joni Mitchell, drums by John Guerin. My girlfriend at the time, Lisa, loved that song, so I did that drum fill to impress her. (Thank you, John!)

The recording is Doug, Billy, me, and Richie playing both soprano sax parts. "Summer Highland Falls" was the first of Billy's songs that made me think, "This guy writes some great music." It's a great tune written in the Jackson Browne style of songwriting.

### "ALL YOU WANNA DO IS DANCE"

This was a silly song and we needed a couple guitar players to do it right. The band Topper comprise the musicians on the track: Doug, Russell, Howie Emerson, and me, with Billy. Mingo Lewis' percussion, as well as the strings, were later added at Caribou Studios. Russell and Billy sing the "oh, la, la la." The song was written in response to disco.

### "NEW YORK STATE OF MIND"

"New York State of Mind" is the only song Billy ever wrote the words and music for at the same time. He had just spent years out in L.A., and loved being back in New York. Living upstate in Highland Falls at the time, he wrote both this song and "Summer Highland Falls" there. I've always loved this song, but it moved me the most when I saw the New York Mets beat John Rocker and the Atlanta Braves in the fourth game of the 1999 playoffs at Shea Stadium. "New York State of Mind" came through the P.A. at the end of the game—it was perfect.

Once again this is Doug, Billy, and me on the basic tracks, with Richie doing his sax solo at Caribou Studios. Strings were added last. It became a very inspiring and spiritually healing song in the days after the attacks on the World Trade Center on September 11, 2001. When we played it then, people wept.

### "JAMES"

About a friend of Billy's, "James" was done really well in the earlier sessions at Columbia Studios with Nigel Olsson and Dee Murray. Their background vocals were superb—they were also great singers—but their track was scrapped and Billy duplicated their vocals when we re-recorded the song. I play a brush on the snare and the bass drum is hit on the "three" count, like you would find in reggae. I'd use this concept again to create the groove for "Just the Way You Are."

### "ANGRY YOUNG MAN"

Billy, Doug, Jim Smith (guitar), and I did the basic track for "Angry Young Man." Jim didn't own an acoustic guitar, so I brought mine. When we were listening back to the track, Billy kept playing the percussion part on his chest with his open hands, while saying, "I want something like this on the verses." "Let's use that exact sound," I responded. We laid Billy on a chair, placed a microphone near him, and I played the percussion part on his chest, doubling it with brushes on a snare. The song was done in three parts: "Prelude," "Angry Young Man," and the end. Billy overdubbed the Hammond organ and Mini Moog synthesizer. Russell Javors and Howard Emerson played the electric guitars.

### "I'VE LOVED THESE DAYS"

"I've Loved These Days" represented the end of the cocaine-and-champagne Camelot days. It was time to get serious. I think this song is reminiscent of the movie *Days of Wine and Roses*. This song is another with Billy, Doug, and me on the basic track, with Richie on soprano sax and strings added at a later date at Caribou.

### "MIAMI 2017"

On October 30, 1975, the headline of *New York Daily News* read:

FORD TO CITY: DROP DEAD.
*Vows He'll Veto Any Bail-Out.*

Years of fiscal fakery, budgetary smoke and mirrors crafted by three mayors, three governors, and legions of state legislators finally pushed the city to the brink of bankruptcy. Disaster loomed and New York pleaded with Washington for salvation. But President Gerald Ford made no secret of his feeling that New York had willfully and wantonly created its own problems. "There would be no federal rescue," he said. The political backlash was immediate and enormous; Ford soon retreated, and the city managed to limp through its crisis, if only barely. "Miami 2017" is a science fiction story from the future of one person's recollection of what had happened to the greatest city in the world.

We rehearsed in between the recordings and mixing at Caribou and left straight from Boulder to start touring. Our first gig was actually right in Boulder, at a club called The Good Earth. The musician's salary for this tour was $400 a week on the road. It would still be a while before *Turnstiles* would be finished and released.

*Turnstiles* sold about 50,000 copies in the U.S. and did very well in Australia, where 36,000 copies constituted a gold record. In 1976 we toured Australia and played to packed houses in all the major cities. With the tour running low on money, CBS president Walter Yetnicoff put up $80,000 to keep us on the road. Eventually, *Turnstiles* sold enough for Columbia Records to give Billy a shot at another album.

When the time came to start planning the follow-up to *Turnstiles*, Billy was again looking for a producer. Sir George Martin, the legendary Beatles producer, was interested. He came to see us play in Glassboro, New Jersey. We were all psyched. Imagine us working with the guy who produced the band we admired the most! After watching us play, George told Billy he was interested in the project, but wanted to use his own musicians. Billy told him, "Thanks but no thanks. Love me, love my band," and passed.

When Billy returned from the meeting, we were all over him, dying to know what George had said. When Billy explained, we were beyond disappointed. I said jokingly, "Ah, fuck him, he sucks anyway. What did he do after the Beatles? I hated the group America and he didn't do anything for Jeff Beck!" It was really bold of Billy to do what he did. After all, this was *the* George Martin. It was then that we knew we were a band.

**Wearing gag t-shirts during the recording of *The Stranger*, 1977.**

# 19

# *The Stranger*

On September 9, 1977, the *Turnstiles* tour ended on a high note with three nights at Carnegie Hall in New York City. The show was recorded live with an orchestra, but was not released at the time. Eventually it saw the light of day in the CD box set of the 25th anniversary of *The Stranger* album. In the crowd one night at Carnegie Hall was producer Phil Ramone. Phil had worked with Frank Sinatra, Paul Simon, Phoebe Snow, The Band, and many other artists. He was also the sound guy at Madison Square Garden on the night Marilyn Monroe sang "Happy Birthday" to JFK, and he designed the Oval Office recording system that took down Richard Nixon in the Watergate scandal. Phil was a major name in New York recording, and he was on staff at Columbia Records. After the show, he came to meet us at the Howard Johnson hotel on 52nd Street and 8th Avenue, where we were staying. Phil said he liked us and that he felt a lot of uncontrolled energy and a raw street sound in the band, and that he didn't want to change it, but felt he would be the person to get it under control. Phil was chosen as our producer.

Billy was signed to Columbia Records, which made him a solo artist, but with us in the studio with him, and with Phil knowing how important our presence was, Billy was acting as if he was in a band. We were paid double union scale, which was about $300 per three hour session, but it would always be a double session. Eventually, we moved up to double scale, double session, so we were making $1200 per session. The budget was tight to the point that my drums and Doug's amp were brought to the studio in the back of an old pickup truck—classy cartage. But we were making real money, nevertheless.

Near the start of Billy's recording dates, Doug and I had booked a session with Russell at Ultrasonic Studios on Long Island. It turned out to be the same day Phil wanted to start recording, but we explained it to him and he was very cool with it. That night I got a call from Billy; he was feeling no pain and was screaming on the phone. "I finally get you guys in the studio and you tell Phil you've got to record with Russell?" "Billy," I said, "Phil's okay with it. He said we'll just start one day later." "I don't care," retorted Billy. "Forget Russell and forget Topper. You're in my band now!" Although Russell and Billy both had a vision, the difference was that Billy had the record deal. We ultimately did the recording with Russell and went in the studio with Phil a day later than scheduled. Russell was not asked to play on *The Stranger*. Phil brought in studio musicians to replace him.

## "MOVIN' OUT"

We played clubs and small theaters on the *Turnstiles* tour. There wasn't a lot of money being made, so we stayed at cheap motels. On days off— which were rare in those days—we would sit by the pool. Richie and I would make believe we were related and still living at home in the city. We'd pretend we were visiting Billy, who had moved to the suburbs like we and our families did on Long Island. At that time, in the 1950s and '60s, we were still waiting for the Long Island Native Americans (the Ustase Indians) to come riding onto our front lawns. For my parents' generation, leaving the city and moving to Long Island was pretty radical.

As we acted out going to visit Billy in the suburbs, Richie would tuck a tissue into the wrist part of his sleeve and act like he was Billy's aunt, and I would be Billy's cousin. We'd say to him, "Oh what a beautiful job you've done with the place. Did you landscape it yourself?" Billy would say, "You think this is nice, later I'll take you in and show you my finished basement." Finishing the basement and making it into the family room was one of the first things the new suburbanite did when they bought their home. We would ask Billy, "Why did you leave the city?" He would say, "You gotta move out here, you're killing yourselves in the city—those people are crazy."

Those dopey little skits, created by boredom, became the premise for the song "Movin' Out," with Anthony and Mrs. Cacciatore. Billy had played me the song in his apartment one day. As he was playing, I thought to myself, "Gee, this melody sounds very familiar." When he finished, I realized what it was. "You shmuck," I said. "That's a Neil Sedaka song!" He was using the melody from "Laughing in the Rain." "Shit," said Billy. He loved the lyrics he had written, so he re-wrote the melody. The next time he played it for me, when he got to the end of the song, I said, "I think a piano piece, like the one at the end of 'Layla,' would fit perfectly here." Immediately, Billy wrote the instrumental ending to the song. When Billy would clear his throat he would make a "huh-uhm" sound, and that became the first two notes of the guitar line.

Doug Stegmeyer had a beautiful 1956 maroon and beige Corvette. It had a 302 V8 Chevy engine with a four-on-the-floor. The starter was on its way out so it had a little trouble starting, but when it did, it had the greatest sound. We took a cheap Panasonic cassette player and taped the microphone to the bumper of the car right over the exhaust pipe. One summer day, Doug and I drove that car around the streets of Northport, Long Island, with the top down, recording the sounds of the car. This is what you hear at the end of "Movin' Out."

This was the first song we recorded with Phil Ramone. I immediately found out how important the two-and-four feel was to him; it would become a huge part of my drumming and the success of Billy's records and live shows.

### "THE STRANGER"

Billy had a battery-powered Casio keyboard with percussion loops on it. He came up with the feel for the "The Stranger" by pressing all the buttons at once:

rumba, bossa nova, rock 'n' roll, etc. When we heard the demo, it was the drum machine and Billy on the Casio keys, with his voice doubled in an octave higher falsetto. Steve Kahn, who played guitar on *The Stranger* along with Hiram Bullock, is a soft spoken gentleman. His father, Sammy Kahn, wrote classic songs like "Teach Me Tonight" and so many others, so Steve gets a lot of respect in the music business, not only because he is a great musician, but also because of who his father was. We had noticed that on another album he'd recorded, Steve was credited as "Mr. Steve Kahn." To bust his chops, we started calling everyone in the studio "mister." Conversations sounded like this: "Mr. Jim Boyer, could you please give Mr. Doug Stegmeyer more of Mr. Liberty DeVitto's drums in the headphones?" We took it so far as to start calling the album *Mr. The Stranger*.

The body of the song was recorded first, and Billy wrote the intro and ending later on during the sessions. He imagined Frank Sinatra in an old movie, standing under a lamp post on a foggy night wearing a pork-pie hat and a trench coat. The whistling on the track was done by Billy. At one point, there was talk about having someone unknown whistle and then having a contest where people would try to guess who it was.

### "JUST THE WAY YOU ARE"

The first time I heard this song, Billy sang it to me a cappella while I sat on the steps outside the bar Sail 'n' Ale in Northport, Long Island. Doug and I had spent many a night there. The drink "miles of smiles" was invented there; it was similar to a black Russian, but with one more added type of alcohol, your choice. This was our favorite drink, and the band kept the bar in business.

"Just the Way You Are" was written on the *Turnstiles* tour and we were already playing it live. We played it at Carnegie Hall in 1977. At that time it had more of a Stevie Wonder feel, like "Sunshine of My Life." My mom was at the show, and afterwards she said, "If you guys put that out, it will be a gold record." "Yeah right," I answered. "If that ever happens, you can have the gold record to hang on your wall." Mom's gold record still hangs there today.

Phil Ramone knew the song was a hit, but it had to get away from the groove it was in. When a drummer thinks he's playing the right part for a song but someone else tells him, "No, that's not what I want," the drummer will often try to play on different drums or cymbals, but will rarely think about playing *with* something else—playing the same groove but with a different implement in your hands, like a mallet or brush. It just so happened that I had some brushes in my stick bag, and when I picked one up and played it on the snare drum, it gave the groove a new sound. Playing all those bossa novas at weddings this way was paying off! At first I was playing the brush and stick combination exactly the way I did on "James," from the *Turnstiles* album. Phil Ramone heard the brush and acoustic guitar together and liked the combination; the sounds had the same timbre. As I was playing, I looked through the glass in the studio and Phil was making hand motions. The tom-tom hit, which we called the "skip/hop" pattern, comes at the end of each of Billy's vocal phrases, or in what I call the "holes." Placing the bass drum on the third beat of the measure completed the beat.

After we recorded the song, we hated it. We were a rock 'n' roll band; the song was too mushy for us. When Linda Ronstadt and Phoebe Snow visited the studio, Phil played the basic track for them. They loved it, saying it was a very sensitive song that women would love and relate to. If we put it on the album, they added, we'd get so many women we wouldn't know what to do with them. The song was immediately added to the album. Later, we did get the women, and we did know what to do with them. There was one time when I was sitting in front of Doug on an airplane and got on my knees to face him. "Let's try not to get laid tonight," I said. Seconds later, a beautiful woman came down the aisle and sat down right next to me. I turned to Doug and, like Kramer in *Seinfeld*, hit the back of the seat and said, "I'm out."

When Billy and Elizabeth broke up, I would yell new lyrics to Billy during our shows. "I love you just the way you are" became "She took the house, the dog, the car." We stopped doing the song in concert after that. "Just the Way You Are" garnered Grammy Awards for Record of the Year and Song of the Year in 1979, and it was our first gold single.

## "SCENES FROM AN ITALIAN RESTAURANT"

Most of the different parts of this song were written at various times during the *Turnstiles* tour. The "Brenda & Eddie" part was actually already written and we were doing it live. Billy wrote the other parts as the tour progressed. Rumor has it that the Italian restaurant in the song was Christiano's in Syosset, Long Island. I don't know about that, but Billy did eat there a lot. At Fontana Di Trevi, on 151 West 57th St, across the street from Carnegie Hall, a waiter came up to Billy's table and asked, "A bottle of white, a bottle of red, perhaps a bottle of rosé instead?"

"Scenes" is about people you knew in school who peaked too early. The most beautiful girl and the most handsome guy in school are not what they once were, and are struggling to hang on to what they took for granted. Everyone wanted to go steady with them, but now their beauty, athletic ability, and popularity are fading.

The song's basic track was recorded all in one take; we had eventually started playing the entire song in concert before we entered the studio. Richie overdubbed his horn parts and I overdubbed the cymbal swells. The accordion was added later, as were the New Orleans-style horns played to the lead horn part Richie had recorded.

## "VIENNA"

Russell wrote a song for Topper called "The Topper Song," which had the same format as "Vienna." This one was really easy for Doug and me. We suggested to Steve Kahn that he choke the chords, which was the same thing Russell had done on the Topper song. The similarity of the two songs is uncanny. The end blues lick on the piano was my suggestion; the idea came from the end of Leon Russell's "A Song for You."

## "ONLY THE GOOD DIE YOUNG"

On a day off in Knoxville, Tennessee, during the *Turnstiles* tour, Billy came running into my hotel room to play me this song. Billy being Jewish and knowing that I was raised a good Catholic boy, I guess he wanted my perspective. He had written it on acoustic guitar with a reggae feel, and played it for me that way. I thought it was great, but the lyrics were trouble. In the studio, the feel changed. It's been rumored that I said I hated reggae and wouldn't play it. This is not true—I played (and loved) lots of reggae with Topper. The groove change happened when Paul Simon came to visit us in the studio. He felt the words were so controversial that the groove should be light-hearted. The listener would get caught up in the fun feel and the lyric would fly by without being noticed. That's when I came up with the first drum fill, which is basically a rip-off of Mitch Mitchell's playing on Jimi Hendrix's "Up from the Skies" on *Axis: Bold as Love*. The whole brush swing feel comes from that record. Doug and I had gone out partying the night before we recorded "Only the Good Die Young," and I was so hung over that I passed out in the broom closet of the studio right after we recorded the track.

One of the greatest things to happen to *The Stranger* album came from the Catholic Church. "Only the Good Die Young" was bombing as a single and falling off the charts when Catholic churches banned the song. The worst thing you can tell a young person is that they can't do (or listen to) something. The Church wound up selling a lot of records for us. I put a couple of extra bucks in the basket on Sunday.

## "SHE'S ALWAYS A WOMAN"

As previously explained, Billy's wife Elizabeth was his manager at this time, and she ruled with an iron fist. Doug and I would always complain to Billy that she was too controlling, and that she would cut us down if we asked for more money. Billy had an uncanny ability to be able to separate the wife from the manager. So when he came in with the song, Doug and I heard what Billy really felt regarding what we had been telling him. How can you complain after a song like that?

The fact is, Elizabeth was nothing like any woman I knew. She was brilliant in the music business, a business that was dominated by men at the time. Elizabeth dared to enter this world knowing the opposition and hostility she would face. She opened the door that made Billy Joel the major artist he is today, and was a trail-blazer in this line of work. Elizabeth is still involved in creating new musical works and theater, and she was instrumental in getting me, Richie, Russell, and Doug inducted into the Long Island Music Hall of Fame. I have total respect for her and love her dearly.

### "GET IT RIGHT THE FIRST TIME"

"Get it Right the First Time" fades in because it took a few go-rounds for me to get comfortable playing the groove. I remember coming up with this beat: I was listening to a tape with just Billy on piano playing the song and I worked out the drum parts in a little room in a rented house in Northport, Long Island. People thought it was Steve Gadd playing the drums on the track—a great compliment.

As we tried to record "Get it Right the First Time," we just couldn't get it. We would do "Movin' Out," and then try "Get it Right the First Time," then we would do "The Stranger" and then "Get it Right the First Time" again, then "Just the Way You Are" and then "Get It Right the First Time" yet again. It was one of the last songs that we completed for *The Stranger*. Every time we tried, we would end up saying, "Why don't you go ahead and get Stuff to play it. Get Steve Gadd to play it." Phil would say, "No, you guys are going to play it. You're already playing it; you just don't have the confidence right now to think that you can do it."

That's the difference between playing something and *playing something*. I was trying to mimic Steve Gadd, but I wasn't putting any Liberty DeVitto in it. Not being Steve Gadd, it didn't sound right. It might have been the same kind of part Steve would play, but that's not how he would play it. Phil knew it was just a matter of time until we finally figured, "We can do it, we recorded the rest of the album, this shouldn't be hard."

### "EVERYBODY HAS A DREAM"

This was an old song Billy had hanging around. It was actually on the tape Doug gave me when I auditioned for Billy, but it had a very straight two-and-four feel. I always loved this song. When Billy needed one more song for the album, I told him to play "Everybody has a Dream" for Phil, who changed it to a 6/8 feel and put it on *The Stranger*.

Russell originally called the album *Old Bug-Eyes is Back*, because of Billy's eyes. It was also called *The Strangler* by an interviewer. The back cover was shot at the Macaroni Factory in downtown Manhattan, a mom-and- pop Italian restaurant.

I didn't realize the popularity and success of *The Stranger* until one night in Washington, D.C. We had just finished a gig at the Daughters of the American Revolution Hall, and Billy and I were leaving through the back doors. Billy walked out first and was jumped by a screaming crowd of girls. I saw his face as he was being mobbed by this frenzy; the expression was saying, "Whoa, this is so cool." I knew at that moment we had made it. Not long after that, *The Stranger* went gold with 500,000 copies sold, then platinum with a million copies. The total sales quickly jumped to four million.

The reason for this fast growth was Columbia Records' new tactic. Instead of taking a new artist and spending money on recording and promoting them, maybe selling 50,000 copies, why not take a million-selling artist, with whom you've already recouped your investment several times over, and make him a multi-million seller without investing too much more. This is one of the reasons why albums by the Eagles and Paul Simon were so huge. *The Stranger* was one of the first records Columbia tried this with; it was very successful.

Billy and the band were gung-ho to tour and Columbia was doing great radio promotion. During this time, the Sam Goody scandal came to light. The Sam Goody Corporation, then a major seller of music, and its president, Samuel Stolon, were knowingly purchasing and reselling bootleg copies of Eric Clapton's *Slow Hand*, the *Grease* soundtrack, *The Stranger*, and several other albums. Billy testified as a government witness in the U.S. Justice Department's trial against the retail giant. Unfortunately, according to court accounts, Billy wasn't able to help much. He seemed nonchalant at the hearings and was unable to determine the difference between the bootleg and authorized copies of his album. The jury convicted Stolon as well as the Goody Corporation. Billy lost thousands from the scam.

*The Stranger* ultimately wound up selling seven million copies. We were becoming more and more popular with each passing day. As the record sales increased, our tours got bigger. We played our first arena show at Maple Leaf Gardens in Toronto. Management was interested to see if we could make the transition from theater to arena without losing the personal touch. After shows, there were always crowds waiting for us at the hotels where we stayed. The hotels were never far from the venue, making it easy for fans to find us, so when we'd get out of our cars, they'd chase us into the hotel to get an autograph or a picture, or just to meet us.

One night, I was being chased by a group of people. Richie was walking ahead of me with two women. I ran up and grabbed one of them by the arm and said, "Make believe you're my wife!" Several months later, that girl and I were married. The marriage was a mistake. I was 27 and wanted someone who was going to be there when I got home, and I was convinced that I needed someone to take care of my finances while I was on the road. The problem was I was having too much fun on the road. I was a "rock star" and she was a New Jersey schoolteacher. The only thing we had in common was that we both loved alcohol; she became a drunken adult and I was a drunken adolescent. I should have never gotten married; the only thing that changed for me was that I now had a ring on my finger and a piece of paper signed by a judge. I was still partying every night and hanging out with strange women. I was a shitty husband.

The partying became a blur. Doug and I would ask ourselves, "When was the last time you didn't drink for two days in a row?" On a plane, traveling to the next gig, I'd say to Doug, "I'm not fooling around tonight; I am not getting crazy tonight." But we'd always fall right back into it.

An amazing thing happened to the way people, especially women, perceived us, as well. We'd be sitting in a hotel bar somewhere and there would be a bunch of women having a "girl's night out." We'd try to start a conversation with them and they'd want nothing to do with us. Maybe one of us would ask where we could find a laundromat. The women could tell from our accents that we weren't from around there, and they'd ask what we were doing in town. "Our band is playing," we'd say, and suddenly we'd have their interest. "Where's your band playing?" they'd ask. We'd tell them whatever "enormodome" was in their city. Then they'd ask the question that would change us from beasts to princes:

"What's the name of your band?."

I'd say, "I play drums for Billy Joel." It would be amazing how we would suddenly be transformed: we were no longer two disheveled guys with horrible New York accents; we were the stars who played on the sensitive hit song "Just the Way You Are." "We can't believe you're here!" they'd say, and then party with us for the rest of the time we were in that town. If you spent the night at a girl's place, as opposed to your hotel room, it was called an "away game." Many a time I would wake up in strange surroundings, panicking for a minute, wondering where I was. Then a strange woman would walk in the room and I'd say, "Who are you?" When one of us brought a woman back to our hotel room, we knew an old joke that explained our feelings perfectly: What is the definition of eternity? Answer: The time between when you climax and she leaves. Some guys liked hookers better. You didn't pay them for the sex; you paid them to leave when you were done.

So, that was *The Stranger*.

# Groupies

**B**ecause they inhabit every part of rock 'n' roll, I felt that groupies needed their own chapter in this book. They come in all shapes and sizes. Some just want to say they met the band, others literally shake when they are talking to you. There was a group of fans in Japan who came to every show and showed up at the train stations in every city. I had befriended this one girl who would wait in front of the hotel to see us, because they were not allowed inside. The Japanese promoters were very strict about this. Out of curiosity, I asked her if she had a boyfriend. She explained that she loved music and the music was her boyfriend. The way she said it and the look in her eyes led me to believe she was totally touched by what we had done musically. I know what you're thinking—but no, nothing happened.

Then there are the ones that go all the way; groupies that want to party and sleep with band members. I will never understand the effect our music had on people; I guess similar things happen in all fields that represent power or position. The backstage pass is the holy grail to some, and they will do anything to get one. We just so happened to have the song "Just the Way You Are" in our arsenal, so women thought we were the sensitive types that understood them. They thought we were playing it directly to them. Before anyone was married, it was insane. I will admit, it did continue even after the ring was on the finger for me. Sometimes if we were simply hanging in a bar, a woman would come over just to say how much she loved our music. If she was with a guy, sometimes this meant trouble.

One time I was in a bar having drinks with a friend and a woman came up to me to say she loved the songs we recorded and the way I played drums. Her boyfriend and his buddies were there, and they were drunk. There is nothing worse than a bunch of jealous drunken idiots, and it's usually the friend of the boyfriend that feels the need to come to the girl's rescue. So this particular time, a guy came up to me and started the usual babbling, "Oh, you think you're so good," or "Your band fuckin' sucks." I tried to explain that I was just innocently talking to the lady, but this time, as I turned back to the bar, this moron put me in a chokehold. While he's choking me, he's saying Billy Joel is going to be looking for a new drummer because he was going to kill me. I immediately did an old trick my mother taught me when I was a kid: I reached behind me and grabbed him by the balls. I squeezed his nuts so hard he had no choice but to let go of me. I can still see him walking away in pain, holding his nuts in shame.

Another time we were drinking in a bar in Georgetown outside of D.C. Again a girl came over to tell us how much she loved our music. Again, the boyfriend's friend was the one who started the trouble. At one point our tour manager tried to defuse the situation, but to no avail; the guy called him a pussy and told him to fuck off. The difference with this situation was that this time I was hammered. I and some of the other band members went to the bathroom. The guy was in there. As he was walking out he said, "Oh look who it is, it's the pussies." I told one of my guys, "I'm gonna take this motherfucker out."

The guy was sitting at a table on a bar stool, so I stuck my arm out and gave him a clothesline right in the neck, knocking him off his stool. As I stood there, he slowly got up. He kept getting bigger and wider, and when he finally stood all the way up (with me holding his throat) I began to realize he was about six feet, eight inches to my five-foot-eleven, he probably weighed in at 220 to my 174 pounds. He must have played football in college. So I did what David would have done to Goliath if he didn't have a rock: I poked him right in the eye. He said "ouch!" and covered his eye, then poked his fingers right through my glasses. That's when all hell broke loose and it seemed like everyone in the bar was fighting. Finally, he was thrown out the front door and the cops were called in.

After the dust settled I told the bartender I was sorry for starting the fight. He said, "Are you kidding? We've been trying to get that asshole out of here for months!" Another advantage to being who we were was that the cops were obliged to drive us back to the hotel in their squad car. I woke up the next morning with a black eye. The moral of the story: always bring an extra pair of glasses while on the road.

*

The worst, though, are the male groupies. Especially if they are your friend. I had a friend who I had met through someone in my family. He was a great guy, or at least I thought he was; he'd do anything for me and my family. What I found out too late was that he was working his way to Billy and then eventually Elton through me. He came to rehearsals with me, flew out on the road to hang with us, befriended the band and crew, and made jackets with everyone's names on them. He even showed up at the Rock 'n' Roll Hall of Fame induction. Eventually he got so close to Billy that he was negotiating my salary. I should have known shit was going wrong when he stole my autographed Elton album. He started to wear my skin and was becoming me. It was like a science fiction movie: the invasion of the body snatchers. His only problem was he couldn't play the drums. I cut him off from my life but he still maintained a relationship with Billy. He eventually blew it with Billy when he threatened to kill one of Billy's best buddies for hitting on his girlfriend.

We were on tour and one of the stops was Louisville, Kentucky. This guy started to send me gifts on the road; he knew where we were playing by checking the internet. He'd send me bottles of Kentucky bourbon; I wasn't drinking at the time. He would contact me on social websites. I was nice enough to write him back and thank him for his gift. Eventually he started to write how he knew the tour was coming to Louisville and he wanted me to get him backstage. This was during a tour with Elton John and Billy, so I wrote back telling him it was too tight backstage to give him access. Not getting the hint, he kept insisting, saying how great it was going to be hanging backstage with us. Because I come from New York, he said, he was going to send a full spread of bagels and lox to the venue for me. I guess he assumed that because I come from New York, I must be Jewish. I kept writing to him saying, "Don't send anything, there is no backstage," but he kept insisting. When I arrived on the day of the show in Louisville, one of the crew guys told me someone who said he was my friend sent a whole bunch of bagels and lox for me. "How much of a friend is he if he doesn't know you are allergic to fish?" asked the crew member. The next morning, this was the email I received:

*Dear Lib,*
*Let me tell you something, you fucking dickhead bastard… I think you are a fucking piece of shit. You, your band, and anyone affiliated with Billy Joel. Fuck you, asshole. I went to the expense and trouble of sending you fucking gifts and pleasantries and I try to come see you guys and it's like fucking Fort Knox, while I stand there and watch all these dignitaries come backstage with nothing more than a fucking good looking piece of ass on their hands with backstage passes and VIP stickers on. I spend hard-earned money on a chance to meet you guys and go the extra mile to try to let you know how much it means to me to have you here, and send you guys bourbon and food backstage, and then you treat me like some fucking pauper. Fuck you."*

This went on for several pages and included some really nasty business involving "devil dick," whatever the hell that means. I did send the note on to Billy and Elton, just to be a sharer. I won't repeat what Elton said, but it still makes me laugh to this day.

About this seafood allergy that I just mentioned: I developed it suddenly while playing one night at JFK Stadium in Philadelphia. I had eaten seafood all my life. I'm Italian, so my mother would always do the gigantic fish feast at Christmas Eve, and I ate everything. This night would change all that. At dinner I had eaten two bowls of pasta with shrimp, then went to my pre-show shower. (We all had rituals for before and after the show.) I stepped out of the shower and was drying myself off when I felt itching from my wrists down to my ankles. I thought it must be the towel. Soon the itching went away so, thinking nothing of it, I started the show. We were a few songs in when the temperature hit 95° and the lights that were on us made it feel like 110° on stage—it was *hot*.

About four songs into the show, during "Scenes from an Italian Restaurant," the full-blown allergic reaction to the shrimp hit me. My lips started to swell up, my eyes started to close, and then I couldn't breathe. I was beating my chest as I was trying to play, then I started getting weaker and began to slow down. Billy looked over at me thinking I was having a heart attack. Barely making it through the song, I began to fall off my stool when my drum tech grabbed me and dragged me onto the drum cases stacked behind the kit. Fortunately, at every outdoor venue there are paramedics on the side of the stage. A doctor came running up to me and started telling me to lay still; they'd be taking me into an ambulance. In a very high-pitched voice, because my throat was almost completely closed, I said, "I have to go back on and finish the set." The doctor responded, "You're not going anywhere but to the hospital." Luckily, Elton's drummer, Charlie Morgan, knew the set, because we had been touring together for a while. They went to Charlie's dressing room, loaded him into a golf cart, drove him to the stage, and before they'd even told him what had happened, he had to go up and finish Billy's set. (He did a great job. Thank you, Charlie.)

They got me into the ambulance and gave me a shot of adrenaline. At the hospital, they examined me, gave me another shot, and said all I could do was wait for the swelling to go down. After a few hours I was driven back to the hotel. The next day, I woke up and the swelling was almost gone. Luckily, it was a day off. I decided to go to the movies; *Forrest Gump* was playing around the corner. Now, I had just had a severe allergic reaction to shrimp. I don't know if you remember the scene in the movie when Bubba talks about all the different kinds of shrimp dishes, but it was killing me!

Soon after that night in Philly, the Billy Joel-Elton John tour was on its way to Japan. In the hospital they told me not only to stay away from shellfish, but to not eat any fish at all until I got tested to find out my specific allergies. This was perfect timing, since I was headed to a country where basically all they eat is fish. Not being a Japanese speaker, I needed a note written in Japanese that said I was allergic to fish, which I would be able to show a waiter or waitress at a restaurant so I would be safe. When we arrived, I went to the bellman at the hotel to ask for this note. I tried to explain that I needed a note that said, "I am allergic to fish." I quickly realized the bellman did not speak any English, so I tried to see if I could get my point across another way. I said, "I cannot eat fish." That didn't work. Then I hit my hand on my chest and said "Me, no fish!" while doing the international hand motion for *no*. "Ah!" he said in the way the Japanese do, which led me to believe he finally understood me. Motioning for me to wait, he went in the back room, and when he came back he smiled broadly as he handed me my note. I said "thank you" in Japanese—one of the only things I knew how to say in Japanese—and went on my way knowing I was now safe to eat in Japan.

When I went into restaurants, I would give the waiter or waitress my note, but I did not get the expected result. Usually they would make a face like it was strange but they understood, then hand me back the note and walk away. This kept happening, and I thought they were looking at me as if to say, "If you can't eat fish, why the hell are you in Japan?" One day, a Japanese friend of mine who spoke and wrote fluent English came to visit me. I told him my story and showed him the note. Laughing, he told me that it said "I am not a fish." The moral of this story? I should have forgotten about the note and just gone down to the Subway sandwich store in the hotel!

**Graphic from back of a jacket given to me by Phil Ramone during the recording of *52nd Street*.**

# 21

# *52nd Street*

The studio where we recorded this album, A&R, was at 799 Seventh Avenue, New York City, but the entrance was on 52nd Street. (This is where the cover photo was shot.) Fifty-second Street was famous for its jazz clubs; in its heyday, you could walk from club to club down the street and hear some of the most legendary jazz musicians of all time on any given night. At the time we recorded, the musicians union (Local 802) was also on 52nd Street, in the Roseland Ballroom. Between all of this, and with the Beatles naming *Abbey Road* for where EMI Studios were located, we called our album *52nd Street*.

Living in South Jersey at the time, I was still married but acting as if I wasn't. I wanted to go back to where I was from; I loved Long Island and it was all I knew. Billy's management wouldn't spring for a hotel room during recording, so I would drive home to Willingboro, New Jersey, every night and then back to Midtown in the morning. It was a two-hour drive that had me closer to Philadelphia than to Manhattan. Also, I missed hanging out with the band. Doug told me it was starting to show in my playing, so I had to get my shit together real quick. If music is my mistress, she was getting pissed. There is no room to be tired. Doug and I eventually got to stay at a hotel down the block from the studio, which really improved things. I got to hang out with the guys, sleep, and even pop in on an old girlfriend a few times.

One day Doug and I were called into Elizabeth's office at Home Run Management. She offered us a deal on *52nd Street*. We'd get double session, double scale, and then a bonus of $10,000 when the album was turned in to Columbia. After the meeting, we went to the studio and told Phil Ramone about the deal. Doug said he would not play for that amount of money. Phil said, "Someone is offering you work plus ten grand, and you're not gonna take it?" He thought Doug was crazy not to agree, but then he said, "Ask her this: If she's willing to give you $10,000 before any records have been sold, ask her for $10,000 after every million are sold." We did and she agreed. These bonuses were based only on American record sales; all foreign sales and singles were excluded. We did not realize that the word "bonus" would eventually bite us in the ass. We should have insisted on the word "royalty" instead. Royalties go on forever, but bonuses can be stopped at any time, which they eventually were. Whatever deal Richie made for the album he kept to himself; he was a good businessman. He'd always say, "Does Macy's tell Gimbels?"

## "BIG SHOT"

Doug and I went to Billy's house on Long Island to rehearse songs for the upcoming album. The house was called "Tips" because Elizabeth always thought the tips of things were the best part—the tip of a slice of pizza, the tip of a piece of cake, etc. I brought my own drums, Doug brought his amp, and we worked out the arrangement for "Big Shot." Billy would sing a verse, then the chorus, then get up to the "uh oh ooh ooh ooh" part and stop. He was having a hard time writing lyrics for that part, he said. We told him he had enough words and he should let Richie do a sax solo there. "You just saved me a lot of work," he said. "Let's eat." We were already rehearsing for the *52nd Street* tour while the overdubs were being done. Billy wasn't happy with the guitar parts, so he brought in David Brown, who had just been hired for the tour, to see what he could do for the end of "Big Shot." David is not credited on the album, but what he played is what you hear. One take.

### "HONESTY"

I forced Billy into writing the lyrics to this song. I don't like to record without words, so as we ran the song down, I'd make up my own words. Through the drum microphones, Billy could hear me singing ridiculous things like, "Sodomy is such a lonely word." Finally he stopped the song and said, "Okay that's all for now, I can't take any more. I'm going home to write lyrics." The next day he returned to the studio with the finished lyrics. "Honesty" is one of my favorite songs. Originally it had a classical section after the bridge, but this was dumped in the final hours of recording. There were also tons more cymbal crashes throughout the song, but Billy hated them and said they sounded like something from Zorba the Greek. Billy only sang the high note in the chorus at the end of the song once, and that's the take you hear on the album. "Well," he said, "that's the last time I'll ever hit that note." He hit every time we did the song.

### "MY LIFE"

The first verse of this song came from an actual phone conversation Billy had with a friend. He started to write lyrics to what is now the instrumental part in the beginning. I made up some really nasty words: "You suck my '—,' what a way to say good morning." Billy couldn't get them out of his head. The part stayed instrumental. Sometimes during live shows, he'd mouth those nasty lyrics to me.

During rehearsal with Elton John for the Face to Face tour, Elton stopped "My Life" and told Billy that I wasn't playing it right. Billy told Elton, "He's not ever going to play it right. He hates this song." To be honest, I still think it sucks.

In the studio I was arguing with Phil about the drum part he wanted me to play. It was a straight disco beat, which I thought sucked, so I told him I wouldn't do it. He got pissed, threw something at the console and said, "You've been in the business for twenty minutes now and you think you can tell me what you'll do and won't do? Get out there and play what I know will work." I think of that story every time I look at that gold "My Life" single on the wall. Later in life, I would be reprimanding my kids and they'd say, "I don't care what you say anymore, this is my life. Go ahead with your own life, leave me alone." Ouch!

While writing the lyrics, Billy had come up with "Then they'll tell you can't sleep with somebody else. Ah, but sooner or later you sleep in your own space." I remember looking at him and saying "Either way it's okay, you wake up with yourself."—not thinking he would use it!

### "ZANZIBAR"

To me, "Zanzibar" is one of Billy's best, musically and lyrically. The original demo didn't have the lyric, "I got a jazz guitar," so there was no jazz section. Once the lyric was written, it was swing time. Phil and Billy flew with the master tape to L.A., so we never got to meet trumpeter Freddie Hubbard, who played the closing solo on the tune. The final solo is a compilation of three solos that Freddie did; Phil put together the best parts to make the one solo. Going into the first solo, you can hear me put my sticks on the floor tom and pick up the brushes. The one-bar rest coming out of the solo section with the brushes was originally two bars, so I could have time to switch from brushes back to sticks, but after the song was recorded one bar was sliced out. If there was no fade, you'd hear me, Doug, and Billy fall apart. By the time we got to the end of the song we had played as much jazz as we could possibly stand.

### "ROSALINDA'S EYES"

"Rosalinda's Eyes" is a rock band trying to play a Latin feel. When other musicians heard "Zanzibar," "Get it Right the First Time," "Just the Way You Are," and "Rosalinda," they were under the misconception that we were jazz guys trying to play rock. There was actually a time when Doug and I were getting more jazz gigs than rock gigs. Sometimes a bandleader would drop a chart on me—that's when I would thank God for Doug. I couldn't read music, but Doug was a great reader, and he would walk me through the tune. Most of the time, the artist we were playing with just liked the way we played and allowed us to do what we wanted; it was our feel they were after.

"Rosalinda's Eyes" was a big part of our show in Havana, Cuba, in 1978. The people were familiar with the song because they were able to pick it up in Havana from Miami radio stations. After we left Cuba, my drum part was taught as an American version of a Cuban beat.

### "STILETTO"

The working title for this song was "Forgiveness." It's us doing our Traffic groove. Traffic was an English rock band formed in Birmingham, England, in April, 1967 by Steve Winwood, Jim Capaldi, Chris Wood, and Dave Mason. Billy and I had a common love for this band.

For the recording, I thought I had come up with a great sound for the finger snaps. It was raining that day, so I had an umbrella with me. It was the kind you fold up and collapse, so it fits in your jacket pocket. You had to push a button to open it and then it would extend and click into a locked position. I went out into the studio and after clicking it about ten times, I got a sound on a mic that was perfect to imitate the finger snaps. When it was time to record, I put my headphones on and started to listen to the track. I pressed the umbrella button for the first click, and the top of it came shooting off the rod, causing lots of laughs in the studio. We went back to our first idea: real finger snaps.

### "HALF A MILE AWAY"

This song almost didn't make it onto the album. Originally sixteen bars, the pre-choruses were very long and repetitive. It felt like it took forever to get to the verse. Phil came up with the idea of just cutting out four bars of the chorus—which in those days was done physically, with a razor blade. He saved the song. Sometimes it's as simple as a little nip and tuck. We never played "Half a Mile Away" live.

### "UNTIL THE NIGHT"

Another one of Billy's best, in my opinion. For this song, I kept telling myself to think of the Righteous Brothers. I would never have made it through the recording had I not known the words. When we finally finished the take I couldn't believe I remembered how the song went. When I heard it back in the control room it was like an out-of-body experience; I didn't remember playing any of it because we had learned and recorded it so fast. It was fun to play this one live. I made a mistake in the tune, but as they say, if you're going to make a mistake, make it loud. It could be the best thing you play all day. Billy loved it.

### "52ND STREET"

This was a last minute addition to the album. I think it was recorded in one take. It's the only tune that's really just the band: Doug, Billy, Richie, and me. I call this vibe "perfectly sloppy."

# 22

# Cuba

The Havana Jam was held at the 4,800 seat Karl Marx Theater, just west of downtown Havana, Cuba. The first Cuban-American collaboration held since Castro's 1959 revolution, it was a series of concerts held over three days. On March 1, 1979, a TWA 707 brought 134 Americans to Havana Airport, including Russell Javors and Richie Cannata. During their flight, Russell yelled out that they were heading to the "Bay of Gigs." Of course, the Bay of Pigs invasion was the failed military counter-revolution in Cuba undertaken by the Central Intelligence Agency. The United States sought the elimination of Castro for his brutal displays of power and insistence on communism.

Billy, Doug, Elizabeth, and I flew from Key West to Havana on a chartered jet. Billy was the biggest commercial selling artist on CBS at the time; *The Stranger* and *52nd Street* had sold over eight million copies in two years. Others on the trip included Kris Kristofferson and his wife, singer Rita Coolidge; Stephen Stills; jazz group Weather Report; the Columbia Jazz All-Stars, which included Stan Getz, John McLaughlin, Herbert Laws, and Jimmy and Percy Heath; and the Fania All-Stars. In between every American act at the festival there was a native Cuban band, which included the eleven-member group Irakere.

When we arrived at the airport, we were transported to the hotel in a "cab": a green 1959 Ford Falcon with bald tires. The driver sped down the rain-slicked roads as we watched zombie like people walk the streets. A soldier with a machine gun sat in the middle of every intersection. We stayed at the Mar Azul (Ocean Blue) Hotel, which was, appropriately, right on the beach. We were all freaked out by the time warp we were experiencing. It seemed that time had stood still in 1959. Either there was a big black market for American car parts, or the mechanics of Havana were incredibly talented in keeping those twenty- to thirty-year-old American cars running. The hotel was so sparse that it had no television, a phone in every room that didn't work, a bed, a lamp, and a bathroom with running salt water. The maids came around to the rooms every day with pitchers of fresh water. The lobby bar had rum and beer. The drink of choice was a rum mint lime drink called a mojito. We consumed these in mass quantities along with other mind enhancers that just seemed to show up.

During the day, we would stand on the balcony of our hotel rooms and throw packs of cigarettes down to the locals. We all ate breakfast, lunch, and dinner at the same time in the same room. On the beach, where there were mostly Russian tourists, we'd give out tee shirts to the local teenagers. They would turn the shirts inside out and put them on that way, so they could pass the military police that were at the ends of the beaches without having the shirts confiscated. The kids would ask us questions about America and American music, telling us how they'd heard us on radio stations transmitted from Miami. They'd ask us for American tee shirts and jeans, but most of all they wanted American dollars. If the day came when they could get a raft or boat and leave Cuba, they said, they'd need our money once they reached our shores.

One American reporter was offered a pretty Cuban girl in exchange for his $35 designer sneakers. He passed—he must have really loved his sneakers. We took Polaroids of the locals and watched their childlike reactions as they saw the photo develop right in front of their eyes. The water was beautiful. When you swam out, you could be anywhere; the Caribbean, Mexico, etc., but when you turned to swim back in, you were immediately reminded where you were. The beach was lined with military bunkers, each equipped with machine guns pointed outwards toward the seas. On a night off we went to the Tropicana. It was like being in a time machine; I couldn't imagine it being any different in the 1950s, when Americans vacationed there and the Mafia was in control of the hotels and casinos. It looked just like a scene from "I Love Lucy," when Ricky Ricardo was there. The décor, scenery, costumes—everything was from the '50s. It was classic.

On show days, the rule was everyone had to go to the shows, whether you were playing that night or not. Buses were our transportation. Weather Report, an influential American jazz-fusion band, featuring Austrian-born keyboard player Joe Zawinul, American saxophonist Wayne Shorter, Jaco Pastorius on bass, and drummer/percussionist Peter Erskine was the first band to perform. They used smoke machines in the first minutes of their act. I watched and laughed as the smoke came over the front of the stage and the first three rows of the Cuban audience jumped out of their seats. Having no idea what was going on, they ran to the back of the theater; they had never seen smoke machines before. Each night the show was five hours long, which is an awful lot of mojitos for those who were not performing. We were drunk every night. One night we watched Jaco Pastorius jump out of a window in the back of the theater into the moonlit ocean filled with boulders. We partied every night as the police watched from a distance.

Billy and the band were the last ones to perform. The people went nuts. They were screaming, "Bee-lee, Bee-lee" while running towards the stage. At the end of the show they bravely yelled at the guards to get off the stage so we could do an encore. Billy moved the crowd with the same intensity as Fidel Castro, who spoke years before in the same theater. Billy was just as charismatic.

The shows were filmed and recorded by CBS for a live album and TV special. Billy's management were the only ones to refuse to have their artist be

Uncle Liberty, 1944.

My Sicilian grandparents,
France Prestigiacomo and
Salvatore Sardisco, 1920.

Dad on his way to Bastogne, Battle
of the Bulge, World War II, 1944.

**Outtake from Supa's Jamboree photo shoot, 1971.**

**My first endorsement, Tama Drums, 1978.**

**Billy and I clowning before a show at Toad's Place, New Haven, CT, during the recording of *Songs in the Attic*, 1981.**

Liberty DeVitto    Doug Stegmeyer    Billy Joel    Richie Cannata

**BILLY JOEL**

Columbia

7810

**Columbia Records promo shot for *52nd Street*, 1978.**

**Billy Joel Band. L to R: Richie Cannata, Russell Javors, Doug Stegmeyer, me, Billy, David Brown,** *52nd Street*, **1978**

**Me and Billy backstage having a laugh during** *The Stranger* **tour, 1977.**

Me and Billy on Phil Ramone's baseball team, "Ramone's Rangers," 1983.

With Billy at a motorcycle rally for Charity Begins at Home, 1984.

**Russell, Doug, and me at dinner in Japan, 1986.**

**The studio mafia: L to R: Jim Boyer (engineer), Phil Ramone (producer), and Brad Leigh (engineer).**

**Waiting for the bullet train in Japan with promoter Mr. Udo, 1980.**

**Recording session with a Beatle! L to R behind Paul McCartney: me, Dave Lebolt, Neil Jason, and David Brown, Power Station, NYC, 1986.**

**Steve Gadd, Richard Marx, me, and Billy, 1989.**

**Recording with Karen Carpenter for her solo album, 1979.**

**Receiving gold albums in Australia for *The Bridge* and *Greatest Hits I & II*, 1986.**

**Old Glory in the Soviet Union, 1987.**

**Performing on *The Bridge* tour, 1986.**

**Italian Americans of Distinction event, June 9, 2014. L to R: Dad, me, Governor Andrew Cuomo, Tony Danza, 2014.**

**My girls: Maryelle, Torrey, and Devon**

**Fifty three years later and still friends: Me and Carmine Appice.**

**With the Queen of Rock 'n' Roll, Ronnie Spector.**

**The one who bumped Ringo off the top of my list, the great Dino Danelli.**

**Reuniting with Mitch Ryder, who I toured with at age eighteen, in 2015.**

**Russell, Supa, and I playing at Recovery Unplugged Treatment Center, Fort Lauderdale, FL, 2019.**

**Some of the cast from the documentary *Hired Gun*, August, 2017.**

**Me with my Liberty drums.**

**Playing at the Cavern in Liverpool, England, with Billy J. Kramer, August, 2010**

**My Sicilian Family.**

**Dad at 91 years old.**

**In concert with the Lords of 52nd Street on Long Island, 2019.**

**Proud to be an American.**

a part of the filming and recording, with Billy saying, "We are not down here on some capitalist venture, I'm here to play music for these people." The next day we left by jet, while the others waited four hours at the airport to depart for home.

"Cuban exiles" refers to the many Cubans who fled from or left the island of Cuba. These people consist of two primary groups loosely defined by the period of time occurring before and after the Mariel boatlift of the 1980s. The pre-Mariel group consisted of the mostly middle and upper classes of the island who fled due to fear of widespread reprisals after the communist takeover led by Fidel Castro from the 1950s to the 1970s. The people in this group were mainly seeking political asylum. The second group consists of those people who emigrated from Cuba during and after the 1980s. By and large, the majority of these people were, and are, economic migrants. The phenomenon dates back to the Ten Years' War and the struggle for Cuban independence during the 19th century. In modern times, the term refers to the large exodus of Cubans to the United States since the 1959 Cuban Revolution.

Some of the kids we met on the beach in Cuba showed up backstage at one of our later shows. After we left Cuba, they said, a lot of the people we had met on the beach were put in jail just because they had spoken to us. Everything we gave them was confiscated. They told us how some of the people we befriended had drowned when their small, overcrowded boats had capsized in the ocean as they tried to make it to the United States. The kid who told us about this had actually been on a boat that capsized, but he held onto the boat and drifted. Some of his family members were lost, but he was able to make it.

In 2006 I met a drummer at the NAMM show in California who was at the show we played in Cuba. With tears welling, he held my hand and told me how he had decided to play the drums after hearing me that night. Now living in America, he is an accomplished drummer touring the world. To touch someone's life like that means more to me than playing Madison Square Garden or winning a Grammy. To inspire is my greatest accomplishment. At a recent Lords of 52nd Street show in Florida I met another Cuban gentleman who was at the Havana show. Hugs and gratitude were in abundance that night.

**Outtake from the liner notes photo session for *Glass Houses*. L to R: Doug Stegmeyer, Russell Javors, me, David Brown, Richie Cannata.**

# 23

# *Glass Houses*

People who live in glass houses shouldn't throw stones. The cover shot was taken at Billy's house in Long Island. Billy hated the shot of the band that was to be on the record sleeve. Feeling that it was too posed, he wrote on the original negative with a grease pencil, listing our names and instruments and drawing arrows to our head. This dressed it down a bit. The photographer said that we were so boring in front of the camera that he wanted us to do something different, so I put my watch on my ankle. David Brown's shoes were so filthy that they had to airbrush out the footprints he left on the white paper floor during the development process.

By now I was back on Long Island, living in an area called Harbor Green in Massapequa. Accountants were advising me to have my wife quit teaching because I'd be paying more taxes if she continued to work, so she did. It seemed like we had a party every night. I had a room with a jukebox and a stereo in it. Doug bought me a neon sign, the kind that hangs in bar windows, that said "The Reptile Room." This was because when people walked in, they usually crawled out. Music was always blasting, and I'd always invite the neighbors so no one would call the cops. David Brown got lost in the neighborhood one time and asked someone on the street, "Do you know where Liberty lives?" They brought him to my house.

Doug and I wanted more money for the album, so we decided to meet with a hotshot music lawyer. We arrived at his firm and the receptionist took us into his office. About two minutes later he came in and positioned himself behind his desk.

He said, "So, you guys want more money!"

"Yup."

"Are you willing to quit?"

"Nope."

"Then there's nothing I can do for you."

He got up, opened the door to his office, and led us out. We stayed at double scale, double session, and kept the $10,000 bonus for this one too. We knew we had a hit with *Glass Houses* because in the middle of recording, we went out and played "You May Be Right," "Sometimes a Fantasy," and "All for Leyna," and all of the songs got tremendous receptions. The tour built anticipation for the new album with the fans.

While recording *Glass Houses*, we also recorded an album with Karen

Carpenter. With Phil Ramone producing, the album was recorded in New York in 1979 and 1980. Some of the songs from the album were later featured on the Carpenters' 1989 compilation *Lovelines* as well as later releases. In the liner notes, Karen dedicated the project to her brother: "To Richard, with all my heart." The liner notes—as well as including comments from Richard Carpenter and Phil Ramone—include Richard's explanation for shelving the album in 1981 and his later decision to release it. Karen was backed by various New York musicians including Steve Gadd, Greg Phillinganes, Louis Johnson, and us. *The New York Times* called us "Billy Joel Ruffians," which included David, Doug, Russell—who wrote two songs on the album—and me.

### "YOU MAY BE RIGHT"

This was the first time we had the full touring band in the studio; no studio musicians. Billy and I played maracas on this track, definitely trying for a Rolling Stones vibe. We did ride motorcycles in the rain, but walking through Bed-Stuy was a bit of a stretch for any white boy from Long Island at that time. I walk my little girl in the stroller through Bed-Stuy now. Boy, how times have changed.

### "SOMETIMES A FANTASY"

The first day of recording of every album starts with Billy laying down all the ideas he has. He always felt that the idea may be good by itself, but the true test was to see if it would fly with the band. When we did the demo for "Sometimes a Fantasy," there was a glitch in the 24-track tape machine that made a high pitched sound right after the guitar solo. The machine played such a perfect part that when we did the final take, the sound was duplicated on a synthesizer. There is an extended version of this song where it doesn't fade out, and at the end you can hear Billy repeating Ringo Starr's words at the end of "Helter Skelter": "I got blisters on my fingers."

### "DON'T ASK ME WHY"

On this song, I only played with one stick, which was in my left hand playing the floor tom, while I held two maracas in my right hand. David, who was playing acoustic guitar, was having a hard time hearing me in his headphones. They mic'd David right next to my drums and he played with one side of his headphones off so he could hear the drums in the room. This made the drum track leak into the guitar track and vice versa, so both tracks had to be mixed as one. There was no isolation at all, which actually led to a better sound on both instruments. The track originally had a flute solo by Richie but that was replaced by Billy's piano solo. Richie played the claves and Billy played castanets on the track.

### "IT'S STILL ROCK AND ROLL TO ME"

"So Bill," I said one day, "How do you really feel about the music reviews in *Rolling Stone*?" This song is based on Billy's answer to that question. He was angry at the reviewers. If we did two shows in a row in the same city, he used to do a thing on stage called "review the reviewer." Billy would take the first night's review on stage for the second show and tell the crowd, "OK, let's review the reviewer!" Then he'd read to the crowd what had been written. Sometimes reviewers got set lists or song titles wrong, or even said that the crowd was boring or subdued. Billy always got a great reaction from the audience when he did this, as well as getting his digs into the reviewer.

On this track, my drums are tuned down and muffled like the drums on John Lennon's "Instant Karma." I even do the straight-four drum fill within the shuffle that the great Alan White played on the Lennon track. I use my cymbals sparingly. This song was Billy's first number-one single and, of course, the press hated him for it.

### "ALL FOR LEYNA"

In the early 1980s the mood in music was very aggressive with youthful lyrics. I had seen the Police in Europe and loved them. Knowing that Billy was inspired by current events, I told him I thought they were going to be the new thing. I think "Leyna" is a result of that vibe. The hole after he says "stop!" is an edit. We played right through it when we recorded, and it was very awkward to play live.

### "I DON'T WANT TO BE ALONE"

Steve Lawrence had a song called "Can't Get Used to Losing You" which was the inspiration for the beginning of "I Don't Want to be Alone." The lyric "But like the song says, being caught by the wink of an eye," is from a song called "Mama Didn't Lie" by the Shirelles. "I Don't Want to be Alone" originally had a guitar solo which David Brown played through a Leslie tone cabinet, a la Jimi Hendrix, but it was replaced with a sax solo by Richie. Billy felt it would sell more with a sax solo than with a guitar solo.

### "SLEEPING WITH THE TELEVISION ON"

This is another song similar to "Leyna." I love the lyric, "Just for the night, boys." Billy was going for that Farfisa organ sound in the solo: the sound that's heard on Del Shannon's "Runaway" and Question Mark and the Mysterians' "96 Tears."

### "C'ETAIT TOI (YOU WERE THE ONE)"

Oh, the French; great food, great wine, very romantic. The Beatles did half of "Michelle" in French, so why not do half of one of our songs that way? The French loved "Honesty," and that was in English. We brought in an interpreter from the United Nations to be sure all the pronunciations were right, but the French hated it. They said it was mispronounced, and that Billy had "destroyed the French language." Billy says his songs are his children, some have done very well, moved on to college, and are successful. "C'etait Toi" still hasn't gotten out of bed. Russell came up with the drum beat on the chorus.

## "CLOSE TO THE BORDERLINE"

Our first venture out of A&R Studios, we recorded this at Jimi Hendrix's Electric Ladyland Studios. Billy wanted the listener to have a hard time finding one at the beginning of the song, which is why I played the spastic drum intro. I think it sucks, but the song is great. Russell and David's solos at the end were recorded in the spirit of the Beatles at the end of "The End." Before he wrote the song, Billy would ask me how much something costs, and I always said, "A buck three eighty." It doesn't mean anything, it was like saying, "I have no idea!"

## "THROUGH THE LONG NIGHT"

This song was a clue of what was to come. It was recorded in the way the Beatles' "Yes It Is" was recorded; the harmonies are to one side, there are guitar effects with volume control, and the drum part is simple. The next studio album, *Nylon Curtain*, would have more of this type of Beatles influence.

My monitors, "Big Marie" and "Gabrielle."
They almost made me deaf.

# 24

# *Songs in the Attic*

**W**hen you have nothing, you'll sign anything. In 1971, Artie Ripp signed a then-twenty-two-year-old Billy to a management contract for $150 a week. Billy then recorded *Cold Spring Harbor*; Artie had a production company called Just Sunshine Incorporated and a record label called Family Productions which produced the album. Artie also had a piece of Billy's publishing. The record was released on Family Productions. While Billy was working at the Executive Lounge piano bar in Los Angeles, Artie introduced Billy to Clive Davis, who was then the president of Columbia Records. Clive offered Billy a deal after hearing him play, and Family Productions was included.

Family Productions is represented on each record by a picture of the Capitoline Wolf, which is a bronze sculpture depicting a scene from the legend of the founding of Rome. The sculpture shows a she-wolf suckling the mythical twin founders of Rome, Romulus and Remus. According to the legend, when Numitor, grandfather of the twins, was overthrown by his brother, Amulius, the usurper ordered them to be cast into the Tiber River. They were rescued by a she-wolf who cared for them until a herdsman, Faustulus, found and raised them. The logo actually represents the twenty-five cents Artie received from each album copy sold.

With the success of *The Stranger*, *52nd Street* and *Glass Houses*, Columbia pushed *Turnstiles* into a gold record, selling 500,000 copies. By this time, *Piano Man* was over a million in sales and *Streetlife Serenade* was catching up. Artie wanted to re-release Billy's *Cold Spring Harbor* album, but Billy hated the recording. Billy said that someone sped up the tape during the mastering of the LP and his voice sounded like a chipmunk, and he also didn't like the fact that if the album was re-released, Artie would be making money for doing nothing. Because of this, Billy scrapped the re-release and the plan changed to Billy and the band doing a live album with a few songs from the old album. This would entice the fans to buy what would become *Songs in the Attic* instead of *Cold Spring Harbor*. The songs we performed and recorded from *Cold Spring Harbor* were "Everybody Loves You Now" and "She's Got A Way."

When we set out on the tour, I had just become a father to a baby girl. My daughter Devon was born on Friday, June 13th. She has the same birthday as Russell Javors. I was a great father, but still a terrible husband, and this tour was to be no different than any of the others. We recorded in arenas and did shows in small clubs. Phil Ramone traveled with us, and we had a great time.

Originally the album was to be called *Foam the Runways*, referring to the now-discouraged aviation safety practice of spreading a layer of fire suppression foam on an airport runway prior to an emergency landing.

Originally, it was thought this would prevent fires, but the practice is no longer recommended. In particular, the FAA was concerned that prefoaming would deplete firefighting foam supplies in the event they were needed to respond to a fire. Also, foam on the runway may decrease the effectiveness of the landing airplane's brakes, possibly leading to it overshooting the runway. The use of the phrase for the album title was a play on the fact that everyone on the tour had beaten themselves up pretty good. Like a disabled plane trying to land, we were coming home fried and ready for a crash landing.

*Nylon Curtain* tour, 1980. L to R: Me, Mark Rivera, Billy.

# 25

# *The Nylon Curtain*

In April, 1980, right in the middle of making this album, Billy had a motorcycle accident. With his Harley Davidson Café Racer, he broadsided the driver's door of a car as it went through a red light. The front wheel of the bike hit the car, and the handlebars turned and crushed Billy's thumb between the grip and the gas tank of his bike, which broke his wrist. He flipped over the top of the car and landed on the pavement. He was very lucky to have only sustained those injuries.

The album was put on hold for six weeks. As a result of the accident, *The Nylon Curtain* took longer to record than any of Billy's other albums: from November 1981 to July 1982. It became the most critically acclaimed album in his catalog, and the content ranged from mushy love songs to the lyrically political. Billy hated being on the cover of the albums and pressed very hard not to be on this one. Overall, the theme of the album is the positive and negative experiences of our generation, the "over-30s" (which we had just turned at the time of the recording). Billy was criticized that *The Nylon Curtain* was too "Beatlesque," but actually Billy never denied this, and said it was a tip of the hat to the Beatles. In fact, it sounded so much like them that John Lennon's son Julian hired Phil Ramone to produce his first album, *Volotte*, after hearing it.

The album was recorded at Media Sound Studios on 57th Street in New York. We had a lot of difficulty recording there. The band was very reliant on Phil's cues to tell us how we were doing. He'd sit and bounce to the groove if it was okay, but he'd stand and really get into it if it was great. At Media Music, the door to the control room was directly behind the board, where Phil sat. Every time the door opened the band was distracted by the bright light that came from the hallway. Phil got really pissed off and instructed his assistant, "You gotta do something about this, get me a buzzer, get me something! Anything! Get me a statue of the Madonna that lights up to tell people we are working." So the maintenance crew at the studio hooked up a giant plastic statue of the Virgin Mary that was wired to a switch on the recording console that Phil could control. This let people know whether the band was doing a take: Madonna on, they could not enter, or Madonna off, they could come in. We did a remote during these sessions from the studio for "Saturday Night Live" in which we performed "She's Got A Way" and "Miami 2017."

Richie Cannata left the band prior to recording, so Billy, Doug, David, Russell, and I recorded the album mostly by ourselves, thus making it Billy's first album since *Streetlife Serenade* not to feature a regular saxophonist. Richie was involved in playing and producing so much that he thought it was time to move on. Eventually he opened Cove City Sound Studio on Long Island, which is still going strong today. Richie never quit and was never fired, and he still maintains a relationship with Billy. It would take two musicians to replace Richie. I believe that it was at this point when management started to think, "If one band member can be replaced, then why not the others." They would have seen how wrong they were, had they thought about the music.

For this album Billy didn't want to think about how we would duplicate the sound of the record live; he just wanted to make a great album. Although *The Nylon Curtain* was well-received by the critics, it was a bomb in comparison to the sales of *The Stranger*, *52nd Street*, and *Glass Houses*. "Elvis Presley Blvd." was recorded during *The Nylon Curtain* sessions, but was dropped from the album and became the B side of "Allentown."

## "ALLENTOWN"

Billy had the first half of the verse done for years but it was originally titled "Levittown." He just couldn't come up with anything to write about Levittown that was significant, but with the closing of Bethlehem Steel near Allentown, Pennsylvania, Billy found a worthwhile subject. The additional sounds on the song are a pile driver from a sound effects record, Billy's voice doing the "ohh che, ohh ahs," and me jumping up and down with two hard-shell percussion cases. These cases were two feet wide, two feet long, and one foot deep, filled with shakers, maracas, and tambourines, with a belt and two latches to keep them closed. The trick was for the sound to hit on the beat. In order for this to happen I had to jump into the air before the beat and hit the floor on cue. When I was done, my arms were locked at the elbows and when we opened the cases, the gear inside was smashed to dust. Billy received a bill from Studio Instrument Rentals.

## "LAURA"

Beatles all the way. I could not find the "1" for the beat on the piano intro; Billy had to cue me each time. Like John Lennon's, "Sexy Sadie," which is really about the Maharishi Mahesh Yogi—who John was very disappointed in—this song is about Billy's mother. The name Laura fit the syllables in "mother." On the album, Billy sings, "Here I am, feeling like a fucking fool." He tried to change it, he tried, "friggin'," "freaking," and all different variations, but that was the ultimate word for the emotional point of the song.

## "PRESSURE"

Recorded at A&R along with the rest of the album, Billy played the demo for us in his car while we were driving to the studio. The piano part sounded like a Russian Cossack dance. The keyboard solo is intended to emulate the sound of car horns.

### "GOODNIGHT SAIGON"

This was a leftover melody from the *Glass Houses* sessions. Originally titled "Together," it was about World War II. Though none of us went to Vietnam, the song and its production brought people to tears; Billy wrote it from the experiences of his friends who went. The helicopter is a combination of a sound from an effects record and a Moog synthesizer. I played drums and shakers; I did not play the buzz roll. The chorus is sung by the band and Phil Ramone. If you listen closely, towards the end you can hear me yell, "You're alright, Sarge!" The drum fill at the end that most people think is a helicopter is actually a dead drumhead.

### "SHE'S RIGHT ON TIME"

This is our Traffic tribute. When Billy played with the Hassles, he covered a Traffic song called "Colored Rain." It started with vocals only, no instruments, like another one of my favorite Beatles songs, "No Reply." I had asked Billy if he could do a song like that, and he came up with "She's Right on Time."

### "ROOM OF OUR OWN"

When we started recording this song, we played the opening lick over and over to try to get the tempo right. This was all cut out, and all that remains is the shot on the snare drum before Billy starts the count. We had just learned the song and barely knew it. In the song, Billy yells "bridge!" to let us know the bridge is coming. The drum part in the last chorus after the solo is a mistake. I actually got lost, but I think I recovered beautifully.

### "SURPRISES"

Uneventful. No surprises here.

### "SCANDINAVIAN SKIES"

The voice is an actual announcement from an airport in Norway, and the jet sounds are from a sound effects record. I overdubbed the same part on the drums three times. A phase shifter is on the fills. We used the percussion cases again, like on Allentown. Billy mumbles in the background, like John Lennon on "Yellow Submarine." The solo is on a Mellotron, an electro-mechanical, polyphonic tape replay keyboard, originally developed and built in Birmingham, England in 1963. It evolved from a similar instrument, the Chamberlin, but could be mass-produced more effectively. The instrument is played by pressing its keys, each of which presses a length of magnetic tape against a capstan, drawing it across a playback head. Then, as the key is released, the tape is retracted by a spring to its initial position. Different portions of the tape can be played to access different sounds. "Scandinavian Skies" was another song influenced by the Beatles, specifically "Strawberry Fields." The song is about a true experience we had after snorting heroin in Amsterdam and playing the blues all night in Oslo. The basic track was recorded with Doug on bass, Billy on Hammond organ, and me on drums. There are no guitars on this.

## "WHERE'S THE ORCHESTRA?"

Being at the top isn't like you thought it was. Maybe it's a little disappointing at times. The summer after the album's release, Billy and Elizabeth split up. After a Mexican divorce, which was popular at the time with Americans because it was far simpler than the legal process in the U.S., Elizabeth left with 50% of what she and Billy owned. Billy got to keep their beautiful English Tudor in Lloyd's Neck, which had a living room and den right on the waters of the Long Island Sound. A year later, when Christie Brinkley moved in, they couldn't keep the peeping toms away. Paparazzi would anchor right outside the living room window and wait to catch a glimpse of the American beauty. And I don't mean Billy!

**Me with Christie Brinkley during the recording of *An Innocent Man*.**

# 26

# *An Innocent Man*

O f all Billy's albums, for me this one was the most fun to make. It took us about two weeks to do the basic tracks, and it was one of the only albums where we just sat down and played the parts. In fact, it happened so quickly and was so much fun that we thought it was surely going to bomb. The songs emulated the bands and singing groups of our youth: the Drifters, the Four Seasons, Motown, and James Brown. Upon hearing "Uptown Girl," Frankie Valli called Phil Ramone and asked, "Why can't someone write a song like that for me?"

*An Innocent Man* was recorded at Chelsea Sound on 42nd Street between 8th and 9th Avenues in New York City, before Disney bought the block, back when most occupations fit the street's reputation. A few of us, at times, took advantage of the extracurricular activities. The studio was old and being renovated. When it rained, the ceiling leaked, but it all added to the fun and the spirit of this record. So much money was spent to make *The Nylon Curtain* that for this album, the management company was literally looking over our shoulders.

By this time, Billy had started dating Christie Brinkley, and during these sessions we met her. We knew she was coming into the studio one day, so we all wore our best outfits. When Billy saw us he said, "Why are you guys dressed like that?" Russell answered, "Because my tux is in the cleaners." We made fools of ourselves when Christie arrived, but the really funny thing was that Billy had started to wear his headphones in a unique way, so as to not mess up his hair. *An Innocent Man* had so many singles pulled from it that the record company had to use songs from previous albums for the flip sides.

## "EASY MONEY"

Recorded for a movie with the same name starring Rodney Dangerfield and Joe Pesci, this song was the greatest recording experience I ever had. Phil Ramone put the band together, and we recorded the whole song at once. The musicians alongside me were Doug on bass, David on guitar, Leon Pendarvis on Hammond organ, Richard Tee on piano, Eric Gale on guitar, Ronnie Cuber on baritone sax, John Faddis on trumpet, David Sanborn on alto sax, Joe Shepley on trumpet, Mark Rivera on tenor sax, and Frank Floyd, Lani Groves, and Yolonda McCullough on vocals. Billy sang lead in a booth by himself. What you hear on the record is what was recorded that night.

## "AN INNOCENT MAN"

Before we recorded this one we listened to all the Drifters records. Mark Rivera played the triangle on the basic track along with us. Billy did the finger snaps while he sang the song live at the piano.

## "THE LONGEST TIME"

This song is not really a cappella. A cappella means only voices, with no musical accompaniment. The basic track for "The Longest Time" had Doug on bass, Billy playing block chords on the piano for reference, and me playing on a reel-to-reel Ampex tape box with brushes. Billy's block chords were later removed to give the a cappella effect. Billy sang all the vocals, and had a hard time because he couldn't remember which part he had done already. The song is in the style of "So Much in Love" by the Tymes.

## "THIS NIGHT"

In the '50s and early '60s, groups would take classical pieces, change the rhythm, and write lyrics for them. For instance, "Lover's Concerto" by the Toys is based on the melody of the familiar Minuet in G Major attributed to J.S. Bach (from the 1725 Notebook for Anna Magdalena Bach). One key difference is that the Minuet in G Major is written in 3/4 time whereas "A Lover's Concerto" is in 4/4. The chorus of "This Night" is from Beethoven's Pathetique.

## "TELL HER ABOUT IT"

The drum part that's on the record is the first drum part that I came up with, but during recording, everyone had their ideas about what I should play. I tried half time patterns, different bass drum patterns; every musician in the room had some drum part they wanted me to play. I played them all until I came full circle and decided on my original. Phil did a real Motown mix on this song that was released as a dance mix. There were a million background vocal parts that never made it to the record. Billy's original piano was removed when Richard Tee overdubbed his piano part.

## "UPTOWN GIRL"

Different drum fills are sometimes related to names or sayings. Examples: bucket of beans, Pat Boone Debbie Boone, blotting paper-blotting paper-blotting paper-blot, etc.. The opening drum fill has as many notes as there are syllables in "Liberty DeVitto." We overdubbed the hand claps and did foot stomps on a piece of plywood on the floor. The song was modeled after the style of the Four Seasons.

## "CARELESS TALK"

Uneventful. After the sessions, we never played it again. However, I do love what I played, and the drum sounds are in a very early-1960s style.

## "CHRISTIE LEE"

Billy thought "Christie Lee" was a great rock 'n' roll name. On the track, Billy does a great imitation of Little Richard on the piano. Although the song is a fictitious story, Billy used Christie's name, and Joe was a pet name Christie had for Billy: When she looked at him, she didn't see him as "Billy," she saw him as an average "Joe." At the end of their relationship, Billy told me he always hated that name, and questioned why she couldn't call him Billy.

## "LEAVE A TENDER MOMENT ALONE"

This tune has a Burt Bacharach feel. Phil and Billy flew to France to record Toots Thielemans on harmonica; Toots came out on the road a few times and played the song live with us. Toots was a very nice man, and was also very funny. One of the times he joined us on the road was at Wembley Arena during the *Innocent Man* tour. Apparently he had read an article that talked about this guy who was friends with singer Boy George who named himself "Susan." Toots thought this was hilarious, especially the fact that this unattractive man didn't look anything like a woman. So Toots decided to change our names: he was Olivia, and all day he kept calling me Evelyn. It was quite funny hearing this older man yelling, "Evelyn, oh Evelyn," and I had to explain he was looking for me.

## "KEEPIN' THE FAITH"

Russell was playing the lick to "Cleanup Woman" by Betty Wright. The next day, Billy came in with this song based around that lick. There is no hi-hat or eighth feel on the drums; basically I played this song with one hand on the snare and the bass drum. When the single came out, the drums were processed through a Simmons electronic drum brain. You can actually hear drum fills that weren't loud enough to trigger the brain. There were also softer notes, known as ghost notes, that didn't register, so they aren't audible. In drumming, a ghost note is played at very low volume, typically on a snare drum. The purpose of a ghost note is to be heard under the main sound of the groove, producing a subtle 16th-note feel around a strong backbeat or certain accents. As a result of the ghost notes being muted, "Keepin' the Faith" has a weird feel, like pieces are missing. T.M. Stevens replaced Doug's bass track on the single.

*The Bridge* tour, 1986.

# *Greatest Hits Parts 1 & 2* and *The Bridge*

**W**hen it came to our royalties for this compilation, Doug and I were paid as if it was one album, earning 2.5 cents per unit for the package—but when the RIAA certifies the sales of the record, they counted it as two units. So if *Greatest Hits Parts 1 & 2* sold 500,000 copies according to the RIAA, we were only paid on 250,000 copies. However, we did get double scale, double session when we recorded the two new songs: "You're Only Human (Second Wind)" and "The Night is Still Young." Hall & Oates put out a new single and included it on a greatest hits album, and this led to a trend where artists would include a couple of new songs on a greatest hits album with a bunch of older material. I always thought it was risky to add two new songs to all the old hits. What if the new songs bombed?

In our case, "The Night is Still Young" stiffed, but we lucked out with "You're Only Human." Because of the subject matter— suicide—Billy received a letter from President Reagan, congratulating him on writing such a positive song. (Mrs. Reagan was very involved with suicide prevention.) The song climbed the charts and eventually reached number nine in the US.

Billy had seen the movie *The Flamingo Kid*, and in the soundtrack was the song "It's All Right" by the Impressions. He loved the groove of that tune, and based "You're Only Human" around that feel. To emulate a drum machine, I played the track using hi-hat, acoustic bass drum, and a Simmons snare.

## THE BRIDGE

This album was recorded in different studios. We started in Columbia Studios, then moved to Chelsea Sound (where we recorded *An Innocent Man*), and ended up at the Record Plant. Doug started to have noticeable health problems around this time, brought on by years of partying. During the making of this album he was hospitalized twice with an enlarged pancreas.

Billy brought in a lot of great artists on these songs. He felt the best parts of his songs were the bridges, thus the name of the album.

## "RUNNING ON ICE"

This song has no bridge. We recorded it at Chelsea Sound. Sting was asked to write a song for the Columbia Pictures movie with Robin Williams called *Club Paradise*, but he passed, so they asked Billy to write a song along the lines of something the Police would have written. In the end, the song never made it into the movie due to financial disagreements. Pete Hewlett ghosts Billy's vocal through the whole song.

## "THIS IS THE TIME"

We recorded this song at Chelsea Sound. The hi-hat and Simmons toms were recorded as an overdub at the Record Plant. David Brown plays some of the best Hendrix guitar on this tune.

## "A MATTER OF TRUST"

Billy wanted to write a song with a beat like "Addicted to Love" by Robert Palmer. He found it hard to write a heavy rock song on the piano, so "A Matter of Trust" was written on the guitar, with the piano playing a similar part to "Every Breath You Take" by the Police. Billy did not play rhythm guitar on the recording, and he used the guitar only as a prop in the video and when we performed live. For live shows, the guitar was only turned on when he'd play an introductory chord to start the song.

## "MODERN WOMAN"

Written for Columbia Pictures' *Ruthless People* with Danny DeVito and Bette Midler, there is an electronic '80s version of this song where the guitars play the bass line. I played on a full Simmons electronic drum kit, which sucked. I don't think we ever performed this song live.

## "BABY GRAND"

"Baby Grand" was recorded with Ray Charles and his orchestra. Billy asked me if I minded if he went and recorded this with Ray's people, as Ray was known to be hard on musicians. I told him, "Whatever sells records." When Billy came back with the recording, he asked me to play some crazy fills to make it less clean and sterile, but it didn't work. Vinnie Colaiuta was the drummer on this track.

## "BIG MAN ON MULBERRY STREET"

We were rehearsing for *The Bridge* album in the Puck Building located at the edge of Little Italy in New York City. When I first played the song, I tried to play it like a real jazz drummer, but Billy said, "You're not a jazz guy. Play it like a rock drummer trying to play jazz." That gave the song the real big band swing that it has. The verse is me trying to do a Bernard "Pretty" Purdie shuffle. The brushes were overdubbed, the horn stabs were written to the drums fills.

Ron Carter was overdubbed on upright bass, which didn't sit well with Doug and affected his attitude for the rest of the album's recording.

## "TEMPTATION"

I can remember being at Billy's house waiting for him to drive to the studio. Christie was pregnant, and she was putting up their Christmas tree. We had to go, and as Billy was saying goodbye, he would sing to Christie's stomach, "She's such a temptation." Fascinated by the pregnancy, he wanted to know who the baby was, and what she looked like. The person he is singing about in this song is his unborn child. I loved what I played on this track; it's weird and different.

## "CODE OF SILENCE"

This is the only song Billy ever co-wrote: Cyndi Lauper wrote the lyrics and really helped Billy on this one with a fantastic vocal. I stole the idea for the "backwards" drums, with the snare on 1 and 3, from Jim Gordon on "Bell Bottom Blues" by Derek and the Dominos. Dan Brooks plays an excellent blues harp on the track. We all have a "code of silence."

## "GETTING CLOSER"

In my high school yearbook, a friend wrote, "Practice, keep your head, and one day you'll play with Steve Winwood." I had always been a big Winwood fan, so I was totally thrilled to play with him on this song. My brother Vinny was also a huge fan, so I brought him along to the session. In the studio, we jammed on hours of Traffic songs, and Steve told Billy that at times he had to look up to make sure Jim Capaldi (Traffic's drummer) wasn't playing drums. I showed Steve my yearbook. He laughed and said, "You're making me feel very old."

**Looking out at Red Square on tour in Russia, 1986.**

# 28

# The Soviet Union

During *The Bridge* tour, Billy was asked if he'd be interested in doing a series of concerts in the Union of Soviet Socialist Republics. He would be the first rock artist to perform under the General Exchanges Agreement signed by President Reagan and Soviet General Secretary Mikhail Gorbachev at their 1985 Geneva Summit. Billy was invited to do a full production show, with staging, lights, and sound. The Russian audience would experience for the first time a live show like we had grown accustomed to in the free world. We'd go there with a show exactly like the one we'd put on in the U.S.; other bands had played in the U.S.S.R., but not with a full production. Santana, Elton John, and Blood Sweat and Tears had all gone there but had only done solo or small shows. Bobby Colomby, the drummer for Blood Sweat & Tears, told us that when they came home and played Madison Square Garden, the crowd did not like the fact that they had played in a communist country and expressed their anger by throwing "bags of shit" at them while they played. Nevertheless, Billy decided he wanted to go.

Billy announced the plans to go to the U.S.S.R. during a show at the Meadowlands Arena in New Jersey. The crowd booed us. It was a very eerie feeling. Billy said, "Hold on, they are people too. When my daughter grows up and asks, 'Daddy, what did you do during the Cold War?' I would like to have something to tell her." The boos gradually turned to applause.

When we played in Washington, D.C., representatives from the Russian Embassy came to see the show at the Capital Center. During the show, they followed along with our set list and graded each song from one to ten. All the songs did well in their scoring system except "Goodnight Saigon," which received only five points. After the show they told Billy they found it difficult to understand. Billy explained that it was about the Vietnam War and all the soldiers that we had lost in a fruitless war. They said they understood, because it was like their war in Afghanistan.

At a meeting after the show, the representatives from the Russian embassy told the band what to expect. They said each of us should bring someone with us if we could: a wife, a girlfriend, or someone close. Steve Cohen, our lighting designer, brought his father. The reasoning for this, they explained, was because we would likely be so moved by what we saw during the day that we'd need to talk about it at night when we returned to our rooms. We weren't allowed to take videos of government buildings, military personnel, railroad stations, or seaports. We could not trade American dollars or English pounds for anything, couldn't bring in *Time* or *Newsweek* magazines, and we were forbidden to have *Playboy* or any other pornographic magazines. We could bring one book to read, which would be checked when we got to the border. A personal bible was allowed if we wanted one—but no more than one. We were instructed to leave with what we came with. Billy made it clear from the beginning that we were going there to play music, and we would leave the politics to the politicians.

Here is all I knew about the place I was going: reds, pinko commies, three-headed monsters that breathed fire, the space race, and Nikita Khrushchev banging his shoe saying, "We will bury you!" I thought of them as the enemy. We used to hide under our desks in school because of them. According to the domino theory, they were going to take over the world one country at a time. I had been to Cuba in 1978, but that was different. The Cubans were familiar with our music and style; they had listened to us on Miami radio stations. From what I had learned in school, Russia was a country with a violent history led by infamous figures like Peter the Great, Alexander the Great, Lenin, and Marx. As soon as they found out my name was Liberty, I thought they'd arrest me and put me away.

Pete Hewlett, George Simms, and Mark Rivera accompanied me on a flight from London to Moscow on Lufthansa Airlines. That plane was to be the last string that connected me to everything I knew in the free world, except for the music I carried within me. Arriving in Moscow, we went through customs, which was a room with a desk where they checked our papers. To our surprise, they kept our passports. My first thought was, "I guess it's true: Once you're in, you don't get out unless they let you out." We were met on the other side by the people who worked for the concert committee. They quickly escorted us to an Aeroflot flight that was to take us to meet Billy in Tbilisi, Georgia.

Billy was invited to meet with the Georgian vocal group Fazisi, who performed religious chants and Georgian folk songs. The ethnic and social aspects of folk songs are important factors that influence the development of creative convictions of the Georgian people, who have carefully been preserving the traditional art of these songs for centuries. They are revered for their physical and spiritual healing power. Born out of both happiness and misfortune, the folk songs have always accompanied the Georgian people's life. Billy asked Pete, George, Mark, and me to join him there to sing a cappella with him as a performance for the Georgian group. Since I wasn't usually a backup vocalist, I asked Billy why he wanted me there. "For comic relief," he replied.

I was the first one to climb the steps to board the Aeroflot plane. The second I walked through the door, I quickly turned around and stepped right out. The odor inside the plane was shocking; it reeked like sour milk, the most pungent odor I'd ever experienced. The floor of the plane was covered in linoleum and half of it was ripped away. I held my breath and got to my seat. The smell was so bad that I went through my carry-on bag, grabbed my toothpaste, squeezed it onto my finger, and rubbed it under my nose.

The flight was very different from the commercial flights I had flown before. There were no inside coverings over the door mechanisms; the gears and latches that operated the doors were in plain sight. There were no announcements to tell you to put your seat in an upright position or to stow your carry-on luggage; there was more of a "ready, set, go!" feel than anything else. The woman in front of me had a huge box on her lap as we took off. Somewhere behind me was a person holding a crate with live chickens in it. When we landed in Tbilisi, we couldn't get up from our seats until the two pilots left the plane. As they walked off, I noticed they were wearing pistols on their belts. They boarded and exited the plan ahead of the passengers to avoid hijackings. I watched as the baggage handlers removed luggage and sacks of potatoes from the belly of the plane.

The next day we were to play in a casual jam session with Georgian musicians at a local theater. A government-controlled radio station announced that Billy was doing a concert, and they gave away tickets to this jam session, so the place was packed. The people that were there were expecting to see "the great American poet and musician Billy Joel" perform his songs. Instead of a jam, we turned it into a concert. Since it was the first thing we did in Russia, we decided to go all-out with the limited amount of equipment that we had. We had no bass player, so a Georgian bassist who was a college professor volunteered to play with us. There was barely a P.A., so Billy blew out his voice before we even got to the main concerts we were there to do. Mark Rivera didn't have his sax, so he played guitar and tambourine, and Pete Hewlett also played guitar. There was a drum kit, so I was set. When we were done, the people stayed and talked to us, asking questions about pop music in America.

That night, after our impromptu performance, the college professor had a party for us. The people were so warm, I felt like I was with my family. Their food was delicious; the tomatoes were the freshest and juiciest I had ever had. We sang, drank homemade wine, talked, and laughed. I said to one of the Georgian singers, "I can't believe how nice you Russian people are!" In a stern voice, he replied, "We are not Russian, we are Georgians." We talked about how there would soon be a change; you could feel it in the air. They said the change would probably start in Georgia (which it did).

The next day we were on a plane back to Moscow. After arriving, we were driven by bus to our hotel, which was beautiful but crumbling. In fact, there were pieces of the building falling off into the streets at times. After checking in, we had dinner at the hotel, but the food was completely different than what I had in Georgia. I said to one of the Russian promoters, "The tomatoes were delicious in Tblisi, why don't they have them here?" "The roads between the cities are so bad," he answered, "that by the time trucks brought them here, they'd all be rotten." At that moment I started to realize that maybe my preconceived ideas about the U.S.S.R. weren't quite accurate. "These are the evil powers that are going to take over the world," I thought, "and they don't even have the roads to move tomatoes?"

Moscow is a beautiful city. Our hotel was right on Red Square. One of our interpreters told us that we were being listened to. They told us, "When you get out of the shower, if you need more towels, just say it out loud, as if you were talking to yourself, and you will see, the next day there will be more towels." I tried this, and sure enough, it was true. The "sprinkler systems" in our hotel rooms, we were told, were actually microphones.

I explored the city, going on every tour I could and seeing amazing palaces and architecture. Red Square was a beautiful place; you can't comprehend the beauty of St. Basil's until you are standing in front of it. I could not get over how red the star was atop the Kremlin. The whole city is painted in grays and steel; color is absent, except in Red Square. I ate everything they put in front of me. There was no air conditioning anywhere. Hygiene was different there; there were no tampons for women—they literally used rags. People had body odor because there was only one government brand of deodorant, but that was a luxury. When it came down to buying bread or deodorant, they chose the bread. The department stores were empty. People waited in line for shoes and bread; sometimes they waited in line and didn't even know what they were waiting for. It may have been something they needed, but if it wasn't, they'd take it anyway and trade it for something they needed. They were monetarily poor, but they were rich in love and family. I was expecting to see the equivalent to the United States: the other world power. Instead, what I saw was a country made into a third world nation by a government preoccupied with funding the military and building rockets.

I brought chewing gum and pins to trade with the people in the street. A pair of my Levi's got me a beautiful black lacquer box. Leningrad was the same. The subways were amazing in Leningrad; they are the most beautiful subways in the world. There were huge paintings of the revolution on the walls. The one thing that was consistent throughout all of the U.S.S.R. was the people. They had inner beauty, both old and young, and nothing to give to us but genuine love. Locked away from the rest of the world, when they met us they embraced us as what was on the other side of the wall. Their love wasn't jaded by how much jewelry they owned or how big their car or house was. Always smiling at me, they wanted to know what was going on in the outside world. The old people had adjusted to communism, and for the middle aged people it was all they knew, but the younger people were asking questions. In their atheist country they were asking, "Who is God?" Seeing the churches that had been left standing, they would ask the elders, "What is that? Who are the people in those paintings?" Slowly they were realizing their country had once been different. At one time they had been free to choose; they weren't told what to believe.

Two veterinary students that I befriended took me to a restaurant. Passing tables and going through a door in the back, we walked down a long hallway into a room that resembled a coffee shop from the 1960s on Bleeker Street in the West Village of Manhattan. The tables in the room were filled with people of college age. I realized that this was their place to talk about the government in secret. Something big was about to happen, they said. Watch for when the Russians stop sending aid to Cuba, they told me. That will be the beginning of a big change. It was reminiscent of the U.S. in the 1960s. Another kind of revolution was about to take place, and music would be a major part of it.

In the U.S.S.R., music was not sold on records like in the States. Essentially it was passed around by smuggling. Someone would sneak a tape into the country, and then play it on his boom box for a group of ten or so. The listeners all had tape recorders and would press record as the guy with the boom box pressed play. A lot of information about the outside world was learned through music. Some recordings were actually copied onto old X-rays. People also tried to smuggle magazines and books into the country, but it was very difficult to get them past the censors, and printed material also took longer to spread among people. I visited the grave of Vladimir Vysotsky, a folk music legend in the U.S.S.R. who was compared to Bob Dylan. Considered the voice of the people, he sang anti-government songs. Since his death, thousands visit his grave each year, in the same way people wait to go to Lenin's tomb.

At our concerts, I watched the crowd be moved from sedate to totally uninhibited through the music. At the beginning of the concerts, no one was allowed to get out of their chairs, but by the end, we had soldiers on the stage, dancing and spinning their hats. There was an amazing spiritual connection in the music. Each side, musicians and audience, were giving from their heart. A change had also come over me from my perspective in the U.S.S.R. Looking back at my own country, I began to see that America was too far into its own way of life for some other country or idea to change it. If the U.S. were to fall, it would be from the inside out. The people in the U.S.S.R. had nothing; Americans had everything. The Soviet people would wake up and be thankful they were still strong enough to work. They would hug their children to keep them in the warmth of their love, and were happy just to have food on their table, instead of BMWs in their driveways. Some Russian people wanted the things that we have in America, but I found that they mostly just wanted freedom to choose. They wanted the choice of the art they could look at, the music they could listen to, and above all to be able to think for themselves and not be imprisoned for it.

I cried when I left the Soviet Union; I thought I would never see those people again. Not too long after we left the U.S.S.R., the Berlin Wall came down and more and more people were able to leave the countries in the Soviet orbit. Eventually I did see some of those I had met; they came to my house and I was privileged to share some of our American ways with them. We had a backyard barbeque, they swam in my built-in swimming pool (something which many of them had never seen before), and we played music on my huge stereo. They picked up on certain American things very fast. One day, my sister Louise took our young Russian friends to see New York City. On the way, they stopped at Burger King and were eating french fries and hamburgers as my sister drove. After one of them was done with his meal, he took the trash and threw it out the window. Louise yelled, "Why did you do that?" "I see a lot of Americans do that," he replied. "Isn't that what you do?" The concept of this new freedom was like looking through the eyes of a child. It was hard to say, "I'm an American, do as I say, not as I do."

The Russian tour cost Billy $2.5 million. He was only paid $2,500 per show, and he was not allowed to take the money out of the country. It sat in a bank account in Moscow until he donated it to the people who were affected by the Chernobyl nuclear power plant disaster.

We did a live album called *Kohuept*—which means "concert" in Russian—to recoup some of the money, and there were also two television specials. In addition, we did a live radio broadcast from Leningrad into the United States via satellite, which was the first of its kind. Many people taped the broadcast and the specials, so the album didn't sell that well. I did lectures at high schools and talked about my experiences with the Russian people. What I had learned was that the Cold War was our government against their government, not their people against our people.

On the twenty-fifth anniversary of our trip to the Soviet Union, we did a documentary, and while I was being interviewed, I mentioned that Billy had asked me to tone down my look a little. I had really gone all- American: I had a shirt with an American flag on the chest, American flags on my drumset, and pins of the flag and Mickey Mouse on my jacket. As we performed in the U.S.S.R., I found that Billy's concerns about this were unfounded. To the contrary, when people saw me on stage, playing my drums with arms wildly flailing and the American flag on my chest, they saw it as an awe-inspiring symbol of the freedom of self-expression. So, I'm pleased to say, Mickey and the flags stayed.

**Checking all lugs and wing nuts!**
**The drums are ready for the beating that is Liberty DeVitto.**

# 29

# Storm Front

The Russian album did very well in Australia, so we went back a second time on *The Bridge* tour. David Brown had left the band by this time due to broken promises from management, and Doug's problems were more evident. Playing the Sydney Entertainment Center, the band was Russell, Doug, Dave Lebolt on keys, Kevin Dukes on guitar, and me. Billy took me aside and said, "What do you think about just me and you going in to do the next album with all new musicians?" What could I say? I felt awful for the other guys, but having a family to support, I was thankful I still had a job. The way that Billy handled the band's termination should have been a sign to me of things to come: they found out when the information was broadcast on MTV. Having worked with Phil Ramone since *Turnstiles*, Billy also wanted a different producer for this record. I was in the studio recording with a band from Italy when I ran into Phil. Because we were all so close, I could tell by his voice that he was deeply hurt.

I called Billy and put Phil on the phone with him. I think this made Phil happy, but probably upset Billy. Later I felt sorry; I may have stepped over the line, because I loved both of them and I think I understood both their feelings. Phil was glad I made the connection and was happy just to speak to Billy, but I understand why Billy was upset at me. It's hard to understand the pressure he was under, and of course he could have blown at any moment. He had to write twelve new songs for an album, with hopefully a few hits in there. This is a huge task, and Billy did it alone. Elton had Bernie. Paul had John. Henley had Frey. Sure, we helped with the arrangements, but the chords, melodies, and lyrics were his. I've known people who have had nervous breakdowns under a fraction of the pressure Billy was feeling. Also, Billy is not like a lot of other artists. Some artists will write maybe twenty-one tunes for a twelve-song album, with nine of them as total throwaways, only to be released on charity records, boxed sets, or after the artist dies. Billy didn't do that. Everything he wrote is on an album—all quality songs. In the end, Mick Jones from Foreigner produced the album.

As we started recording, Billy was dealt a financial blow from which he would never mentally fully recover. Phil Ramone had brought Billy's accounting to John Eastman—Paul McCartney's lawyer and brother-in-law—to review his salary. After looking at the books, John called Billy and told him, "As a solo artist, you should be making more and have more than Paul, but according to what I see on paper, you can't even shine Paul's shoes. I think you have a problem." Billy went to see John, who explained what was going on.

Frank Weber was Elizabeth Joel's brother. When Elizabeth and Billy divorced, she handed Home Run Management over to Frank and it became Frank Management. Frank had "borrowed" an exorbitant amount of money from banks against Billy's catalog, leaving Billy responsible for all the paybacks. Having acquired power of attorney, Frank had signed Billy's name to all his "investments" without Billy's knowledge. Like many white collar criminals, he was so brilliant that he covered his tracks in such a way that no one realized what he was doing.

Frank made individual deals with all the band members. Unbeknownst to us, at one point Doug and I were getting more money for *The Nylon Curtain* than Billy was, because our deals were percentages from the first album sold. Billy, on the other hand, was still paying the costs of making the album and wouldn't see any profit until that had been recouped. I should have seen the writing on the wall when Frank got tipsy at Billy's bachelor party at the Plaza Hotel and came up to me and said, "I hate you for one reason: One day they will find me out, but you will be here forever. I hate you for that." At a show at Nassau Coliseum, Frank was there with his wife, who was dressed casually in a sweat suit but wearing a stunning diamond necklace. A friend who was a jeweler pulled me aside after meeting them. "Is there something going on with Billy and his manager?" he asked. "If that woman is wearing that necklace with that outfit, what does she wear when she gets dressed up?" He priced the necklace in the six-figure range without even touching it.

*Storm Front* (which had a working title of *House of Blue Lights*) was recorded at Chelsea Studios, which had been overhauled to state-of-the-art condition and called the Hit Factory Times Square.

### "THAT'S NOT HER STYLE"

The Rolling Stones had signed a multimillion dollar deal with CBS, but their album at the time was tanking. Someone at CBS said that Billy Joel had a better Rolling Stones song on his album than the Stones had on theirs.

### "WE DIDN'T START THE FIRE"

This was one of the last songs recorded for the album. Sony Records came into the studio to hear what we had. They said they heard a second and third single release, but they hadn't found the first yet: the one that would jump out and take the album straight to the top.

The lyrical content was inspired by a conversation Billy had with an eighteen-year-old kid. The kid's generation was coming of age in a tough and turbulent time, he said, but Billy's time growing up was the perfect time to be alive—nothing bad happened back then. Billy asked the kid if he knew about things like Vietnam, JFK, the Cold War, etc., and tried to explain that we didn't start this stuff; it's always happened and will continue to happen. The events span Billy's life from 1949 to 1989; he flipped through a book called *Chronicles* and took the events right off the pages.

The percussion parts on the track were played by Billy on timbales, me on a snare drum with the snares turned off, and (in her debut with us) Crystal Taliefero on congas.

## "DOWNEASTER 'ALEXA'"

A good captain names his boat after a female, and the Alexa Ray was named after Billy's daughter. Its hull style is a downeaster, which is a fishing boat with a long transom and a short bow. The song is sung in the persona of an impoverished fisherman off Long Island and the surrounding waters who, like many of his fellow men, is finding it increasingly difficult to make ends meet and keep ownership of his boat. The fisherman sings about the depletion of the fish stocks ("I know there's fish out there, but where God only knows") and environmental regulations ("Since they told me I can't sell no stripers") which make it hard for men like him to survive, especially with the conversion of his home island into an expensive summer colony for the affluent ("There ain't no island left for islanders like me"). The lyrics reference Block Island Sound, Montauk, Martha's Vineyard, Nantucket, and Gardiners Bay, amongst other locations.

While the song is about a fictional person, the song brought attention to the real-life plight of the Long Island baymen—known locally as "bubbies." The baymen represent a dying breed of people who, like small farmers, work with the environment to provide for their families. These men and women were being forced out of their livelihoods by industrial overfishing that depleted the traditional fishing grounds as well as the creep of urban society and government regulation. Billy was always sympathetic to these people, even getting arrested during a protest supporting the baymen.

## "I GO TO EXTREMES"

The working title for this song was "Woman Like You," and it was recorded at Right Track studios. I had come up with a syncopated drum beat and asked Billy if he could write a song to it. The next day he came in with the music and melody but no words, so this became the first song I ever recorded without lyrics. After we recorded it with the syncopated beat, however, we felt it was too hard and jerky; it didn't flow. We cut the track over with me playing it straight, but the syncopated rhythm is in Billy's lyrical phrasing. Billy said that he would have never written the song if it wasn't for me.

Mick Jones convinced me to go to the bell of the cymbal on the outro. He said that's what an English drummer would do. We recorded this song to a cowbell click track, which is something we hardly ever did. ("Running on Ice" was recorded to a shaker click.) Sometimes Phil Ramone would start us off on a click, but would pull it out of our headphones if the song got faster and we were off the click. The click was there so if we needed to do another take of the song, we could go back to the original tempo that felt best. An example of a song where the click was pulled out in mid-song is "Sometimes A Fantasy" from *Glass Houses*.

### "SHAMELESS"

Billy was always a huge Jimi Hendrix fan, but found it really difficult to play Hendrix on the piano. "Shameless" was written in the style of "Bold as Love" by the Jimi Hendrix Experience, with me doing my best Mitch Mitchell. David Brown is fantastic on guitar on this track, and Garth Brooks had a huge country crossover hit with the song. This is one of Billy's children that did very well.

### "STORM FRONT"

This song idea was inspired by "Sledgehammer" by Peter Gabriel. Billy and I were driving to the studio when it came on the radio. I immediately thought it was Steve Winwood; we were both very impressed by the tune. Billy was working on lyrics with his boat as inspiration. He called me one night and sang the first verse over the phone:

> *Safe at harbor, everything is easy*
> *Off to starboard, daylight comes up fast*
> *Now I am restless, for the open water*
> *Red flags are flying from the Coast Guard mast*
> *They told me to stay, I heard the information*
> *I motored away and steered straight ahead*
> *Though the weatherman said*
> *There's a storm front coming (mood indigo)*
> *White water running and the pressure is low*
> *Storm front coming (mood indigo)*
> *Small craft warning on the radio"*

"That's cool," I said. "But I don't think your fans want to hear about your boat. Why don't you make it sound like it's about a woman and the storm front is a bad relationship that's going on." Here's what he came up with the next day:

> *I've been sailing a long time on this ocean*
> *Man gets lonesome, all these years at sea*
> *I've got a woman, my life should be easy*

*Most men hunger for the life I lead*
*The morning was gray, but I had the motivation*
*I drifted away and ran into more*
*Heavy weather off shore*
*I'm still restless for the open water*
*Though she gives me everything I need*
*She asked me to stay, but I'd done my navigation*
*I drove her away, but I should have known*
*To stay tied up at home*

### "LENINGRAD"

Billy captured the true feeling of our Russian tour experience in the lyrics of this song. "Leningrad" was written in the studio during the recording of the *Storm Front* album, with Billy writing the lyrics during an in-studio break. As we were running through the song and got to the end, where Billy sings, "We never knew what friends we had until we came to Leningrad," he stopped playing. I remembered a little piece of music he had in his "bits and pieces" file and suggested he play it at this point. (Billy never threw anything away; unused ideas would go into the bits and pieces file to be used at some other point.) This bit became the intro to the song and the musical tag out.

### "STATE OF GRACE"

One of my favorite songs, I think "State of Grace" gave us our first look into the end of Billy and Christie's relationship. I watched Billy spend a lot of time on one note; it was on the word "grace." It kind of makes me sad when I hear it now.

### "WHEN IN ROME"

"When in Rome" is real blue-eyed soul reminiscent of the '60s. Billy sings about having to play by the rules of others to be successful, but when the day is over, you can be yourself. When you're in Rome, you have to do as the Romans do, but when you're home, all you have to be is you.

### "AND SO IT GOES"

This song was written during the *An Innocent Man* sessions, but was shelved because (not sounding like an oldies song) it didn't fit with that album's concept. It missed *The Bridge* and finally made it onto *Storm Front*. "And So It Goes" has a similar lyrical theme to "Leave a Tender Moment Alone." Billy is saying that he has to try not to say too much, that he could ruin it all, but if he doesn't say anything, that would also be a mistake. The song was written either for Elle Macpherson or Christie Brinkley.

*

Billy started coming to tour rehearsals really, really out of it. He was going for depositions constantly, building his case against Frank. Financially in the red and borrowing money to finance the *Storm Front* tour, Billy was advised by his accountants that he should take back what was his in order to recoup some of the losses that Frank's management had created. This impacted me by having my income cut from a percentage of gross to a weekly salary. They also took all my record royalties, except *Greatest Hits Vol. 1 & 2*. I guess I was just thankful that I still had a job.

At the same time, a tragedy was unfolding in my personal life.

My brother was dying.

**My brother, Vincent DeVitto.**

# 30

# My Brother, Vinny DeVitto

My mother once ran into one of my brother Vinny's high school teachers. The woman asked how Vinny was doing, and my mother told her he was fine. The teacher asked if Vinny was married and if he had any children. He was married and had two children, my mom answered. "Do they have his eyes?" the teacher asked. Vinny had beautiful eyes.

Vinny was my parents' third child. He was different from me, my sister Louise, and our baby brother, Sal. We had dark skin, brown eyes and dark brown hair. Vinny had lighter skin, hazel eyes, and light brown hair. He looked more like my mother's father, whereas we looked like the DeVitto side of the family. My parents loved all their children equally; no one child got more than the next—but I was "the oldest son," Louise was "the only girl," and Sal was "the baby." Vinny was Vinny. As he got older, he was known in high school as Liberty and Louise DeVitto's younger brother—and he was judged on what was known about his older siblings. On Vinny's first day in eleventh grade, the teacher, Miss Stoddard, walked over to his desk and asked him if he was related to Liberty and Louise DeVitto. Vinny said yes. Miss Stoddard pointed to the door and said, "Get out of my classroom."

When I had my automobile accident, a lot of people came to visit me. Vinny got so tired of hearing about me that he would just leave the house. At about sixteen years old, Vinny was becoming a "tough" guy. He thought he was invincible, wearing a chain from a mini-bike around his waist and never hesitating to cut you down. When he belittled someone, it made him feel bigger—Vinny was the shortest in the family.

I don't know where he got the balls, but one night at the dinner table he challenged my father. Doug Stegmeyer was there; his mother had sold her house, so he had been living in our basement. My father had just taken the last glass of red wine from the bottle on the table. While drinking his wine, my father asked Vinny to go upstairs and shut the light that he had left on in his room. Vinny made a crack and said, "Take it easy, I'll do it later." This caused my father to lose his temper, and he got so mad he stood up and said "Take it easy? Take it easy, you son of a bitch? I'll take it easy; I brought you into this world, and I'll take you out of it." At this, Vinny said, "Yeah, right!" My father stood up, and while holding the empty wine bottle by the neck, he tried to break it over the back of the kitchen chair. My parents' early-'70s kitchen set had green vinyl-covered padding, so every time my father hit the bottle on the chair, it would just bounce off without breaking. Each time the bottle didn't break, Vinny would make another remark and laugh harder.

While this was happening, my mother, who was giggling at what she was seeing, kept motioning for Louise, Sal, and me to look at Doug, who was just staring straight down at his plate. Finally, my dad got so mad that he slammed his fists on the table, which sent the food and everything else flying. Doug got splattered with sauce, but not even for a second did he lift his head or say a word, nor did he put his fork down; he just continued to eat. We all looked at Doug and laughed, and Vinny finally went and turned his light off when my mother asked him to do it.

When Vinny turned eighteen he was running with a tough crowd; they were hitting the bars hard. Vinny left a bar in Seaford Harbor called the Hi Lo one night and ran his '68 blue Chevy into six parked cars. He said he was looking down to tune in his radio. Another time, after leaving for work, he came running back into the house two seconds later yelling, "My car has been stolen!" Sal volunteered to drive him back to the bar where he was the night before, and on the way they found Vinny's brown Cadillac wrapped around a telephone pole. Another night, he came home so fucked up that he ate two uncooked pork chops that my mother had breaded and had left to cook the following day. When my mother found out she called poison control. They asked her if he was sick. She said no. They said the alcohol must have killed all the bacteria.

Vinny and Sal shared a bedroom; Vinny's bed was on one side of the room and Sal's on the other. Vinny would get out of his bed in the middle of the night and think he was in the bathroom. He would be so fucked up that he would sometimes piss or puke on a sleeping Sal.

I had a friend in high school named Eddie. We used to get drunk a lot and cause trouble in the local bars. One night we were in the Hi Lo shooting pool and drinking with another friend, Randy. Eddie had just gotten out of jail for robbery and was on probation. There were these two guys from another town in the bar that night, and one of them kept hassling Eddie about how to shoot pool. Eddie was trying to stay cool, but all of a sudden, out of nowhere, as Eddie was leaning across the table to make a shot, the guy hit Eddie over the head with the bottom of a beer mug. Getting up slowly, Eddie put his hand on his head, and there was blood all over it and dripping onto the floor. Eddie turned, jumped on the guy, and started beating on him. Seeing this, Randy started beating on the guy, too. Then the guy's friend, who had been sitting at the bar, got off his bar stool and started heading for the fight. I noticed that he had pulled a knife out of his pocket.

I immediately went after him. Because of my drumming, I never used my hands to do anything that could hurt them, so I hit the guy in the head with my pool cue. I broke five cues over the guy's head before we finally threw both of them out of the bar. Eddie was in bad shape, so I drove him to the hospital, where he received a couple of stitches on his head. The next night, the manager of the bar asked me what had happened. I played dumb, and then he showed me the garbage pail full of broken pool cues.

The more I got involved with bands, the less I saw Eddie. He was getting a bad reputation in Seaford as a drug user who was into heroin. Around this time a friend of mine, Kevin, overdosed on heroin. Kevin and I met when we made our Holy Confirmation at Saint William the Abbot Catholic Church in Seaford. We were assigned as partners to walk down the aisle together towards the altar. Even years later, when we would run into each other, we still called each other "partner." Kevin was found dead in Eddie's brother's car. Eddie's brother was in the military, and his car had been left on the lawn at his mom's house; Kevin "nodded off" in the car.

I had just gotten home from the *Turnstiles* tour and went to the White Whale, a small bar in Seaford Harbor, to check out a band I used to play with called Blue Hair. It was one of the first nights I'd been out in my hometown since I got the gig with Billy, and it was great. I was like a local hero. The bartender who used to hate me for causing trouble loved me now and was giving me free drinks. There were songs on the jukebox on which I played drums. I was enjoying all this at the bar when Eddie came in and sat next to me. "You better watch your brother Vinny," he said. "He's foolin' around with shit he shouldn't be." I looked at Eddie and said, "Get the fuck outta here. You're crazy." There's no way that could be true, I thought. Vinny always thought Eddie was fucked up. He wasn't stupid enough to turn out like him. Just the same, I spoke to Vinny a few days later about what Eddie said, and just as I thought, he said Eddie was crazy.

The truth was Vinny and his small circle of friends were shooting heroin. Why didn't I tell my parents what Eddie had told me? Why was I in total denial? There were signs. I had noticed his eyes were sometimes glassy. He always wore long sleeve shirts. He would stumble into his room and sleep all day. My mother thought it was because Vinny worked so hard. Sometimes he would be scratching like he had fleas. It seemed so unbelievable to me; this couldn't be happening to my family. My father was a cop, surely he would see it.

Vinny was a follower. He went the way of the crowd. I did stupid things too. I tried it all with my friends: LSD, methamphetamine, uppers, downers, cough medicine, and glue. In the 1960s, my friend's father was a doctor. We used to go over to his house and go through his father's sample drawer. There were uppers and downers; we would read the suggested dosage and double, triple, or even quadruple it. But it was recreational for me. I wanted to play the drums and if anything was gonna screw that up, I was over it quick. Eventually some of the guys I hung out with started to rob houses. I started seeing a whole lot less of all these guys, who were now messing with heroin..

One of my best friends and I used to like to do all the "up" drugs: speed, acid, Black Beauties. My buddy got in trouble with the law and spent some time away. When he got out he only hung out with me and my drum, because he knew he had to remove himself from the destructive crowd. We'd smoke pot and listen to records in his bedroom: Cream, Jimi Hendrix, and his favorite, the Doors. One day, we got really stoned and listened to the Beatles' *White Album*. Before we parted ways, he gave me a Chuck Berry record which showed me the beauty of simplicity in rock 'n' roll.

My friend was not a musician but loved that I played the drums. He would come to all my gigs, all my rehearsals, and would even sit in my parents' basement and play air drums while I practiced. He would help me with my drums when I needed to bring them to a gig. Once he surprised me by taking a train to Baltimore and showing up at the club I was living and playing at, bringing my desperately needed eyeglasses. He followed me and my drum around everywhere until he met the woman that introduced him to the Hare Krishna religion. He totally cleaned up his life: no more drugs, no booze—not that he ever really drank much—and he became a vegetarian. Some days he wouldn't talk; it was a practice in self-control. He became a pillar in the ashram. I kept my Catholic ways. We eventually stopped hanging out.

My career as a drummer was taking off big-time. The albums I played on were all smash hits: *Turnstiles* had done well and *The Stranger* had sold millions. I was touring and had become a respected drummer all around the world, and had just gotten married and was looking for a house on Long Island. Everybody loved me now. I was a star. My parents were proud of me, and I thought the rest of my siblings were.

I was wrong.

In the beginning of 1980, Vinny held up a gas station with a gun. The bizarre thing was that it was the gas station he had worked at for years. He even knew Brad, the guy who was working there at the time of the robbery. After taking the money, he drove down the Wantagh Parkway and threw it out the window, then drove back to my parents' house where the police arrested him. My parents bailed Vinny out of jail, and while he was out awaiting arraignment he hooked up with his friends and they all stuck the same needle in their arms one more time. When he went in front of the judge, she noticed the tracks on his arms. She told him she was probably going to save his life by what she was about to do. Before the gavel hit the bench, Vinny was sentenced to one year in jail. A few weeks later, I had to see my lawyer about becoming an incorporated business. He knew my family, and told me something that shocked the shit out of me. He said, "Your brother did this because of you. He did it to get attention." I was terrified. Did that mean my brother hated me? He held up a gas station with a gun. Would he have used that gun on someone? Would he have used it on me if I was there that day?

Vinny remained at the Nassau County Jail on Long Island. When someone is arrested in Nassau County, they go to the Nassau County Jail before they are sent to an upstate facility. It didn't matter what your crime was, or what jail you were ultimately sent to, this is where you went after you were sentenced. But Vinny was never transferred. My parents had a friend who worked for the judicial system in Nassau County. She lived two houses down from us back in Seaford, and she knew all the judges in the Nassau County courts. Between the efforts of my parents' friend and Vinny's lawyer, Vinny only spent four months in jail.

Jail was a frightening and enlightening four months for Vinny. He had robbed a gas station to get attention, and was now getting more attention than he had bargained for. He was grouped in with thieves, rapists, and murderers. There were guys from the Mafia, motorcycle gangs, and black guys who hated white guys. My parents would visit Vinny all the time, and he would tell them how scared he was and how they had to get him out of there. I went to visit him once. It was hard to see my brother dressed in prison-issue clothes because he had committed a crime out of jealousy of what I had accomplished with my drum. We didn't talk about it; we both knew how stupid he had been. "I gotta get out of here," he said. "You don't talk to anyone, and you don't make eye contact with anyone." My visit with Vinny didn't last long. I felt distant from him. He was my brother and I loved him, but as I was traveling the world, directing my energy into my drum, Vinny had been directing his energy into his anger. The anger led him to stick a needle in his arm, which would ultimately get the best of him.

My family used to say Vinny went away to college because we didn't want anyone to know he went to jail, and when he got out, he totally cleaned up his act. He met a woman named Debbie, they got married, and he got a job working for Grumman Aircraft in Farmingdale. Debbie and Vinny had two children: a girl named Tarin, and the only DeVitto grandson, Eric. Vinny was happy and all was forgiven. He was coming to Billy Joel concerts and even started to like the music (although he did admit that whenever we played "Piano Man," he would always wish he had a fast-forward button so he didn't have to listen to it).

All was going well, but a strange thing started to take place. All the friends from Vinny's old crowd were dying. They were overdosing on heroin. Vinny was scared by having to go to all his friends' funerals. When we asked him if he was all right, he would nervously say how glad he was that he stopped doing dope, because that could have been him. One by one all the friends from his circle were gone. Vinny tried to maintain a normal life. When he would come home from work in the evening, his wife would leave to go to her part-time job and Vinny would make dinner for the kids. After dinner he would bathe them, and then put them to sleep. All this would not have been a big deal for a healthy man, but Vinny was calling my mother and telling her how tired he was. With his friends dying and him feeling tired all the time, Vinny was under a lot of stress.

He knew something that he couldn't tell anyone.

AIDS is transmitted through the exchange of blood. It was being spread from intravenous drug user to intravenous drug user through the use of the same needle. When Vinny and his friends found this out, they said if they ever got AIDS they would kill themselves. Could this be why all his friends were dead—and if they had AIDS, could he have it too?

Vinny's attitude changed, especially towards gays, since AIDS had ravaged the gay community. Vinny was one of the biggest joking ballbusters I had ever known, but now, when a joke was told about gays, Vinny would say, "Don't say that. They're good people too." He told us we shouldn't say derogatory or racist things about anyone. This was not the same Vinny whose friends went to Disney World and kicked Goofy in the balls as a joke.

Vinny began to get sick more often. He was having coughing fits that had him spitting phlegm, and he was always tired. I was divorced from my first wife and remarried by this time; my second daughter, Torrey, was three years old. My first wife had custody of my seven-year-old daughter, Devon, and my wife was pregnant with my third child. I was living in a house in Fort Salonga, Long Island, and my career was doing great. I had played on nine multi-million-selling albums and after performing in the Soviet Union, we had become one of the biggest acts in the world. I was sleeping at home when a call came in the middle of the night. It was my sister, Louise, but she was so upset I couldn't understand what she was saying. "Lou," I said, "slow down and tell me again." "Vinny couldn't breathe so Debbie rushed him to the hospital" she replied. "They took a blood test. He has AIDS."

Although technically he had been admitted to the hospital for a severe case of pneumonia, Vinny and his wife had known he had AIDS for a year, but they didn't tell the rest of the family. They had been seeing a psychologist to help them. When my parents arrived at the hospital, my father brushed past Vinny's wife and their psychologist friend, and stayed with Vinny for a while. Upon leaving, he overheard the psychologist say, "You'd better tell him his son has AIDS." My father could not believe it. To him, this was his son's death sentence. I went to the hospital right away. Vinny kept denying the truth, saying, "I don't have AIDS, it's just pneumonia. I'll be okay." Somehow we all kind of believed him. Isn't that crazy? In total denial, we just kept thinking that he couldn't have AIDS. It would be a long time before our family accepted the truth.

Louise, meanwhile, was getting worried. She used to mess around with heroin, and had shot it in her arm using the same needle as Vinny. She immediately went for a blood test, but, thank God, she tested negative for HIV and AIDS. Vinny was constantly in and out of more hospitals over the next two years. This became an exercise in total chaos. The extent of my AIDS education was as brief as the skit Eddie Murphy did about it in *Raw*. All the doctors could tell us was that it could be transmitted through sex and intravenous drug use. Then, articles in the newspapers started coming out saying a dentist got it from a patient's blood. Then the big scare was blood transfusions. It was just all mixed up and no one knew anything for sure. In the first hospital to which Vinny was admitted, the staff was so uneducated about AIDS that they would not enter his room. His doctor told us to get him out of there, that he deserved a better place, so we moved him to Nassau County Medical Center; which had a floor designated for AIDS patients. We still denied that he had it, and we didn't tell anyone his true diagnosis—we told everyone he had cancer.

When someone has AIDS, there is the hopelessness of there being no cure and the horror of watching the person disintegrate in front of your eyes. Hospitals make their money from insurance companies, so there was a lot of "experimenting" going on in the hospital with AIDS patients. The longer the hospital kept them alive, the more money it would receive. One of the most painful things they did was take bone marrow from Vinny's leg. The results came back and Vinny was diagnosed with cancer. They put him on chemotherapy. He lost his hair and they sent him home. Because he got pneumonia repeatedly, he was constantly being sent back to the hospital. His immune system was so compromised that if he was around anyone who was sick, he would also get sick. In the end, he was confined to the hospital.

Vinny's condition would change like the weather. My sister Louise took my parents to North Carolina to get away from everything. She told me to call her if Vinny took a turn for the worse. When they left, Vinny told them to go and have a good time, he was fine. I visited my brother while they were away and found him lying in a bed full of his own feces. He asked me in a weak voice if I would get someone to clean him, and the hospital staff came immediately. I panicked, called my sister and told her, "Come home, it doesn't look good." They drove all night from North Carolina. When they arrived at the hospital the next morning, Vinny was sitting upright and said to them, "What are you guys doing here? I thought you were on vacation."

Vinny would say one of the worst things about being in the hospital was the food; he hated it. His wife told him that he had better get used to it, because she had two children to care for and no time to be running out to get him a hamburger. We DeVittos, however, would bring him whatever he wanted: deli sandwiches, Italian, Chinese, Greek, steaks, hamburgers—if Vinny wanted it, we brought it. He loved stuffed artichokes, so my mother made some and brought them to the hospital. Vinny was in bad shape by this time, and had lesions on the roof of his mouth. When the lesion specimen was sent to the lab, the report that came back said that these lesions were usually found on dead people. When he bit down on the artichoke leaf, he couldn't get his mouth back open. A nurse had to come in and help him open it. This was when my mother said she knew it was the end; Vinny was too weak to eat his favorite food.

Towards the end of Vinny's life, "spiritual" things started to happen. My sister Louise and I were visiting with him. We were having a normal conversation when he said, "I saw God." We were like, "Yeah, right." He said, "No, I really saw God. He was right out that window." He pointed to the window in his room. "His presence was so bright, I could hardly look at him." I could feel the calmness in Vinny's soul.

One night I met Billy's lighting designer in the city for dinner. As we were talking, I told him that my brother had AIDS. He slapped me across the face and said, "Why didn't you tell me? I know people who know about AIDS and could have helped!" The gay community was far more educated about AIDS than we were, and as a gay man, he had friends that had gone through it. I felt horrible. I could've done so much more for Vinny through people who were within my reach.

I decided not to go see Vinny anymore. It was just too much for me, and I couldn't take it. Plus, it was a constant battle with my wife. She didn't want Vinny around, and she was paranoid because my second daughter played with her cousins (Vinny's children). What if they were infected? One Sunday we were all at my parents' house for dinner. Vinny was in the TV room, and we could all hear him coughing and spitting his phlegm into tissues. He would toss the tissues into a little garbage can that was in the room. After dinner the kids all went into the TV room to play. On the way home, my daughter Torrey said that when the kids were playing they accidentally kicked over Uncle Vinny's garbage pail. My wife panicked and asked Torrey, "Did you touch any of the tissues?" Torrey said, "Yes, we didn't want to get in trouble, so we put the tissues back in to the garbage." Horrified, my wife yelled, "Don't put your hands in your mouth, and don't touch your ears or eyes!" Then she started to cry, which made Torrey start crying and say, "I'm sorry, Mommy, I didn't know I did something wrong." When we got home, my wife took Torrey to the sink and scrubbed her hands with a brush like a lunatic. We called the AIDS hotline. There had to be blood involved for transmission of the disease, they told us. I called my mother; she checked the garbage pail and found no blood.

My wife had had enough. The pressure of being pregnant and being around Vinny was too much for her. She packed her bags and drove to her family in Michigan. I headed back on the road. One day I was back home when there was a knock on the door. It was Vinny. "I know how you feel," he said, "but I've got to see you." We talked for a long time. He just had to see everybody as much as he could, he said, because he knew that his time was short. After many hours of talking with me, Vinny left. I was so happy that he came to see me, but I felt like a horrible person. I was running from Vinny and his disease. I was mad at him for getting sick, and mad that he was going to die. I knew what I needed to do for my brother.

Knowing what it would mean to him, this is when I brought Vinny with me to the recording session with Steve Winwood. I can still see his face looking through the control room window with a big grin of joy and disbelief on his face, watching his brother play with Steve Winwood. He was such a big fan that we buried him in his Steve Winwood tour sweatshirt. Vinny also loved Eric Clapton; in fact he named his son after him. I was able to arrange for Vinny to meet Clapton. Backstage at the Clapton show in Nassau Coliseum, Eric was so kind to him. We told Eric that Vinny had cancer. Eric told Vinny, "Don't worry, you'll beat this." They took photos and Eric hugged him goodbye. My brother Sal got married, and Vinny was able to be best man, but soon after that he started to deteriorate fast.

Meanwhile, I was juggling loss of income from Billy's predicament, and we had a major tour starting. It was now only a matter of time with Vinny; he had full-blown AIDS. My sister-in-law was losing her husband, and legally had the last word in all hospital decisions as far as Vinny was concerned. My mother was losing her son but had no legal rights. The doctors loved Vinny. They knew he had tried heroin. There were other dope addicts with AIDS that were still getting dope brought to them in the hospital, but the doctors knew Vinny had tried to straighten out his life. One doctor told my mother, "I know there's a God, but does this boy deserve this?"

Coming out of the hospital elevator one day, I came upon my mother talking to my sister-in-law. Vinny was in a coma and the doctors had told my parents that he was not going to last too much longer. The hospital had found cancer in Vinny's brain and my sister-in-law was telling my mother that she was sending him for radiation treatments. My mother said, "Why are you making him go through radiation? Please, don't do that. The doctor just told us he doesn't have long to live. They told us not to put him through anything else. He had been through enough, let him die in peace." For reasons only she in her heart knows, my sister-in-law insisted. "Please don't put him through that," my mom implored. "His hair just grew back." My sister-in-law had the last say in the matter: "I've made the decision." My mother said, "But please, I'm his mother." My sister-in-law responded, "And I'm his wife." Mom snapped and started beating her, screaming, "I want him back, I just want my son back!" I grabbed my mother's arms, and we both fell to the ground as I begged her to stop, but she kept yelling, "I want my son back!" over and over again.

Every morning my parents went to the hospital and watched the staff take their son for the radiation treatments. It was killing them. At the end, Vinny was in a coma. Whenever they arrived at the hospital, Mom and Dad always went straight upstairs to Vinny's room. One day when they got there, my mother decided to stop for a cup of coffee in the cafeteria, and then they took the elevator to Vinny's floor. When they got close to his room, a nurse stopped them and said, "I'm sorry. Your son is gone. He died fifteen minutes ago." My mother still feels that if she didn't stop for the coffee, she would have seen her son alive one more time. Even though he was dead, the nurses let my parents go in the room and hug their son for the last time.

The hospital asked my father if he wanted an autopsy done. "Please don't," he said. "We know how he died. My son has been through enough." The hospital understood and no autopsy was done. After my brother died, his doctor wrote a letter to my mother that said he was sorry he had lost Vinny. The doctors met the Vinny that we all knew; the Vinny who was funny, kind, and tried to turn his life around. Everyone was sad to see him go.

As the *Storm Front* tour approached, I can remember how selfish I was. What if he dies when I'm on tour? What would I tell Billy? "Hey Billy, could you cancel a few shows? I gotta go home." Billy would probably have said yes, and found another drummer to fill in. I was feeling so insecure at the time, things being cut off left and right, that I worried Billy's accountants might suggest he could save more money without me. I prayed my brother would die before the tour started. I am ashamed of myself for having done such a selfish thing. In the end, Vinny did die before the tour started. Maybe it was a last sign of his love for me.

I was at rehearsal when I looked up to see one of my bandmates standing in the doorway. The look on his face was unmistakable as he said, "Your sister is on the phone. It's time." I went into a room alone and Louise told me Vinny was gone. He was just thirty-two, leaving two small children and a wife. I hung up the phone, put my head in my hands, and cried. After I pulled myself together, everyone expressed their condolences, and Billy asked me if I wanted to go home. I told him no. I knew I'd feel better if I banged on something.

After rehearsal I went to my parents' house. They were, of course, devastated. This was the second son my mother had lost. My father was out of it. Near the end, when Vinny was in a coma, I had watched my dad hold him like a baby. The tough World War vet and New York cop was telling his son to go; it was okay, he should go with Jesus. Dad whispered to Vinny that his grandmother was waiting, he should go be with her. As I watched my father dying emotionally and my brother dying physically, "Angelia" by Richard Marx was playing softly in the background on an inexpensive radio. I still have a hard time hearing that song. It brings back the memory of that day so vividly. It was surreal, I was a spectator, and the mighty giant was holding his dying son, weeping. My soul was screaming, "This can't be true." No matter how much you prepare, you're never ready to let somebody go.

Later that night I went home and played "Cavatina" by John Williams and

Liona Boyd, and I cried by myself. To us, AIDS was some gay disease that someone else got. When Vinny was diagnosed, he realized why most of his friends had mysteriously died or ended their lives. In 1986, the disease was shrouded in fear and misunderstanding. We didn't know how long he would live or what he was going to go through. There was a time when it was thought that AIDS could be transmitted through saliva and sweat. I didn't care. I held and kissed my brother every time I saw him. Vinny's wake was insane: Italians crying all over the place, throwing themselves on the casket. Russell, Doug, and even Billy came to my brother's funeral. When my parents thanked Billy for coming, he said, "It's family."

In June 2004, I watched Vinny's daughter Tarin DeVitto graduate Summa Cum Laude from the State University at Albany. His son Eric graduated from high school a few weeks later. My sister-in-law did a great job with their children. I know Vinny is proud of them.

**Yankee Stadium,** *Storm Front* **tour, 1990.**

# 31

# The *Storm Front* Tour

This album and tour were appropriately named considering what was looming. I was not ready for the Storm Front tour; I was emotionally shot, physically out of shape, and I arrived in Boston to start the tour with nothing to wear on stage. The tour started at the Worcester Civic Arena in Massachusetts, and we rehearsed there for three days before the first show. Every night when I returned to my room, I found myself thinking about Vinny. Feeling emotionally beaten, I would toss and turn in my sleep all night. I had been going to church and praying for answers. In my prayers one night, I said to God, "My heart is broken. I feel like there's a big hole in my chest. What should I do?" I heard a loud and clear voice that said, "Fill it with me." I didn't.

The night before the first show, Billy and the band were hanging out in the hotel bar. I got drunk on champagne. Having stayed away from alcohol for four years, I was fucked up for the whole next day. Still needing stage clothes, I ran out and bought two silk shirts. By 4 PM we were on our way to the gig. I tried to sleep during the ride, but had no success. When I got to the venue I tried to eat, but had no appetite. We hit the stage at 8:20 PM. The combination of the hangover, the hot lights, and my silk shirt made me drenched with sweat by the end of the first song. I didn't realize that silk didn't breathe, so my body had begun to heat up. The shirt clung to my body and I started to dehydrate. I kept drinking water to try to save myself, but I drank more water than my body could handle and I started to feel sick.

While playing the last song, "A Matter of Trust," I looked at Crystal and motioned for her to come over to the drum set. I handed her the drumsticks, got up from the set, and raced down the stairs behind the stage. I threw up in a garbage pail under the stage while she struggled through the song for me. The stage techs said so much vomit was coming out of me that I looked like a fountain that wasn't going to stop. I thought this was the end of Liberty DeVitto. My brother's death was doing more damage to me than I knew. I felt alone and scared. My body had no choice but to build up a tolerance to alcohol, because I continued to drink, and I started to build up a tolerance for playing while I was hung over, because I had to continue to tour. It was becoming harder to do shows, but it was getting easier and easier to drink. I was starting to avoid people and stopped taking phone calls, especially from those close to me who knew me as a God-fearing and sober person.

Mylon LaFever was one of these people. Mylon was a minister and had a teen outreach ministry in Atlanta, Georgia. He used to be a rock 'n' roller who wrote songs for Elvis and hung out with the Allman Brothers and plenty of drug-eating bands. He had given all that up for a life as a minister. I met Mylon when I appeared on "The Scott Ross Talkback Show," which was part of the 700 Club. Scott interviewed me, Mylon, and Dez Dickerson from Prince's band on the subject of being a believer working in a secular business. We had a meeting before the show and decided not to get spiritual, but at one point during the interview I was asked about my brother Vinny. He was in a coma at the time, still in a Long Island hospital. I said, "There is no doctor, no hospital, and no medicine that can help him; it's in God's hands. I believe Vinny is ready to let go of this world and is saying to Jesus, 'You'd better be there on the other side, and I'm putting everything in you.'" The interview got very spiritual after that, and Mylon and I became very close friends. He was someone I could talk about spirituality with, while he understood the business I was in.

Now, though, I was drinking, and I had different priorities than Mylon knew me to have. I was embarrassed, and was avoiding his phone calls and ignoring his messages. Mylon was persistent but patient, because he knew the tour would bring us to Atlanta, where he lived. After weeks of people telling me, "He just wants to talk to you," one day I felt sober enough to finally call back. When we spoke, he never even asked me why I didn't return any of his calls; he immediately went into what he had on his mind. Having recently had a slight heart attack, he was reading a book about healing; how to heal yourself through prayer. In the book was a line that read, "You can have liberty in Christ." Upon reading this, he began to think about me and got the feeling that he needed to lay his hands on me and pray. I thought this was just one of his wacky ministry things, but I decided to let him see me, if only just for a few minutes.

It was July 3 when we arrived in Atlanta, and there were at least ten messages from Mylon at the hotel. Without retuning his calls, I went out that night with the crew guys and got hammered. The next day was Independence Day and the crew was having a baseball game with a local radio station with a night off. I had a terrible hangover, but I went to the ballgame. "I can call Mylon now," I thought to myself. "He'll probably be busy with the Fourth and I'll tell him I have to be at the game and I don't even know where I am." He answered the phone and said, "Describe the park you are in." I told him, "There are a couple of ball fields, a statue to a fallen hero, and a fountain." He said, "You're right around the block from my house. I'll be right there." Five minutes later I got into his car and was on the way back to his house, where a few of his band members were having a barbeque. On the ride he continued to say that he kept getting this spiritual feeling that he needed to lay hands on me and pray. I told him what had been going on in my life: I told him about Vinny and my drinking. He listened closely but didn't say much.

At Mylon's barbeque, his bandmates were all around, swimming, eating, and hanging out. After about an hour, he asked them all to go inside the house with him so they could lay hands on me and pray. "Okay," I thought to myself, "I have to try something. I'm losing myself and my life." Without hesitation the whole crew was inside, and I remember being surprised when I heard what Mylon was praying for. He didn't pray for me to stop drinking; he prayed for God to lift the time of mourning for my brother off of me. The moment he said that, I realized that grief was the cause of my behavior. I immediately felt like someone lifted a manhole cover from my chest. It was incredible. I would continue to miss my brother forever, but I was finished mourning his death—I would remember the good things.

That night, I watched Fourth of July fireworks and suddenly felt fully alive and like myself again. I stopped drinking and played great from that day on. I also kept myself busy by doing drum clinics on my days off. There was even one month when I did more clinics than gigs. Mostly I ignored what the other guys did on the road.

The tour was based in San Francisco for a while. Rumor had it that Billy had met a girl. *The Enquirer* ran a story saying he was wining and dining her at the best restaurants in town. One day my phone rang, and without so much as a hello, I heard Christie's voice on the other end, reading me the article. After finishing the entire story, she said, "Well, Lib, tell me about it." "Christie," I responded, "I've been doing drum clinics. I haven't been around on the days off." She said, "I'll get to the bottom of this," and hung up.

*River of Dreams* touring band L to R behind Billy: Tommy Byrnes, Crystal Taliefero, me, David Rosenthal, T-Bone Wolk.

# 32

# *River of Dreams*

Right before we were to start recording a new, as yet unnamed, album, I was called into Billy's accountant's office for a meeting with Ed London. He informed me that I was only to receive one and a half cents per album and my usual double-scale, double-session pay. "I was getting four and a half cents on *Storm Front* before you took it and everything else away," I replied, "And now I am only going to be getting one and a half cents on this? You bought the other guys out of their bonuses and you just took mine away and gave me nothing? For me to swallow what you are telling me, and to make it easier knowing that I am getting fucked, tell me that you screwed up with the others!" "We had our reasons for doing what we did with them," Ed responded. "We didn't really screw up." I said, "You fucked up, didn't you?" He denied it one more time, and when I repeated the question, he finally said, "Yeah, we did fuck up." I said, "I'm going to Billy to tell him what you are offering me." "Don't bother," he said. "Billy already knows." I found out much later that these accountants were offering me less money than Billy thought I was being paid. This later led to a lawsuit that was actually caused by paperwork errors on the part of the accountants.

Billy was living on the east end of Long Island. He hated the idea of traveling to the city to record; Billy is a real homebody. We used to tour so much that we'd say we never took vacations; we took home-cations. He loved being home, being around his things. Sometimes on the road he'd bring stuff from home to make the time away easier. He'd often take his drawings and design boats, or his nautical charts to plan a trip he'd like to take on his boats. If pressure got too much at home and he needed time to himself, he'd go out on his boat. "You don't have to go far out in the ocean to find solitude," he said. So the prospect of going into New York City to record an album at this moment was out of the question.

First Billy tried to build a studio in a church in Southampton. With the high ceilings in the church, the sound was great, but it was on a main road, and anyone who passed by heard us playing. We did manage to get two Elvis covers done in the church, which can be found on the soundtrack for *Honeymoon in Vegas*. "All Shook Up" was done in one take while testing to see if the tape recorder worked. Billy's idea essentially worked; he was able to go home every night, but there was always someone knocking on the door to see what was going on. The studio was just in a bad spot, so the seclusion of winter on Shelter Island sounded like a better option.

Shelter Island is an island between the North and South Forks of Long Island. Billy built a studio in a boathouse on the island. Everyone tried to talk him out of it, but he was locked in on the idea of being able to go home every night. Carpenters and electricians were hired, and the studio came together very quickly. Each day we would drive our cars onto the Shelter Island ferry and take the fifteen-minute commute to the island, then the boathouse was a fifteen-minute drive from there. The studio was large and well-designed, with a nice-sized control room up a few stairs (similar to the early pictures of the Beatles recording with George Martin looking down on the group). There was a restaurant and bar within a one-minute walk from the studio. This was where we planned to make the next album.

Billy was wearing a lot of hats in regards to this album; he was the singer, piano player, producer, and songwriter. We recorded eight songs at the boathouse: "No Man's Land," "Blonde Over Blue," "The Great Wall of China," "A Minor Variation," "Shades of Grey," "Lullaby," "River of Dreams," and "You Picked a Real Bad Time." Billy had fired Doug and Russell (more about that later), so the band consisted of Schuyler Deale on bass, Tommy Byrnes on guitar, and me. Billy Zampino was the album coordinator; he'd call to tell us where we had to be and what was going on.

At first, things went well. For every album, we always had a chart hanging in the studio listing all the songs and the progress on each. It would show what still had to be done to finish the songs: needs vocal overdub, add guitar solo, etc. There was one song on the chart called "In the Middle of the Night." I was listening back to the take we had just done and asked Billy to repeat a line of the lyrics for me. He said, "We're all carried along in the river of dreams." "River of dreams," I said. "That's great." Seeing the look on my face, he knew what I was thinking. "You think it should be the title of the song?" he asked. "Yes," I said, "but I think it should also be the title of the album."

Right in the middle of things, Billy decided he couldn't produce anymore and that he needed some help, so he started to look for a producer. I think Billy would have made a fine producer, but he just runs out of patience and gives up on himself too easily. That's the downside of Billy that I've seen often. I think it's the perfectionist in him that doesn't like to settle. Billy felt he settled on *The Bridge* album, and I guess with the pressure of writing and performing the songs being as high as it was, he was spreading himself too thin. Ready to give the producer's chair to someone else, he chose Danny Kortchmar.

I had worked with Danny before, when I recorded with Stevie Nicks in L.A. At the time, Danny was playing guitar and Jimmy Iovine was producing. Danny had produced some things for Don Henley, who was a friend of Billy's, and Don was the one who recommended Danny to Billy. Danny came out to Billy's studio one day to check things out. He was smoking a huge cigar and brought his own engineer. We were playing a song and he kept stopping us and making suggestions. Tommy, Schuyler, and I thought the suggestions sucked, so after a while we stopped listening to him. Schuyler was so hung over from the previous night that the smell of Danny's cigar was making him sick, so he said to Danny, "Would you get that fucking thing out of here?" Danny was not very happy with that. Billy just laughed.

With Danny there, the vibe got very uncomfortable. Everyone went out for dinner that night at the American Hotel in Sag Harbor. Schuyler, Tommy, and I sat at one table, while Billy and Danny sat at another. We watched them talking, but we were too far away to hear their conversation. Amongst ourselves, we were saying, "This guy Danny sucks! There's no way Billy's gonna use him."

After dinner that night, Billy said he needed some time to write more songs, so we all went home for a few days. At home one night shortly after that, I got a frantic phone call from Schuyler. He said he had just seen Billy Zampino, who had let it slip that Billy Joel was in a studio in Manhattan with Danny Kortchmar—*and a whole new band.* "There is no way Billy (Joel) would do that," I replied, "I'll call him and call you back. Billy Z. is bullshitting you." I called Billy and got his answering machine, so I left a message: "Bill, its Lib. What's up? What's going on? Call me." A few hours later, Billy called back. I said, "What's going on?" "I don't know, what's going on?" he replied. "You called me." I said, "C'mon Billy, I spoke to Schuyler, and Billy Z. blabbed something I don't think he was supposed to say." "Okay," said Billy, "I'm in the studio in Manhattan with Danny and a bunch of his guys." I said, "Then it's true?" He said, "Yes, but I didn't say anything because I am only trying it for one song. You're still my drummer and you'll still be going on tour with me, but I just have to try this." I asked who he was using. It turned out I knew the guys he was talking about. "Couldn't you have at least gotten someone better looking to replace us? And what about the boathouse?" He said, "It's over."

Every day I waited to get the call to tell me that it was time to go back to the studio to continue what we were doing, but it never came. When the old band heard about this, Doug called me and said, "You'll see! That's it! This is only the beginning. This is how the beginning of the end was for me! Billy will be done with you too."

Every time I spoke to someone who was involved with the album, they'd say things were going great and Billy was moving along. It seemed things had gone from one song to two songs to three songs, etc. Tommy Byrnes called me one day after he was called into the studio to do some guitar overdubs. He said Billy was worried about me because he had heard that I was freaking out. I sent Billy a fax:

*Billy, I'm alright, I understand what you are doing. I support you one*

*hundred percent, and if you need anything, you can always call me.*
*You can tell Danny that if he needs anything, he can kiss my ass.*
*Love, Lib*

Billy told me that the note hung in the studio for the rest of the time that they were there. I understood that Billy had a pattern of trying something new on every album. I was the only consistency through each album since *Turnstiles*, but this time he wanted to try something without me. The funny thing was that when Danny would use the boathouse tracks to play for his musicians as "demos" of what they were about to record, they'd ask, "What's wrong with that?" He'd scream, "That's not how I want it done!" Most of the arrangements that made it onto *River of Dreams* were an exact rip-off of what we had done in the boathouse. People who were hearing the new tracks said that without me, they were stripped of the Billy Joel sound.

Before the album was released, Billy asked me to come out to his house and listen to it. Driving out there, I prepared myself to hear a great album with stellar musicianship, and Billy would be proven right in his thinking and changes. Sitting down in Billy's living room, he handed me a Walkman and a set of headphones and told me he'd be in the kitchen. I was afraid to hit the play button. I sat there alone in Billy's living room listening, and when half the album had played, I started to laugh. The production sucked. After it was over, I went into the kitchen and Billy said, "Well?" With a smirk on my face I said, "It's nice, when are we going on tour?" I couldn't wait to go home and call Schuyler to tell him how bad it was.

*River of Dreams* actually turned out to be a win-win situation for me. If it sold a lot of copies, then we would tour forever. If it bombed, I could say, "I told you so." As it turned out, Billy's fan base made the album sell well. Only two singles were pulled from it, but by this time, Billy's loyal fans would have bought anything he put out, especially following *Storm Front*— which had so much success that Billy actually told Sony records to let it die. He asked them to stop putting singles out.

The tour for *River of Dreams* went on for a long, long time. I thought Danny's recordings were pretty bad; maybe Billy agreed somewhat because he decided to put "Shades of Grey" from the boathouse sessions on the record. The record label sent two songs, "River of Dreams" and "All About Soul" to producer Joe the Butcher in Philadelphia to remix and reproduce. Joe gave them a hip-hop sound by re-recording and replacing instruments while adding samples. Billy openly admitted that he had made a mistake and that he would never record like that again. *River of Dreams* turned out to be Billy's last pop album. I had made my session money for the boathouse recording sessions, but lost my one-and-a-half cents when Billy changed his mind and didn't use the tracks, even though I played on "Shades of Grey." In addition, my income from *Greatest Hits Volumes 1 & 2* had gone down to just a few hundred dollars a year. At least when I look at *River of Dreams*, I know the title of the album was my suggestion.

After the fiasco around the making of this album, I had to figure out a way to cut my expenses. I had always enjoyed warm weather, and I knew with airplanes and computers I could live anywhere and not miss a beat. It was 1994, and I asked my accountant how much I would save if I moved to Florida. At least $25,000 a year, he said, just in state taxes. When we played the Orlando Arena on the River of Dreams tour, I called a realtor in Winter Park, and within two days I found a house and bought it. I didn't know a soul in Florida, but feeling confident about the move, I put my Long Island house up for sale. I knew the end of my career was near and Billy could pull the plug at any time, so now I wouldn't have to wonder where I'd retire.

Unfortunately this decision turned out to be a disaster and ended with me drinking, smoking pot, and chasing waitresses with my friend who was an Elvis impersonator. Other than the fact that it led to my second divorce, the best part of it was that my friend was quite good at being Elvis!

Doug Stegmeyer and I: the engine that drove Billy Joel.

# 33

# Losing Doug

Douglas Allen Stegmeyer was born December 23, 1951, into a musical family. His father, William, played clarinet with Glenn Miller and Benny Goodman, and was an arranger for television shows including "The Jackie Gleason Show" and "Your Hit Parade." His mother, Peg, played piano, sang, and gave lessons. His older brother, Al, was a studio engineer. (Sue, his younger sister, was the only non-musical member of the Stegmeyer family; she had a great passion for horses.) The odds were stacked against Doug because both his parents were alcoholics. In fact, Doug lost his father at an early age from complications due to excessive drinking. Fortunately his mom escaped the same fate, and today celebrates her sobriety.

Doug started playing guitar and bass at the age of fourteen. He was a student of the Beatles and Motown, and along with his mother's influences of classical and show tunes, he fit like a glove with Billy Joel. He joined up with Billy in 1974, and Billy built his band around Doug—he was the anchor of the group; the bottom and the foundation of the Billy Joel sound. Doug loved music, women, and cars equally—vintage Chevy Corvettes, to be exact. He owned a few different ones, including a beautiful two-tone maroon and beige model with a 302 V8 engine and a four speed on the floor. (This is the car we recorded for "Movin' Out.")

Besides music, Doug also picked up the passion for alcohol that was in his genes, and this led him to leave a couple of those cars sitting on the tops of guard rails. In truth, we all had the love for booze. When we started to play together in Topper, it was a party every night. Many times we'd drink all night and wind up going to Russell's house for breakfast. I got Doug a gig at the Narragansett Inn playing weddings with me. The waitresses would pass us drinks on the bandstand. After the gigs, we would race down Merrick Road from Lindenhurst to Massapequa to the local jazz club.

Doug's nickname, given to him by Dean Krauss (the keyboard player in Topper), was "the eel." When Doug got the gig with Billy and was about to leave town, we were all very happy for him, but sad at the same time. The night of his last gig with us, we all got drunk, but Doug was smashed. I'm talkin' hammered. He could barely speak. After the gig we went to the diner to try to soak up some of the booze. As we passed the diner window on the way in, there were a few women seated at the booths. Doug was so trashed he decided to expose himself to them. The next day, Dean drew a cartoon and called it "the eel." It was a sketch of Doug with his fly open and his penis coming out. His penis had the same head as the head that was on his shoulders. The little head spoke to the big head, and Doug took all his advice. Doug was always listening to the wrong head.

Doug had a heart of gold. After he went on the road with Billy, he called me every night to tell me he was going to get me the gig—and sure enough, he did. Soon we were on top of the world, making records and touring. Doug complemented Billy's left hand on the piano; he knew both his craft and what Billy needed. The bigger Billy and the band got, the more we partied. Even though drink was our favorite pastime, drugs also became prevalent. There was pot, of course, but then coke, Quaaludes and Valium started showing up more and more. One of the crew guys would buy ludes (also called 714s) by the gross. They were very entertaining with a female companion; they'd loosen things up a bit. When "Just the Way You Are" came out, women could not believe that a bunch of guys could be so in tune with women's feelings. They loved us, and we returned their love. It was a tough job, but someone had to do it. We had our share of mishaps when we were high, like falling and getting black eyes, or girls who would stop breathing, but luckily everything always turned out okay.

As the years went on, Doug became more and more of a recluse. He was using cocaine to wake up, and booze and Valium to get to sleep. Doug once told me the invention of the ATM machine was one of his downfalls: it allowed him cash availability to buy a gram of cocaine at any time of the day or night. Doug had always been thin, but was now starting to gain weight. Billy had stopped using the band in videos and told me it was because of Doug's excessive drinking.

Doug was also starting to get lazy, and his attitude was becoming very negative. When we played together we had the time of our lives, but he always thought of us as being the "workhorses." Doug would point out that piano players, horns, and singers usually had time in a song to sit back, enjoy the groove, and rest a little, but the bass and drums were always playing. "We're always working," he said—and he told people how he felt. Once he was asked to play on a shuffle and told the bandleader, "Don't play this too long, I don't want to be your workhorse." Doug and I were always the first to finish our studio work, laying down a sold groove without the luxury of the overdubs and fixes the rest of the band would employ. When Doug and I were paid union scale, we got paid the least in the band because we were done the quickest. Doug called us "the budget boys."

While we were making *The Bridge* album, Doug's chemical dependencies were becoming very noticeable. The hospitalizations from pancreatitis were kind of a last straw; Billy was growing impatient and started bringing in other bass players for recordings. Doug seemed to always be depressed now, and only came out of his room to go to the gigs. One morning on our second visit to Australia on *The Bridge* tour, I was the last one to check out of the hotel. As

I left my room, a maid was already cleaning the room that Doug had been in, and I glanced through the open door into the room. There were eight empty beer bottles on a room service tray. Doug had been drinking alone. The problems kept getting worse, and finally Billy felt that Doug was just not pulling his weight any more, and decided to let him go.

Unfortunately, Russell became a casualty along with Doug. Billy decided that while he was getting rid of Doug, he might as well get rid of Russell at the same time. Rhythm guitarists are the most underrated musicians in a band. I think Russell was up there with John Lennon as one of the all-time greats, but Billy had people in his ear all the time, telling him what to do and who to hire or fire. We used to call these guys "the flies" because they were on Billy like flies on shit. They just didn't like Russell, so they got in Billy's ear to get rid of him.

When MTV broadcast the news that Billy Joel was going back into the studio with longtime drummer Liberty DeVitto and a whole new band, the other guys couldn't get in touch with Billy, so they called me. Not knowing what else to do, I called Billy and told him the guys were freaking out and that people were asking how he could be using a new band, but Billy had already made up his mind—this was a new album and time for a new sound. Doug never recovered. His pride as a musician and person was damaged, and he was angry that someone else was playing his bass parts. When he would come out to see us play at Nassau Coliseum, I felt terrible seeing him. He'd try to look happy, but I could see the hurt and the rage in his eyes. After the show he would always say, "That sucked." Deep down inside, I know Doug was always waiting for Billy to call and ask him to come back and play bass again, but he was slowly starting to realize it was never going to happen.

For some time after he had been let go, Doug would call me to vent. His conversations would start off calm, but would inevitably escalate to the subject of Billy, how he had fired him, and how at least I still had my gig— and then he'd remind me that I was playing with Billy because he had gotten me the gig. There was also financial strain. Billy had bought out Doug and Russell from their royalties, and the wording on the agreements was such that they received one payment, and then Billy owed them nothing more. (As I explained, I experienced the same thing when my "bonuses" were terminated.) Confronted with this situation, Russell used his money to pay bills. Doug, thinking that it would make him happy, bought a new Corvette. As time went on, he went broke, and he was angry.

Doug sank deeper and deeper into depression. In the end, I guess there were two roads he could have taken. One would have been to get help, pick up the bass, and go on. The other was to look for someone to blame and end his life. At the end of the day, he couldn't be happy as "Doug, the great bass player." He had to be "Billy Joel's great bass player." He was offered other gigs but turned them all down. He didn't want to commute from Long Island into New York City to work. He talked about moving to Nashville, but never followed up. If he had only held on tight to his bass, maybe things would have worked out.

I was living in Florida when I found out that Doug had died. He killed himself in his studio. Working with unfamiliar people, some of whom owed him money, Doug was nervous and had recently bought a shotgun. When he couldn't take the pressure any longer and his depression got the best of him, he rolled himself up in a carpet, put the gun in his mouth, and pulled the trigger. Dean Krause, who had known Doug since he was fourteen, was the one who found him. Doug knew that Dean was going to be at the studio the next morning to talk about a recording project they had in the works. Doug wanted everyone to know what he had done. When Dean arrived at the studio, the door was locked, and Dean started to get worried. He knew something wasn't right because Doug's car was there, so he called the police. When they arrived, they knocked the door down and found Doug's body. Dean says he'll never forget the sight of his friend's brains splattered across the control room glass.

Guilt was my first feeling. Was I indirectly involved in what he did? In the days before his death, Doug had called me twice. I stood over the answering machine, listening to his depressed tone as he left a message, "Liberty, it's Doug. Call me please." I would say to myself, "I'm not going to call him. He always brings me down. He's so depressing." Now he was dead. I felt, as his friend, I should have called him back—but I just would have never believed that he would do something like this. I could only see the world from my perspective. I still had my drums.

Could I have stopped him from doing it if I had just picked up the phone? Doug had been there for me. He got me the gig of a lifetime. He was my best man at my first and second weddings. He let me live at his house when I had nowhere to go in between marriages. He came to the hospital when my daughters were born. Above all, he was bass and I was drums. We had become a huge part in the sound of one of the biggest-selling recording artists ever. We had burned our names in musical history. Doug had joined AA and had stopped using alcohol and drugs, and he had his own studio, but it wasn't good enough. With his depression, he had a hard time keeping relationships together with women, and ultimately lost his spirit; he left that spirit in the music that someone else was now playing. Doug didn't decide to stop, someone else made that decision for him. When he realized he could never get back the part of his life he had lost, he just lost the will to live.

When I spoke to Billy, he asked, "How low does someone have to be to do something like that?" When Russell called, I could hear the horror in his voice; he loved Doug. The day before Doug was to be cremated, there was a memorial dinner at his favorite Italian restaurant, Christiano's in Syosset (the town where he grew up). Before I booked my plane ticket to get to New York, I called Richie Cannata to ask him if he was going. In an "I don't know how to tell you this, but…" voice, he said, "The family is blaming you, Billy, and Brian Ruggles for Doug's death." I got the chills. Not only had I lost my friend, but I was being blamed for it. If I had only picked up that phone. Was it really my fault?

Billy went to the dinner. Brian and I didn't go. The funny part was that the people who went were people from Doug's distant past. Richie said people were checking each other out like it was a high school reunion. It was a kind of opportunity for them to grab a bit of the spotlight, somehow. I have no idea where these people were while Doug was alive. The next day there was a small funeral with only Doug's family. His ex-girlfriend and Brian's wife were invited. Brian was told he was not allowed to go.

Billy was quoted in the Long Island newspaper *Newsday* on Saturday, August 26, 1995, as saying, "I am just in shock. I heard about it Thursday night and couldn't believe it. He was a very talented player. He was with me from the 1970s through 1988 and was the leader of the nucleus of the group that was the band. We called him 'the 'sergeant-at-arms.' He was committed to what he was doing and very serious about anything he did." About five years before Doug's death, during rehearsals for the *Storm Front* album, Billy wrote a song about Doug. It was called "Money or Love," and was released in 2005 in Billy's *My Life* box set.

*Money or love, which one are you doin' it for*
*Everybody has to make that choice sometimes you know*
*Something is wrong; I can tell the feeling is gone*
*Do you still remember when we started long ago*
*Wasn't love that kept us here driven in a rented car?*
*Who would have known that endless road*
*Would ever have come this far*
*Money or love, it's all decision when it's all alike*
*Everybody has a soul they can control or compromise*
*When did you start, when did I press upon the pain in your heart*
*When did I become the reason for the sadness in your life?*
*You could have asked me anytime, I would have told you why*
*Maybe if I had changed your mind, now it's too late to try*
*Goodbye*

*Often I have asked myself, could have I been closer to you*
*When you needed someone else*
*Could a friend who really knew you tried*
*When you decide*
*Money or love, what you're gonna do with your life*
*Everybody needs a passion or they cash in while they can*
*Make up your mind before you realize you've run out of time*
*You need a reason why you got to justify to make a stand*
*You could have asked me anytime, I would have told you why*
*Maybe if I had changed your mind, now it's too late to try*
*Goodbye*

A lot of bass players have come and gone since he passed away, but there will never be another Doug.

**Big People (L to R): Ben Orr, Jeff Carlisi, Pat Travers, Derek St. Holmes, me.**

# Big People

Big People consisted of Jeff Carlisi from .38 Special on guitar, Derek St. Holmes from Ted Nugent on guitar and vocals, Pat Travers on guitar and vocals, Ben Orr from the Cars on bass and vocals, and me on drums. Our tour manager, roadie, and stage manager was Joe Delerio, an all-around nice guy we lovingly called "Joe Joe."

This was one of my favorite bands to play with. Everything we did was based around food, and most of the money we made with this band was spent on expensive and excessive drinking and dining. I truly loved these guys. Big People was based in Atlanta, Georgia, and our song list consisted of songs we had played on, sang, or wrote with other respective bands. The set included "Hold on Loosely" from .38 Special, "Just What I Needed" from the Cars, "Hey Baby" from Ted Nugent, "Boom, Boom, Out Go the Lights" from Pat Travers, and "You May Be Right" from Billy, of course.

Ben Orr was Big People's rock star. Famous for his romantic, sexy vocal style, he played bass and sang on the Cars' hits "Just What I Needed," "Let's Go," "Bye, Bye Love," and "Drive," among others. He was especially noted for the silky vocal on "Drive." A man's man, Ben smoked Marlboro cigarettes, drank alcohol, drove a four-wheel-drive SUV, and chopped wood at his house in the mountains of Vermont. But when he went on stage in his black leather pants, brightly colored shirt, long black trench coat, and black cowboy boots, he drove the ladies wild. I'd look out into the crowd when we played "Drive" and watch all the women smile at Ben, hanging on to every word he was singing.

Ben could have had any woman he wanted, but what he wanted most was to be loved. He had two failed marriages. The second marriage brought him the love of his life, a son. Little Ben looked exactly like his father. With the bitter breakup of the Cars—Ric Ocasek and Ben hated each other—and two divorces, Ben was lonely. The group of people he hung out with turned all Ben's solo gigs into a party—one that he paid for. He longed for someone to love him. Big People were the first people that Ben considered family. Ben met Julie the night Big People played a benefit for cancer research in Atlanta, Georgia. They bonded immediately; Julie was a single mother who loved cold beer, music, and motorcycles. She soon found, like we had, how easy it was to love Ben.

Big People was doing a two-week tour of the South by bus. One day I walked into the back lounge of the bus and saw Ben and Julie dancing a slow dance. Ben looked at me and said, "This is the first time I have ever danced slow with a woman." It amazed me that this man, who had swooned thousands of women from the stage and was the envy of every guy in the audience, had never danced slow with a woman before. At that moment I understood that even with all his fame, Ben had been lonely for a long time.

In between our tours, I went to see Ben sing with a group called the Voices of Classic Rock. He had lost a lot of weight and I thought he looked great. I asked him how he did it, and he told me he just cut back on his intake of food. Actually, he said, he found it hard to eat a lot any more. A few weeks later, Big People started rehearsing in Atlanta. By now Ben and Julie were living together and were very happy. Ben's skin color was turning yellow. I told Julie that Ben looked like he could have hepatitis and she had better get him to a doctor, and she promised that she would.

About two weeks later, Ben was diagnosed with pancreatic cancer. A friend of the band's, Dr. Mayfield, was a heart surgeon at an Atlanta hospital, and he immediately took charge of Ben. He put the finest doctors on the case, and Ben was scheduled for surgery. When they opened him up, the prognosis was not good. The cancer had spread and was so wrapped around the pancreas there was no way to remove it. The doctors gave him six months. Ben's only wish was that Big People would continue to perform. We agreed, and with Julie on the bus, we did whatever it took to make Ben happy.

Ben gave his all for every show. For a while we shared the bill with Gary Puckett from the Union Gap and Spencer Davis. These guys had known Ben for a long time, and were shocked and saddened at Ben's appearance. Now very thin and sickly, Ben continued to get weaker, but never gave into the fact that he was sick. We continued on for a time, and then in Fairbanks, Alaska, Ben could barely stand up. Still, he insisted on playing. When he turned to me in the middle of the set and said, "Don't do 'Drive,'" I knew it was over. When I said goodbye to Ben at the airport in Atlanta, I knew it was the last time I was going to see him.

A few weeks later I was in Phoenix, Arizona, sitting in my friend Chainsaw's backyard for a barbeque. I was flying to Atlanta the next day to visit with Ben. A Cars song came on the radio, and we all lifted our glasses to toast Ben. "Here's to Benjamin Orr," I said, "a great musician and a great friend." A second later my cell phone rang. It was Jeff Carlisi. He said, "Ben's gone."

I believe Ben's spirit passed through us in Phoenix, Arizona that night. He stopped in to say goodbye to me. That's the kind of guy he was. Big People continued to perform for a long while, and all the members have remained the best of friends. We still keep in touch with Julie, who is now living in Vancouver, Canada.

# September 11, 2001

About three days after the World Trade Center towers fell, Billy called to say he received a bunch of requests to do benefit concerts. There was one in particular that he thought looked legitimate and properly organized. It was called America: A Tribute to Heroes. Planes were back in the air again, and he asked if I would be willing to fly to New York should the show happen. I responded that from the second I saw the towers fell, I had wanted to go back to New York. I felt helpless sitting in Florida, and I wanted to see my mom and dad, my daughter Devon, and the rest of my family. I wanted to go home.

My sister Louise worked for AIG Insurance Company in a building in the financial district on Water Street. She traveled two and a half hours from Riverhead to Manhattan every morning, and her office had a great view of the World Trade Center. When she arrived at her desk, she'd always look out and think about how awesome those towers were. She took it for granted, as I'm sure we all did, that they would always be there.

On September 11, 2001, my sister's view was horribly different. She looked out that morning and saw smoke coming from one of the towers. Thinking the building was on fire, she called my house in Florida and spoke to my wife. "It looks pretty bad," she said. "I think we should start evacuating. It looks like a really bad fire." Then she screamed, "Oh my God! Oh my God!" and the phone went dead. Unbeknownst to us, Louise had just witnessed the second plane hitting the other tower.

I was returning home from dropping my youngest daughter, Maryelle, off at school and the story was all over television. I immediately called my family, but my mother told me they couldn't locate Louise. Panic set in fast. My father got on the phone, and as a World War II vet, he could not believe the enemy was here; he was crying. Hours later we found out that my sister ran to a co-worker's apartment in Midtown. I wasn't able to speak to her until she returned home the next day.

It was raining in Florida on September 11th. People from the neighborhood who knew I was from New York came by to offer me condolences as if a friend had died. It was as if everything that was me— my attitude, my accent, my music, my country, my people—had all been assaulted. Feeling a deep need to get back to New York, I jumped when Billy asked about the benefit and told him I'd book the ticket as soon as he gave the green light.

When I boarded my flight from Orlando, the airport and the plane were empty. The pilot came out of the cockpit and shook everyone's hand to thank them for flying. I arrived in New York the day before the show, checked into my hotel, called my sister, and then jumped on the subway downtown to see her. I got off at Chambers Street, and that's when the smell hit me. It was eerie and disturbing; I had never smelled death before—not like this. I walked the streets around Ground Zero and got as close as I could. The sight was beyond the news coverage we were seeing in Florida. At my sister's office, she pointed to the empty space outside the window where the towers used to be. It was hard to believe they were gone. We went to a restaurant with some of her friends from work, but it was hard to eat with the thought of what had happened.

The next day I had rehearsal with Billy at Sony Studios, where the show was to take place. At lunch I told Billy what I had seen, and suggested he should see it for himself. Billy asked his security man if he could arrange for us to see Ground Zero after the show that night, and the trip was set up with the New York City Police Department. There were two police officers, Billy, the security man, and Billy's tour manager, which left no room for me in the police car, but Billy said, "I'm not going without you," so the police squeezed me into the back of the car.

They took us down the West Side Highway to Canal Street, then we had to walk the rest of the way because of the lines of dump trucks waiting to be filled with debris. As we were walking, we passed through tents. Each tent was different: tents with bottles of water, tents with gloves and shovels, tents with socks, tents with food—and then they walked us through the morgue. You had to go through the morgue to get out to the site. There was a gurney with an orange bag on it containing a lump of something. The police officers explained that the bag contained a body part which had been found that day.

Accompanied by one of the police officers, I was the first to round the corner into the World Trade Center site. The destruction took my breath away; it was at a level I never thought could be possible. The images I'd seen on TV didn't come close to capturing the reality of it. The smell of the rubble was haunting: a burnt odor of human flesh, steel, wood, paper, electric wire, jet fuel, concrete, and everything else that had been in the buildings. The smell burned itself deep into my memory such that I will never forget it. It was the smell of hatred, loss, tears, fear, broken hearts, vulnerability, and confusion. It was what the air smells like when there is a loss of hope and you question faith. I felt for the first time what someone must feel when they are violated. How could this have happened?

I ran back around the corner, saw Billy coming, and said something trivial to try to prepare him for what he was about to behold. When he rounded the corner and saw the smoldering pile of twisted steel in front of us, he said, "Oh, my God. Those bastards did that?" We were all in shock. Just one hour before, we had played "New York State of Mind," a song about the greatest city in the world. We hoped it would partially heal the spiritual damage that had been done. Now we were looking at the physical result of that damage.

As we walked around Ground Zero, we signed autographs on construction workers' helmets. We stopped in at the firehouse right across the street from the wreckage. I asked one fireman, "What kind of building do you think they should build to replace the towers?" "They can build anything," he said, "just as long as it isn't over three stories high." After viewing nearly the entire site, we all agreed that what people were seeing on television was only part of the destruction. The police took us back to our hotel, and as I followed Billy up the stairs, I noticed a gray powder on the back of his pants. As I looked down, I noticed it all over my shoes, too.

Billy and I sat at the bar alone and ordered drinks. "If I had gone down there before we played tonight," he said, "I would have never done the show. Those guys are down there twenty-four hours a day trying to rescue someone's loved one, and all I did was play a song. I am so insignificant to them." "Don't be so fucking hard on yourself," I replied. "Let me try to put this in perspective for you: If you have a heart attack, you call E.M.S. and they'll take you to the hospital. If your house is burning down, you call the fire department and they'll put it out. If you're in trouble, you call the police and they'll help you. That's their job, and they love it. When their day is over and they go home, maybe they sit back in their favorite chair, crack open a beer, and put on your music. That's how they relax. They listen to what you do, and it's like one hand feeding the other. You do what you do, and maybe it makes them happy. You can feel a fireman's bravery when he walks into a fire. They can hide inside music when they need to escape from their reality. If you stop doing what you're doing, you'd be cheating them out of something they love and need." Billy looked at me and said, "Thanks for saying that. We'll go on the road again in February."

We also played at another benefit, the Concert for New York City at Madison Square Garden on October 21, 2001. Aside from performing for charity, the concert was an attempt to honor the first responders from the New York City Fire Department and New York City Police Department, their families, those lost in the attacks, and those who worked in the ongoing rescue and recovery efforts. The concert was organized by Paul McCartney and included many music legends. English artists The Who, David Bowie, Elton John, Eric Clapton, Mick Jagger and Keith Richards, and American artists Bon Jovi, Jay-Z, Destiny's Child, the Backstreet Boys, James Taylor, Billy Joel, Melissa Etheridge, Five for Fighting, Goo Goo Dolls, John Mellencamp, and Kid Rock performed. Paul Shaffer acted as musical director, Adam Sandler put on a humorous performance as "Operaman," and various celebrities and political figures including Howard Stern and Rudy Giuliani spoke between the acts. Sports figures also appeared, including Joe Torre, whose Yankees were on their way to competing in their fourth consecutive World Series, and the event also included several short films made by New York City's most notable filmmakers: Woody Allen, Martin Scorsese, Spike Lee, and Kevin Smith. All of the stars signed memorabilia that was auctioned off to help those affected by the 9/11 attacks.

I think at the Concert for New York, Billy saw and felt what I was saying to him that night at the bar. Unfortunately, the sight of the fallen towers affected both of us so much that I believe it caused a lot of the problems and bad situations that became part of our lives.

**From a Tama drum ad, 1999.**

# Burn It Down

**W**hile I was standing ten feet away from the biggest pile of destruction I had ever seen, many things flashed through my mind. Just the day before the attack, the towers were massive monuments to our decadence. Now they were two heaps of smoking, twisted steel and over 2500 lives lost for no good reason at all. I had always seen the World Trade Center towers as an amazing engineering achievement, and was often amazed at what mankind could achieve when we put our heads together. Looking at the wreckage, though, something changed. I realized a terrible event like this could happen anywhere, anytime, to anyone. I could even do something like it to myself.

I suddenly realized that I already had.

Sitting behind my drum set has always been a safe place for me. I imagine being protected by a wall of fine maple wood with metal lugs and plastic heads. No one can penetrate that wall. I can share every aspect of my life completely with another person—except what goes on behind the wall. That wall is my sanctuary and my salvation— but it has also blocked my view of things I should have seen coming.

The Billy Joel-Elton John tour ended unexpectedly. We had toured for three months, and on March 15, 2002, we were performing the first of two shows at Madison Square Garden. With vocal cords that were already strained, Billy had also come down with the flu. He should have never taken the stage that night. I guess there comes a time in one's life when all the pressure one has been dealing with builds and makes you explode. Billy had been given decongestants for the flu and allergies, steroids for his vocal cords, and Dewar's scotch for his insecurity. The combination was lethal. We had done shows where he had strained his vocal cords so much that he had a tough time singing, but I had never been with him when he couldn't play the piano. The combination of what he had ingested had him so fucked up he could neither sing nor play. As he struggled to perform that night, he knew he sucked, and he snapped. Billy was shot. The tour was postponed until October of the same year.

With my alcohol consumption at its peak, I was blinded by my ego, which was reinforced by the alcohol, and had turned into a total asshole. Maybe standing on the edge of what once was the Twin Towers now in a pile of twisted metal, or feeling that my seat at the top of the musical world was about to collapse had quickened my descent into becoming the "Angry Not-So-Young Man." In the nine years since we moved to Florida, my wife and I had started to go our separate ways. I was able to beat the drums on the road, but at home, she was receiving the brunt of my anger—and she was sick of it.

I had met Mary on tour with Stevie Nicks in 1983; she was creating and selling the tour merchandise. Stevie knew that with Billy, the band played hard on and off stage, so one of the first things she said to me was, "We (meaning the women on the tour) are like delicate butterflies and need to be treated that way." After eighteen years of marriage, I realized that I was crushing one of Stevie's butterflies, in large part due to my alcohol abuse. With the abrupt ending of the Billy-Elton tour, I packed my things and went home. After about two weeks, my wife said to me:

"You know, I can do this without you."

"What can you do?"

"I don't want you anymore. I need space."

"What the fuck does that mean?"

"You're suffocating me. You're drinking too much, you're mean, sarcastic, and have become the most opinionated man I know. I seem to have lost something for you that I don't think I can ever get back, and I don't want you around anymore."

The very same road which had brought us together was now driving us apart. Our lives as individuals had changed so much. My being on the road gave Mary the opportunity to do things like take tennis lessons, go out with her friends, or do crafts. She and my daughters loved the two dogs we had, but when I came home, I would complain that I hated their pets at every opportunity. I'd complain if things were out of order in the house. My actions and words made it seem like I thought everything Mary did was worthless, while I was working to keep everyone living in our beautiful home—only what I did mattered.

Other factors took a toll as well. When I would come home after having been gone for weeks, all I would want was a nice dinner with my wife, but it never worked out. I had become the celebrity pet in Winter Park, and everywhere we went, it would be, "Oh look, it's Billy Joel's drummer." I would be stuck with these blabbering assholes, and my wife would be off dancing with some dude. Mary had found a new life and loved the attention she was getting on her own. She was sick of living in Billy Joel's drummer's shadow— but she wasn't sick of the drummer's money, house, cars, and everything else that went along with him. I didn't know at the time, but she had already met with a lawyer and knew that Florida divorce laws were in her favor.

I can remember being hammered at a bar one night, and Mary came over and said, "Don't you think this band is great?" I said, "No, I think they suck." She got pissed off and said, "Why don't you lighten up and have fun?" My problem was I was living in a bubble—an egotistical, rock 'n' roll, "I'm the greatest" bubble. When I went on the road, we essentially had separate lives. Mary loved her "space" when I was gone, but also probably envied some of the experiences I was having, and I did nothing to make it better. She hated it when I would call and say that I was going to dinner with the crew, or someone was taking the band out to a great restaurant. Sometimes the promoter of the show would get us tickets to basketball or baseball games. I told her once that I was watching Michael Jordan play basketball from two rows away. She knew how much I hated sports and I think she got a bit jealous that I was there watching Michael Jordan and she wasn't. Eventually, she started to resent me. She found new friends and went to new hangouts in Winter Park.

I also felt she wasn't raising my daughter the way I would have done it. It was another example of "if you're not doing it my way then you're not doing it right." I was so into my world that I had no idea what living in her world was like. We all see life from where we are standing. I thought I was on top of the world, so it made it hard to put myself in her shoes.

When I stumbled across a receipt from the lawyer that my wife had retained, I asked a friend if he knew anyone who could help me understand where I stood if my wife continued the divorce process. One of his pool teammates was a lawyer, and he said she might be able to help. I went to the bar where they were shooting pool that night, and while playing pool with the lawyer, I said:

"My wife wants a divorce, where do I stand?"

"You're fucked."

"But she's the one that wants out."

"You live in the state of Florida. It's a fifty-fifty state. Everything is split in half. Plus, you have been married for almost twenty years, which means she is entitled to lifetime alimony."

"I'm fucked"

"Yes, you're fucked."

I beat her at two games of pool and left.

To get away from me when I was between tours, my wife started to travel a lot. She would go visit her sisters and their families in Kalamazoo, Michigan. My older daughter had moved to California by now to pursue a career in acting, and Mary would take my younger daughter to Michigan for most of her summer vacation. In May of 2002, Mary went to California to visit Stevie, who was doing a few shows around the country. Stevie and her entourage would fly on a private plane, and Mary went with her. She was slowly getting her life back—the life she had before she met me. At the same time, I was losing mine. In a sober moment with Mary, I said, "I know the way I act sometimes. Maybe I could fix it before you lose all your feelings for me." She said, "I think it's too late, the feeling is gone, and I don't think I will ever get it back."

I went back on the road with Billy and Elton on September 13, 2002 and that tour ended on October 14, 2002. Mary and I were separated and I was sleeping in the guest room. On October 18th, I went into the hospital as an outpatient to get an operation for a hernia that I had gotten from exercising too hard. The hernia wasn't that bad, but the doctors thought I should take care of it now rather than having something happen on the road. Back home, I was recuperating in the guest room. The most painful part of the operation was when I would get in and out of bed; the stitches would pull and give me a sharp pain in my groin area. I didn't schedule any work for a few weeks after the operation. The doctor told me I would have to take it easy for a while, with no heavy lifting for at least a month. He also said I couldn't play the drums until I was fully healed.

My next scheduled gig was on November 9 in L.A. for the Rock n' Roll Fantasy Camp, but I was thinking about calling and canceling. I tried to hold out on taking the prescribed pain pills, but I figured what the hell, I was stuck in bed anyway. With my Walkman, headphones, and an excuse to legally get high, I put on my headset, popped a few pain killers, and listened to some of my favorite CDs. I lay in that room for five days, listening to music watching three of my favorite movies: *Casino*, *Raging Bull*, and *A Bronx Tale*. All the pain medication had me feeling good, but my failing marriage hung over me. I wrote a song about it called "How Did We Wind Up Here."

*What ever happened to thick and thin*
*What happened to the love we're in*
*I don't understand how did we wind up here*
*Seems like yesterday we said "I do"*
*And now I must get over you*
*I don't understand how did we wind up here*
*Sometimes I think it's me*
*Was I too blind to see*
*That I was losing you my dear*
*While you were losing me*

*How did we wind up*
*Oh how did we wind up*
*How did we wind up here*

*I remember when we first met*
*And now it's you I must forget*
*I don't understand, how did we wind up here*
*And how it felt to make love all day*
*And how it feels to feel this way*
*I don't understand how did we wind up here*
*I guess I'll never know*
*What makes that cold wind blow*
*That brings the change in you my dear*
*That brings the change in me*
*How did we wind up*
*Oh how did we wind up*
*How did we wind up here*

*I'm not trying to tell you that I'm wrong or I'm right*
*I'm just a fool who could never believe*
*That love would leave me overnight*
*So now you're gone and you ain't coming back*
*I guess this scene can fade to black*
*I don't understand, how did we wind up here*

On the evening of October 23, feeling no pain thanks to the medication, I decided it was time to tell Mary that I wanted to reconcile our relationship. I pulled myself out of bed, walked into the kitchen, and said, "I want my wedding ring back." She said, "Why? We're broken up!" I said, "I want my life back, I want to try to save our marriage." When I got divorced from my first wife I felt terrible about leaving my daughter, Devon, and the guilt never left me. I had promised I would never put my other two daughters through a life of not having their dad with them. "Even if I hated your guts," I told Mary, "I would not leave the house where my children lived." Looking blankly at me, she said, "There's nothing to save. We're done."

At that moment the pills, the violent movies, my overblown ego, and the trauma of seeing the Ground Zero site combined into a volatile mixture with all shit in my life, and it hit the fan. What happened next led Mary to dial 911. As soon as they answered, she hung up, but they knew where the call came from. They immediately called back, and there was a knock at the front door before the 911 operator could say the police were on their way. In the state of Florida the law states that if the police are called to a house and are told it's a domestic dispute, someone is going to jail. I was taken to the Winter Park police station, where they took my statement, and then transferred to the Orange County Correctional Facility.

When the police took me away, I didn't have my wallet, cell phone, or any cash. I was wearing cargo shorts, a long-sleeve shirt, and sneakers, but I didn't put on socks. They took the shoelaces out of my sneakers and put me in an eight-by-ten jail cell with about ten other guys who were arrested that night. Some of them were still drunk, pissing on the floor. One guy was yelling at the cops, "You fuckin' pricks planted that shit on me!" Another guy was such an asshole that the officers took him out of the area. Eventually, they took me out of that cell and put me in one by myself, an all-cement one like a bomb shelter that was about twice the size as the first cell. There was a small window in the door that looked out into the hallway, and a cement bench that ran along two walls. It was freezing.

I shivered as I sat alone on the bench, and began to think about what I had become. "Last week I was on stage with Billy Joel and Elton John," I thought. "Tonight I'm in jail, and all my money and fame can't even get me a blanket." I knew then that I needed someone who would let me bury my face in their shoulder and hold me so I could cry about the person I had become. I needed to start a new life. Although all my possessions were gone, there was still hope; I still had the capability to start again. I still had my drum. I was hitting bottom, but my outlook on life was about to change.

Twenty-four hours later, I was released from jail. I stayed at a friend's place because I was not allowed to go back to my house—the house where my children and all my possessions were. All I had was my passion and ability to drum. No one could take that from me, and with it, I could start all over again. I realized that I didn't need all the shit that goes with being a "rock star." Mary had been telling me I needed to go see a shrink, and by this point I was willing to try anything.

The first thing the psychologist asked was for me to tell her about myself. "I'm an Italian from New York, and I play the drums," I said. "My wife thinks I'm angry and that I talk too loud, I hate everything, and I complain too much." The shrink said, "Well it all goes with the territory. These would be the traits of a New York Italian who plays drums." Then she asked, "What makes you angry, and what do you hate?" I said, "*People* magazine, the TV shows 'Sex in the City' and 'Ally McBeal,' the fact that Billy Joel thinks he's done with music, and what the terrorists did on 9/11." "You hate *People* magazine because it over-dramatizes and is full of the dirt in your business," she responded. "You hate the TV shows because they are empty with no real social value, you're mad at Billy because you want to go on with what you love the most and you hate the fact that he's in control of your destiny. As far as 9/11, everybody hates what happened then."

After meeting with the shrink, I started to look at things a little differently. I now felt that I was not that bad a person, maybe the divorce wasn't solely my fault, and that I did like myself, after all. I had to accept that my reactions do come from being passionate. One passion drives another, and I had made it this far in life because I was able to direct my passion into a positive place most of the time. The passion I get from my drum makes me feel complete, and the passion I get from a relationship with a woman runs parallel. To be able to do what I love and share it with someone I love, and who loves me, is to be totally complete. I realized that to be complete, I needed to play my drum and I needed to be loved by a woman. This was the very beginning of my rebuilding.

While on the road I had seen my musician friends eaten alive because of problems they were having at home. At the same time, I had seen other musician friends have the love of another but be miserable because they didn't have a gig. Country singer David Allen Coe's wife left him when he was right in the middle of writing and recording his album. It changed his attitude so much that the side of his record before she left was called "the happy side" and the other was called "the suicide." You can really see an example of the strain of a breakup in Billy's *Shades of Grey* video, which was a concert recording from Germany. The absence of love and the confusion of divorce had taken over his passion for his music. You can see it in his face.

There is, however, a positive side to having to rebuild one's life. As you dig out from the rubble and start to rebuild, you get to choose what you want to keep and what you want to discard. As I faced my split from Mary and the process of starting over, I knew I had to leave Florida and go back home.

When I was younger my family would always be around the table at 2:30 on Sunday afternoon. The big meal in the afternoon was one of those traditions from the old country. The smell of the sauce would sneak under the bedroom door in the morning while I was still sleeping. It smelled so good that it would wake me up. That's when I would hear Jimmy Roselli singing on the radio; my mother always listened to "The Italian Hour" while she cooked. I would drift downstairs to the kitchen like one of those cartoon characters floating on the air while following a delicious scent.

On the kitchen table would be a big box of buns that my father had picked up from the bakery on his way home from church. If the top of the crumb bun was missing, then I knew Vinny had woken up first. My dad also bought two loaves of Italian bread. One was for dipping into the sauce and one was for the dinner table. Dinner would start with a macaroni dish, then a meat dish, and then salad, and it would always end with some kind of dessert. My mother wasn't much of a baker, so cakes and pies were always store-bought. My family was emotional and passionate, and conversations were like great operas at the dinner table. They would start out at a relatively normal level, and then there would be a great crescendo in which everyone would be yelling with hands flying—then it was back down to normal again without missing a bite.

There were other things I missed about New York as well. Orlando had its population of African-Americans who made great barbeque, but I missed the family-owned ethnic restaurants in New York. I didn't care to eat Mickey Mouse burgers or chain food at theme restaurants. Orlando wasn't a city like New York. It was basically a small town where everyone knew everybody else's business, and where you stopped your engine at the train crossing and watched a hundred box cars go by. On many levels, I needed to be back where I belonged.

I also needed to meet a woman that didn't give a shit that I was Billy Joel's drummer. I never dreamed how that would happen, and when it did, it would blow me away.

**My love.**

# 37

# Finding Anna

**M**ary was gone and I was struggling through on my own. After debating pulling out due to the hernia operation and the stress of my divorce, I had agreed to take part in the Rock 'n' Roll Fantasy Camp. Masterminded by David Fishof, it was similar to a baseball camp, where sandlot baseball players would pay top dollar to play with and learn from legendary pros. The Rock 'n' Roll Fantasy Camp was where fans and weekend musicians would play, learn, and hang out with their idols in the music business. All of the professionals were players in currently or formerly popular bands—I can't use the term ex-rockers because, as we all know, rock 'n' roll never dies. I had already participated in the first camp David had staged in Miami in 1997, and now he was ready to do it again in Los Angeles, California.

Because of the divorce, I was a little disorganized as my trip to L.A. was being planned. After a period of uncertainty as to whether the camp would be happening, I finally started getting calls about it from David Fishof's assistant just as the shit was hitting the fan with my wife. At the time I was thinking "Do I really need to do this?" Things were so fucked up with my life I felt I just didn't want to have any fun. Feeling depressed, I didn't return the phone calls from David's office. His assistant told Mark Rivera, who had been working closely with David on the camp, that she was having a difficult time getting in touch with me. Mark told her to be patient and explained that I was going through a tough time. Her response was, "I don't care what he's going through. I'll be in trouble if he and his drums don't show up at this camp."

With Mark's prodding, I finally called David's office and spoke with his assistant. Having been spoiled by Billy Joel tours where every detail was taken care of, I was confused when the assistant asked me if I wanted to book my own flight or if I wanted her to do it. On a Billy tour, the band's tour manager would always book our flights; I had never done it myself. Trying not to seem dumb, I played it cool and told her she could do it. After the call I started to feel a little better and began to think the trip to California would be good for me—plus I would get to see my daughter Torrey, who was living out there.

On November 9, 2002, I arrived at Orlando International Airport, walked over to the ticket counter, handed the ticket agent my driver's license, and said, "I have a pre-paid ticket to Los Angeles." Looking darkly at his computer, he said, "I'm sorry, but no you don't." My brain was so jammed from home stress that I couldn't remember what details I had arranged. Maybe I imagined David's assistant said she would book my flight? I was getting a good salary for the camp. Maybe it included the price of a ticket? I immediately tried to call David' assistant, but she was already on a flight from New York to Los Angeles.

"Great," I thought, "I knew I shouldn't have done this gig. Now I'm going to wind up losing money." Luckily, I had the production manager's number and was able to reach him. "Buy a ticket and the camp will reimburse you when you get here," he explained. "But just get here!" One $1500.00 roundtrip coach ticket later, I was bound for L.A.

Lodging for the camp was at the infamous Hyatt House (better known as the "Riot House") on Santa Monica Boulevard in Los Angeles. For years, this was known as "the" rock hotel in L.A. More rooms were trashed, TVs thrown from windows, and bands banned from this hotel than any other. It had quite the party reputation. Fried, I checked into the hotel at about ten in the evening. My room was decorated in black-and-white stripes and checks, including the bedspreads, floor tiles, and everything else. I thought, "I'll puke if I get drunk in here. I'm going to concentrate on what I need to do, get my money, and go home." Thinking of home, I then remembered that I would be moving into an apartment in Longwood, Florida, when I returned to Orlando. I was a refugee; my home had been taken.

I slept well that night, maybe because I was back in a familiar environment: a hotel room where I could see my drumsticks sticking out of my suitcase on the floor. The next day I went to breakfast with Mark Rivera and the rest of the "core" band; this was the band that played all the jams and with every featured artist. The band consisted of Mark on sax and vocals; Bobby Mayo from Peter Frampton's band on keyboards, guitar, and vocals; Derek St. Holmes from the Ted Nugent band on guitar and vocals; Mark Farner from Grand Funk Railroad on guitar and vocals; Jack Blades from Night Ranger and Damn Yankees on bass and vocals; and me on drums.

After breakfast it was back to the hotel for the campers' auditions. The idea was to audition these campers and to place them in bands with each other based on skill levels. They were then assigned to a celebrity camp counselor who was responsible for their progress throughout the week as well as coordinating rehearsals and working on any problem areas. During the course of the week, the campers went through training as well as attending lectures and workshops given by celebrities who were day counselors or guest speakers. These were industry producers or agents, along with musicians who would play, lecture, and hang out with the campers. The dominant demographic at the camp was middle-aged men who were successful as lawyers, doctors, and computer programmers. They all had a love for music. They were the guys who played guitar or drums when they were younger, but took the safer road, the one with more security. They often dreamed of what it would have been like if they had taken the other road. They had seen us play in one form or another and lived vicariously through us and our music. Now their money would allow them to take a giant step forward and, for five days and nights, live the life of a professional musician.

I accompanied some of the campers during their auditions. As I sat behind a blue set of Ludwig drums, I glanced out the door and saw a tall, red-headed woman with her hair in a ponytail walking towards the room. Wearing a "Fantasy Camp" tee shirt that she had customized into a tank top for herself, she had a blue notebook in her arms. The way she carried it reminded me of the way the girls carried their books in high school. I'd heard that David Fishof's assistant had red hair, so I figured this was her coming to introduce herself to me. She smiled as she got closer to me, and as I stood up from the drums, she reached out to shake my hand. "Liberty?" she said. "Yes," I replied. Referring to the mix-up with my plane ticket, she said, "I'm Anna. Do you hate my guts?" "No," I said, "I don't hate your guts, it was no big deal. I bought my own ticket and was told I would be reimbursed for it." I guess she was expecting me to be difficult, because I sounded mean on the phone. Little did she know I had hit rock bottom. I didn't have any mean left in me.

Anna had worked for David Fishof for three years and this was to be her last project with the company. She had given notice before the camp, but David asked her to stay on until it was over. In addition to filling every capacity she could at David Fishof Presents, Inc., she also handled other jobs within the company. David also managed the Monkees and Ringo Starr. Anna basically did everything. She started as David's assistant, but then began to fill the role of temporary road manager and sometimes publicist for David's clients. She had traveled with the Monkees and sat at airports with Ringo Starr. She was able to develop personal relationships with these clients and remained close with them and their families. She treasured those experiences and wouldn't trade them for the world, but still felt it was time to move on.

In between the camper evaluations, I would stroll into the room where Anna was working. We flirted with each other, and at one point she caught me taking a stack of CDs. The CDs were given to the camp as gifts for the campers by Time Life Music. I'll admit I took more than I should have, but that was no reason to call me a "CD whore."

After the evaluations of the campers, there was a jam at a Sam Ash Music store a few blocks from the hotel. In one room there was a catered buffet and in another was a stage full of equipment and folding chairs for people to sit and listen to the music. The core band would start by performing a song or two, then one by one the campers would be called to the stage to take the place of one of the members of the core band. I might turn over the drum set to a drumming camper and the next thing they knew they were playing "I'm Your Captain" with Mark Farner. As the night went on, more campers would come on stage until the entire band was made up of campers.

I found myself looking across the room in Sam Ash Music at the most beautiful red hair and white skin I had ever seen. She looked great when I met her that afternoon, but now, with her hair down around her face, she took my breath away. There's a line in the movie *A Bronx Tale* that says, "You have three winners in a lifetime. You get to love three times." I had a first love in high school. The eighteen-year marriage that I thought would last forever had just ended. I wondered, does God love me so much that he would allow my drumming to lead me to what I need and desire the most so soon?

I had to tell her how beautiful she was.

Anna Maria Leath is Irish-Italian from Brooklyn, loves to eat, yells at people, and is Catholic. As I walked from the drum set, off the stage, past the rows of folding chairs and all the instruments piled up next to the walls over to Anna, the irony of a drummer falling in love in a Sam Ash store in L.A. was completely lost on me. When I was a young, unknown drummer, I would frequent the Sam Ash store in Hempstead, Long Island. The sets of Ludwig, Rogers, Gretsch, and Slingerland drums would be displayed in a rainbow of colors. I'd gaze at my favorite kit and dream about owning it, thinking, "This is what I need to be happy." Now, thirty-five years later, I was walking towards Anna thinking the same thing. To be happy, I needed her. Later that night I was surprised to find that Anna had felt the same way when we had met for the first time that afternoon.

After the jams, it was back to the hotel. Although it was around midnight, the excitement of the day's events had everyone wired. The hang at the bar was one of the best parts of the camp. Everyone, including the counselors, was booked at the Hyatt, and every night the lobby bar was packed with campers, counselors, and professionals hanging out. This was where you'd find Mark Farner and I going joke-for-joke surrounded by awed campers, or Derek St. Holmes quizzing the campers on whether they were hearing his voice or Ted Nugent's on Ted's records. The more drinks the campers bought for the counselors, the more stories the counselors told the campers. More drinks made the counselors eventually compete with each other for who had the best sex, drugs, or rock 'n' roll story. One night with the bar already packed, Anna walked in to a scene with Eric Burdon, the lead singer for the Animals and War, singing "Oh, Anna" to the melody of "Oh, Donna" by Ritchie Valens. Eric was surrounded by empty pizza boxes and martini glasses, and literally did "Spill the Wine" that night.

Every night after the bar, Anna and I would hang out. We talked about everything: her job, my kids, music. She told me about the relationship with her boyfriend back in New York. I told her about what had happened to me and my wife. We would talk until five in the morning, even though we knew we had lobby call at nine. Anna took her work seriously. She was and always has been a professional.

At twenty-seven years old, Anna was very mature for her age. At fiftytwo years old, I was young at heart and not willing to get old. From the start of our relationship our age difference was never an issue. One night I told Anna that I had spent some time in jail and almost didn't make it to the camp. At this point, I knew I was falling in love with her and I needed to be honest. At the risk of driving her away, I told her what I did to end up in jail. She knew I was broken and sorry for what I did. Moved by my honesty with her, and knowing she had nothing to fear, I think she fell in love with me that night.

I needed someone to love me for who I was, and this is what I had been waiting for. Anna was falling for the person who is Liberty DeVitto—not "Billy Joel's drummer." For Anna, who was used to spending time with Ringo Starr, hanging out with Billy Joel's drummer was no thrill. I had bought *Introducing... The Beatles*, with the song "Anna" on it, for her. When I gave it to her, she told me, "I know this song, Ringo sings it to me over the phone." Yes, Anna was falling in love with me—the real me.

The camp ended with a battle of the bands at L.A.'s House of Blues. Before we walked across the street to the event, I sat Anna down and said, "Look, there is something we have to talk about." She knew what it was before I said "us." She told me she was very confused and needed to go back to New York to put all her ducks in a row. I told her I loved her and that I would not get in her way, but made it clear that I wanted her to come to me when she had sorted things out. "I know what I want," I said. "You call me when you're ready."

At the House of Blues, the bands played and were given awards and musical merit badges for their participation in the camp. They were then entertained by all of the week's counselors and special guests, like Spencer Davis, John Waite, Eric Burdon, Shelia E, Carmine Appice, Sam Moore, and Simon Kirke. The next day, with the success of a second Fantasy Camp behind me, I sat on a plane that was taking me back to Orlando. I put my seat back, closed my eyes, and dreamed of the girl who took my heart—a girl I might never see again.

When I got back to Orlando, I was picked up at the airport by friends and went straight to a bar. Nothing had changed except that when my friends dropped me off it was at my new apartment. Depressed again, I kept checking my phone, thinking maybe I had missed Anna's call, but there was nothing. Every night I'd go out to try to get her off my mind, only to wake up the next day smelling like smoke and feeling a stronger desire for her. A few nights later I went out and got really drunk. A bunch of friends came back to my apartment after the bar closed, and we smoked pot. I started to think Anna was never going to call me. A wave of sadness came of over me, I got quiet, and eventually asked everyone to leave. Maybe this was the way I was going to spend the rest of my life—alone. That night, I cried myself to sleep.

Anna would not leave my thoughts. I'd drive around in my car listening to Elton's "This Train Don't Stop There Anymore" over and over again. I began feeling like I was falling from an airplane. Anna was the plane, and she was getting further and further away. I knew that the ground was getting closer and I was afraid of hitting it, but if I kept playing that song over and over again, I would be all right. Soon I would be back on tour with some of the guys on that record, and this meant I would be with my drum again. That song kept me from hitting the ground.

At about four o'clock one afternoon, I had just pulled into my driveway when my phone rang. A woman's voice on the other end said, "It's Anna. What are you doing?" I responded, "I'm getting off my knees now, because I can stop praying." It had only been five days since the camp, but they were just as depressing as the twenty-four hours I had spent in jail. The following weekend, Anna came to visit me in Florida. She flew back to New York on Sunday and I followed her on a plane the next day. We've been together ever since that day. I even wrote a song about her.

> *When I met Anna she knocked me off my feet*
> *Smiled at me and said my name and made my life complete*
> *True blue is what I'll do, I'm never gonna cheat on my Anna*
> *When Anna talks to me she looks me in the eye*
> *Makes me feel that love is real and I'm her lucky guy*
> *Like a cool breeze through summer trees*
> *She makes me wanna fly, She, my Anna*
> *Hey Anna what can I do*
> *When I'm here I wanna stay with you*
> *You give me love that's filled with new emotion*
> *Hey Anna, it's in your touch*
> *And your lovin' that means so much*
> *I never knew a girl with such devotion*
> *Now me and Anna we'll build our perfect world*
> *I'll be her perfect boy, she'll be my perfect girl*
> *It can't be no other way, cause we're in love*
> *And here I'll stay with Anna*

On February 18, 2003, I was back in New York to be closer to my mom and dad, but I was spending most of my time with Anna. On the next ten-week tour with Billy and Elton, I was able to tell Elton how his song got me through this tough time. My old love—my drum—was back in my life, and my future was mapped with my new love, Anna.

**L to R: Richie Cannata, me, and Russell Javors.**

# 38

# Rebuilding Liberty

O ne of the hardest things for me to do was to recreate myself. It was a lot tougher than you might think. After all, I wasn't today who I was yesterday. Yesterday I was Billy Joel's drummer, playing around the world and recording albums with one of the biggest artists of our time. Today I am not. I became a man without a country; a musical refugee, if you will.

When Billy announced he was going on the road, I was getting phone calls and emails, "Hey, I just heard you will be in my town, let's get together." I had to explain that I wasn't in the band any more. Those conversations drove me nuts. Billy's people were using "musical differences" as the reason he was replacing me. That statement was the sugar-coated way out. Many bands use "musical differences" to cover up the real reason for a member's replacement, which could be anything from alcohol or drug abuse, the person had an affair with the lead singer's wife, or even the rest of the band simply hates his guts. For me, the funny thing was that when Billy went on tour with his new drummer, the guy played, and still plays, my drum parts. Musical differences was bullshit.

I was broke due to the divorce from wife number two, and I could feel the reaper breathing down my neck. I thought of the car in my garage; that was how my cousin killed himself. Doug did it with a gun, and now I knew what he was feeling. Things got dark, but then I thought about the people I loved, and who loved me. There were my three daughters: Devon, Torrey, and Maryelle; I loved them too much. My mom and dad were still alive; they had already lost Vinny, how could I possibly do something like this to them? And there was Anna, who was there to pick me up after my divorce and was now supporting me in this loss. I wrote a heartfelt letter to Billy as he was pushing me out of his life, and maybe I was too open about my feelings and it did more harm than good.

One night I fell asleep on the couch listening to *The Mission* soundtrack by Ennio Morricone, and drifted into a nightmare. I dreamed I was held by the devil. His arms were wrapped around me and I couldn't break his grip. He started to carry me into the air, high above the ground, as I fought to free myself. As we ascended higher, the devil turned into Billy. I said to him, "If you are going to destroy me, I'm taking you with me." I managed to turn us around and we were heading head first back down to the ground, with me now holding him in a bear hug that he couldn't break. Right before we hit the ground, I started to wake up. Anna heard me moaning and sweating, and came running downstairs to console me. From that point on, I knew I had to beat this.

I was better than him. At some point, people will know the truth.

The next day I started to call around to associates and friends I knew in the business. One of the people I called was Wayne Blanchard from Sabian cymbals. Wayne told me to stop saying that I used to play with Billy Joel or that I was Billy's former drummer. He reminded me that I was the drummer that Billy chose to help him create all those hit records and unforgettable tours, and nothing would ever change that. When Wayne said that, it was a huge revelation for me. That's who I am, and will always be. The name and drumming of Liberty DeVitto is on those records. Anyone who had seen Billy in concert has heard him say, "On drums, Liberty DeVitto." That is my calling card, and I can build a new life and career from that statement.

Now is a great time to start.

I recently went to my Aunt Mary's ninetieth birthday party at a diner in Valley Stream, Long Island. My dad and mom, Uncle George and Aunt Rose, Aunt Millie, and my father's cousins Pat and Lucille celebrated with my aunt. They talked about people who weren't there and how time had flown by. We took pictures and then the DeVittos did what they did best: eat. They told jokes and reminisced about family members both dead and living. They told the story of when their Uncle Tony died, and how the funerals at the time were held in the house of the deceased's family. Their Uncle George was kneeling in front of the coffin when a cat jumped on the open lid and it closed on his tie. As he tried to pull it out of the coffin he was yelling, "Oh my God, he's trying to take me with him!"

As I sat listening to this story, time stood still for me. I could have been seven, fifteen, twenty-eight, or fifty-three, it was always the same—my family never lost their sense of humor. There sat my mom with my Aunt Mary, who years before had threatened my mom's life if she married her brother—my dad; my Uncle George, who wept when my brother Vinny died; my Aunt Rose, who had lost the use of her hands from terrible arthritis; and my other aunts, Mary and Millie, who had lost their husbands; and all were hysterically laughing.

This is how it always was in the DeVitto family. My mother used to say she felt sorry for people who don't have a sense of humor, she didn't know how they could make it through life. I think it's *mangia bene, amar molto, e ridi spesso* (eat well, love much, and laugh often). Whenever I was in the middle of a crisis in my life, my father always said, "Son, this too shall pass." I don't know what the future will bring, but I do know that when it becomes the past, I will remember all the things that made me laugh.

I might even laugh so hard, I'll cry.

Not the end.

I'll let you know when it's the end.

-Lib.

# Epilogue

Life never stops unless you make it. God has given me a second lease on life. I have been sober for sixteen years, and I believe the things that have happened in that time would have never happened without my sobriety.

Anna and I married and we now have Mae, my fourth daughter, who was born on Feb 10, 2017, and she rocks.

My older daughters, thankfully, love me for who I am and understand the things that happened between their mothers and me.

I have settled an enormous debt with the IRS and the State of New York thanks to my brilliant accountants that came along right at the time of my last divorce and my breakup with Billy.

I now live in a great apartment in Brooklyn, and I love my hood and my life.

I have reunited with my old bandmates, Richie and Russell, and along with Doug (R.I.P.) we were inducted into the Long Island Hall of Fame. We are now playing together all over the country (and beyond) as the Lords of 52nd Street.

I also have my all-original band, the Slim Kings, which has again led me in new directions with amazing people and artists. I was part of a hit documentary on Netflix entitled *Hired Gun*, where I felt somewhat vindicated that I was able to tell my story.

I am an honorary board member and longtime supporter of Little Kids Rock, a nonprofit that puts music back into the schools where the music curriculum has been cut.

I am part of the Sessions Panel, whose mission is to provide the bridge between dreams and reality by enriching artists' lives through education, focusing on empowering and sharpening their business skills in the pursuit of excellence.

I have become best friends with Billy J. Kramer. I think it's the closest I'll ever get to hanging with the Beatles.

I have reunited with my family in Sicily.

There is, of course, that dark side that never goes away. But I've learned to deal with it better. Maybe I am finally growing up.

Most of the greatest generation that I grew up with are gone. I lost my mom on March 16, 2015, at the age of 89. My Dad passed on April 15, 2016, at 91. Aunt Millie, the last to leave, passed in 2019. Many of my friends have passed too soon, but so far, I am still here and loving it.

I am blessed, lucky, fortunate, or whatever you want to call it. Thanks to modern medicine, doctors have managed to replace a few bits and have kept me at the constant age of 28 (at least mentally). I always try to walk on the positive side of the street, and on occasion, when life starts to get the better of me, I just think of Paul McCartney's exuberant "1,2,3,4!" as he counted off "I Saw Her Standing There" and launched me into the adventure of a lifetime.

Oh, and I have reconciled with my lifelong friend Billy Joel.

**With daughter Mae, 2020.**

# Afterword

They say life can change in a New York minute. That's exactly how it came to be that Billy Joel wound up writing the foreword for this book.

My right knee was shot. I would feel pain when I walked, and I could tell you every time it was going to rain just by the pain in my knee. My ankle was swelling up like a softball. I ignored it. One morning I woke up and my knee was swollen. I could barely bend it, and it hurt like hell. I told my wife, "I think I need to see a doctor now." I made an appointment with Dr. Stephen Fealey, an orthopedic surgeon at Hospital for Special Surgery here in NYC, and one of the best in his field. After a few shots, x-rays, and finally an MRI, the doctor said I was a candidate for total knee replacement surgery. So, on July 7, 2019, I checked into the hospital to fix my knee. I was assured I'd be drumming in no time.

The operation went well, with no complications. I stayed in the hospital for two nights and went home with twenty-two staples in my knee. I have to tell you, the pain was some of the worst I have ever experienced. I was taking 1000 milligrams of Tylenol and an opioid. Physical therapy started immediately in the hospital and continued as soon as I got home, with a therapist coming to my apartment daily. I was told the pain would be so great that I would need to take the opioids just to get through the physical therapy. They were right. But the pain was the worst at night. I would spend all night rolling around in bed trying to get comfortable, with no luck. (My wife was sleeping on the couch.)

The pain and the pills started to bring on dark and depressing thoughts. I kept wondering, "What did I do to myself? Why did I do this?" I thought my career as a drummer was over. I had gigs lined up in a couple of weeks with the Lords and the Slim Kings, and had committed to sessions in Richie's studio. How could I do it? I'd never be ready. I kept thinking "Liberty the drummer" was done. I went way deep into a dark place and started to imagine what the world would be like without me in it. I started to cancel gigs and recordings; I was done. My wife got worried when I told her what had been running through my head night after night, and suggested I speak to a psychiatrist, so I did.

The doctor helped me by telling me that humans are totally affected when our age runs into our occupation. People tend to believe life is over—and for me, my career depended on that right knee. But through physical and mental therapy, she told me, I could push through it. She asked me who I played with, which lead to questions regarding the circumstances around my departure from

Billy. The more questions that came, the more those answers led to more questions, and I quickly realized I'd have to go back and explain everything about me and Billy again.

I couldn't do it.

I told her I couldn't go back to the past, back through that pain. It was my first and last appointment. That one appointment turned out to be a great blessing. See, that's when it all hit me. I needed to get over the bitterness and hurt that I still had for Billy—not keep harboring it. I was concentrating on the loss all the time, but I needed to think about the great times we had, the legendary music we made together, and all the lives we touched together. It was time to let go.

As I built up my stamina for playing again, and started to play like the drummer who played for Billy Joel all those years, I felt it was time to reach out to Billy. When people ask me, and they've asked a lot over these fifteen-plus years, "What would you do if you ran into Billy on the street?" I always say, "I would hug him and tell him I love him." Kind of an odd response, right? Now it was time to put my money where my mouth is.

I sent Billy an email saying that I wanted to bury the hatchet, and asked if he would like to get together for coffee or a meal (I would pay) and talk about our days of wine, women, and loud, happy songs. I also wrote that if he wasn't into it, I would totally understand; no expectations. Less than twenty-four hours later, to my surprise, he responded. He said he was good with getting together and he too was unhappy with the way things ended between us. We made a plan to meet for breakfast in the coming weeks.

I won't go into too much detail about it—it was a personal time between two (very old) friends; two friends who had a massive, life-changing falling out and were now ready to reconcile. We talked about having little children in our sixties (he has two and I have one—all under five at the time of this writing), and about our adult children and their achievements. We spoke for about an hour and a half, about people we both knew who were doing well, those who are sick, and those who had passed away—and about the good things life had granted us. The actions of the past that pulled us apart were like turbulent waters under a bridge, a bridge that had now brought us together after all these years. He is still Billy and I am still Liberty. As we ate our breakfast, I asked him how the residency at the Garden was going and about his future plans. I told him about the Slim Kings and the Lords of 52nd Street (which he already knew about).

Then I said I was writing a book; had been working on it for years. I explained it was about me; a story that starts with Italian immigrants that came to America with nothing and how, eventually, their grandson became the drummer on one of the top five albums ever created. Also, I told him it was a story of awakening—how my views had changed with age; that I understood more of the reasons why certain things in life had happened. He said it sounded interesting. I asked him if he would like to write the foreword. He graciously said yes, and asked me to send him the book when it was done. Then rain clouds started to roll in, and since Billy had arrived on his motorcycle, soon it was time for him to leave. We said our goodbyes like no time had passed at all.

That night as I lay in bed thinking about our breakfast gettogether, I realized that Billy and I never shook hands. Our first greeting was a hug. Then, when he was standing by his motorcycle with his helmet on, ready to leave, we hugged again, and I kissed him on the cheek and said, "I love you, Billy," and he said, "I love you too, Lib."

**Me and Billy, Florida, 2020.**

**Modern Drummer Festival, Montclair, NJ, 1989.**

# Appendix

## The DeVitto School for Music Business

The difference between a professional and an amateur is that one makes money and the other doesn't. It is the same difference between your dream and reality. Learning the music business cost me millions, so I thought I'd share my multimillion-dollar lessons with you here. Pay attention, because there could be a test at the end.

A band is a partnership between two or more people. The more people, the less your percentage of money will be. Tears for Fears splits a hundred dollars two ways between two members. Blood, Sweat and Tears splits those same hundred dollars ten ways between ten members. Fifty bucks each between Tears for Fears, ten bucks each for BS&T. The more members, the less money for you. But on the other side of the coin, it is easier to split band expenses when there are more members in the band. Rehearsal space, gas for the van, and the cost of a P.A. isn't as much out-of-pocket money when ten people are reaching into ten pockets.

Let's say a club owner hires you to play his club one night. He says he'll charge ten dollars at the door for an entry fee and he'll keep 20% and give your band the rest of the money. 20%? You don't care, you're playing because you just want to play. But if you have four guys in the band and the take is a hundred dollars at the door, your pay has just gone from $25 a man to $20 a man. The band has taken on another member when they agreed to give the club owner 20%. You could have said no to the deal, but then you probably wouldn't be able to play at the club. Now you have gone from the love of music to the business of music.

Let's say no one shows up at the club the night you perform; you don't conform to the "Top 40" format, so most people can't relate to your sound. The funny thing is that your band needs to have its own sound to be successful and rise to the top, but until it is crammed down their throats on the radio, no one really wants to hear it. You only want to play hip stuff, not the crap that's on the radio, but without an audience the club owner is unhappy. He thinks your band sucks, and he refuses to hire you again.

The next thing to do is to rent an American Legion hall or an empty store and pass out fliers with the band name, date, time, and how much it will cost to get in at the door. Get as many people as you can to come and start to build a fan base. Get together a mailing list and send postcards or emails telling the fans where your next gig will be. The more people, the more money. Your silent partner this time will be the people you pay to rent the room where the gig is held.

You're still living at home and eating McDonalds. The next thing you should do is to make a recording with the extra money you are making: something that represents your sound that you can sell at your gigs. Make a five-song CD and sell it for $10. A fifteen-song CD could sell for $15. But make sure it's your best stuff. Next, you'll need a web site so you can post your gigs and sell your CD. It's a good idea to put pictures of fans on it. It will make them come back to the gigs. After you have sold at least 2500 CDs yourself, start shopping them to record companies. They won't want to know about you unless you have sold a bunch of your recordings yourself. Once you have done that, however, they will pay attention; if you can sell 2500 copies in your small town, think how many you could sell with their help. If they like your songs and think you have a hit in the bunch, they will send someone to come out to see the band play live.

When management steps in, everything changes. There are three different "band" scenarios for a management to deal with.

1. A band where each member shares the pie equally except for writing and publishing royalties. In this case, if one guy has a hissy fit, it's a nightmare for everyone, especially the manager. It's like having four or five partners in one business. Example: the Eagles.

2. A situation where things start out as a band—one unit—but the record company only signed the singer/songwriter. The other members of "the band," led by the sugar-coated words of the manager, have now become "sidemen." Now the manager speaks for the artist, and will negotiate with "the band" when tour salaries and record royalties are concerned. The manager's job is to isolate the artist from the band, while at the same time, keep the carrot dangling in front of the band's eyes. Example: Peter Frampton, John Mellencamp.

3. A solo artist. This is ideal for management. There is only one person to deal with; everyone else is hired help. It allows the artist to use whomever he/she wants in the studio; he can hire the best of the best and be done with them after they're paid. He holds auditions for a touring band and can hire and fire whomever he wants and whenever he pleases. The management only needs to deal with the artist. Example: Cher, Celine Dion.

These scenarios were explained to me by a "way-up-there" guy in Billy's office, one of the guys who ripped him off for a good part of sixty million dollars. In the end, I guess Billy went to the same school as me.

# Drum Clinic

(Note: This is a piece Liberty wrote as an outline of his drum clinic presentation.)

My clinic is not about how to play rudiments or how to play in seven-zip time. I am not now (or ever have been) into that kind of drumming. There are plenty of guys out there that do that kind of stuff and are really good at it. If you want to learn how to play a paradiddle, go to your local drum shop and ask the guy behind the counter (who is probably a drummer). I'm sure he'll be glad to show you while he's selling you a pair of sticks. Now go home and lock yourself in a room and practice that paradiddle for a year. You will become the best paradiddlist in the world. I believe the drums are a group instrument. You can never be fulfilled or take them to their complete potential unless you are playing with other instruments. I believe the drum creates a groove that is best understood when it is played in the parameters of a rhythm section or a band. I am doing clinics to tell you what it is like to be in a band.

When I was first asked to do drum clinics, I didn't know what they were all about. I heard that a drummer from a group that I really liked was doing a clinic at the local music store, so I thought it might be nice to see this guy in action. I'd get to see the licks he does on the records, in person—maybe find out what he's all about. When I got there, the place was wall-to-wall drummers. They were as excited as I was to see this guy play what they had heard so many times on record. They were hungry for the knowledge this guy had about the business. This was an advanced part of their schooling with a guest speaker, who would hopefully give them information that would take them to the next level.

The guy finally came out to a huge round of applause. He didn't acknowledge the audience at all, and proceeded to do what I took as twenty minutes of self-indulgent bullshit. He played rolls that were so fast, they were a blur. He played them on the snare drum, he played them from the snare to the tom, from the snare to the tom to the floor tom. Then he raised his hands in the air and played a roll so fast on his bass drum with his double pedal that it sounded like one note. He got up from his drums, said good night, and left. I thought, "What the hell was that?" I called my companies the next day and told them I couldn't do clinics, based on what I had just seen. "I don't play like that," I said. "And if you consider that guy a drummer, then I'm no drummer. I saw 'Machine Gun Kelly' last night. I don't do that kind of stuff. I have nothing to show these drummers." They said to me, "Hold on a minute. You have played with the biggest single artist in the world for thirty years; you've played on Grammy award-winning records; both singles and albums. Billy chose you to help him to make those songs hits. With you he has sold over one hundred and fifty million records. You were the drummer that played in the first full-production concert that was ever performed in the Soviet Union. It's not about chops and speed; it's about entertaining the masses. The drummer you heard may think that's what the young drummers want, but if you ask them, they want to be part of musical history. They want to be in a band that's a household name. In reality they want to be you. They want to be in a band."

Let me set the record straight by saying this: I believe that a band is only as good as its drummer. If you disagree with me, then you must be a bass player, guitarist, or a key board player.

Example One: You're in your car driving down the road with the radio on. Your friend is in the passenger seat. A song comes on the radio and your friend says, "This is a great song, turn it up." You turn it up and say, "Oh it's great, what is it about?" Your friend says, "I don't know what it's about, just listen to that beat!" The first thing that usually gets a listener's attention is the groove to a song; the beat.

Example Two: Many couples like to go out to bars on the week end. The girls are off together talking about girl things while the guys are sitting at the bar having a few drinks, talking about sports. All of a sudden a guy will feel a tap on his shoulder. When he turns around he sees his date signaling him to get out onto the dance floor with her. She is feeling the beat. The guy gets out into the middle of the dance floor with her and he notices her lips moving. She is now lip syncing the words to the song. This is a phenomenon that is universal. I have asked many women about this strange happening. They tell me that the beat drives them on to the dance floor. Next, they love what the song is about. I always ask if all the chords that the guitar or keyboard are playing really matter to them. Unanimously their answer is no.

Example Three: How many times have you seen a band and thought, "Man, the guitar player is great, but the band sucks." The band sucks because the drummer isn't moving you. I've heard great drummers make shitty bands feel good. A band is only as good as its drummer.

There are two reasons why guys take up an instrument. One is to be in a band. The other is to get chicks. You're not going to get chicks if you're soloing in your parents' basement. You get chicks when you're in a band. When I was thirteen years old, I saw the Beatles on "The Ed Sullivan Show." The girls in the studio audience were screaming and crying. My sister and her friends who were standing in our TV room watching were screaming at the TV screen. I thought, "This is a great way to get chicks! I want to be in a band like the Beatles." My mother said, "If you want to play the drums, why don't you take lessons?" So I signed up with this drum teacher in a local music store. He sat me down with a practice pad and a set of sticks and started to teach me rudiments. I asked him, "When are you going to teach me how to play like Ringo?" He said, "Why do you want to learn how to play like Ringo? He stinks." I said," Well, I saw him on TV last night and all these girls were screaming for him, and I don't see any girls knocking on your door." That was the end of my lessons. I had to learn myself. Records became my books. I would set my drums up next to the record player, put on a record, and play to it. I would turn the record player up loud so I could feel like I was actually in the band. While I was learning the drum parts I would learn the lyrics, and that's how I would follow along with the song. As I sang along with the song, I noticed that the drummer did his drum fill when the singer stopped singing, or when a transition was coming in the song. His fills would accent or take the listener to another place in the song; he would set up different movements in the arrangement.

I am from the school of "less is more." I see the song and try to remove everything that doesn't fit, like a sculptor sees the statue and chips away all the stone or material that isn't part of the statue. I love to know the lyrics because it will set the emotional pace to the music. This gets me emotionally involved in the song. There's a story to be told, so I need to know what the song is about. My purpose is to enhance the story with my drum part without stepping all over the song. A conversation between two or more people will go from one level to another depending upon what the people are talking about. A song is a melodic conversation with emotional ups and downs that eventually gets to a level that drives a point across. The drums need to know where those levels change, so they can change with them. For an instrumental I'll go by the title. I'm going to play a song called "Gonna Love You like an Angel" different than one called,"Gonna Smash My Car into Your House."

A lot of young drummers today listen to one type of music. Metal drummers only listen to metal, jazz drummers only listen to jazz, and so forth. I feel it is important to listen outside of your favorite style of music. This is how you learn, and it also helps you to come up with something that is your own style. A lot of ideas in rock 'n' roll come from other styles of music. Good drummers borrow, but great drummers steal. Great drummers take from many different styles of music and incorporate it into their own. Stewart Copeland of The Police took reggae and incorporated it into his rock drumming. Steve Gadd took a drum corps rhythm and placed it on Paul Simon's "50 Ways to Leave Your Lover." John Bonham took a Bernard Purdie groove and played it his own way on Led Zeppelin's "Fool in the Rain." Jeff Porcaro of the group Toto took a mixture of the Bonham beat and the Purdie beat to come up with his own feel on the hit "Rosanna." These were all groundbreaking performers who influenced thousands of drummers.

I meet so many young drummers that are one-dimensional when it comes to listening to music. The worst culprits of this are the Neil Peart fans. Now, certainly what Neil did with Rush is incredible, but all these young drummers see is Neil Peart, all they hear is Neil Peart, and all they study is Neil Peart. I met a guy once that was so into Neil Peart that he said, "I know every drum lick Neil does, I use the same drumsticks Neil uses, and I have the same drum setup that Neil has. My drums are the same color and the same sizes as Neil's, and I use the same cymbals as and drum heads as he does. I drive the same car as Neil, which is also the same color as his. My house has been modeled after Neil's house, inside and out. In fact, I am so into Neil Peart that my girlfriend looks just like him." I looked at the guy and said, "That's great, but I don't think Rush is looking for a new drummer."

It's cool to have a favorite drummer. But don't stop there. By listening to other drummers you will open yourself up to new ideas and new music. If a drum teacher has fifty students, and they are all learning the same thing, there will be fifty clones of that drum teacher. Your drum set is your musical world, and just like in the real world, don't do something just because someone said it has to be that way. Think differently. Be original. Ringo Starr of the Beatles and Larry Mullen, Jr. from U2 are two great examples of thinking differently and having their main focus on the song. What they bring to the song makes the recording better. Contributions like this explain why the Grammys have a "Song of the Year" category for the songwriter and a "Record of the Year" category for the arrangement—which comes from the band and the producer. It's all about how the song is put together.

Why is it that the greatest drummers are considered great because they play fast? When you ask someone to name the greatest drummer ever, the answer is always Buddy Rich. Why? Because he plays so fast. When I was a young drummer trying to find my place in the drumming community, I was very insecure because I could not play fast. Many times someone would come up to me and say, "I heard this drummer the other night. He was great." I would ask what made him great. The answer was always the same: "He was so fast." Sometimes a friend would go to a wedding and say," The band sucked, but when the drummer did a solo, he was so fast that he blew everyone away." I would think, "I'll never be a great drummer, I don't play fast."

I started to think about speed and drumming compared to other activities. Why is it that a runner that runs a quarter-mile sprint in twelve seconds is considered the greatest runner in the world? If that runner was on a marathon team and ran like that, he'd drop out of the race from exhaustion after three miles. So is he really the greatest runner in the world? Or take a baseball player who excels in center field. He can catch any fly ball and can rifle the ball accurately into home plate to throw out a runner. He might be considered one of the greatest players in the world, but put him on the pitcher's mound and he might not be able to throw that same ball straight for ninety feet over home plate.

Physically, people's muscles are different. There are different "twitch" fibers; both slow and fast. Some of us are born with more fast-twitch fibers and some are born with more slow. If you have more fast-twitch fibers, you are able to do things very fast in short bursts. If you have more slow-twitch fibers, you would be able to do the same thing at a steady pace for a long time. You can develop your "lesser" twitch fiber, but only to your fiber's physical capability. That may mean that you might not have enough of that one kind of twitch fiber to let you achieve what your idol is capable of doing.

For every "fast-twitch" drummer that was famous, there was an equally influential "slow-twitch" drummer around at the same time. For Buddy Rich (fast-twitch), there was Gene Krupa. In the sixties, for Mitch Mitchell (fast-twitch), there was Ginger Baker. For Billy Cobham, there is Kenny Aronoff. Joe Morello and Steve Gadd have developed both twitches equally. If there are "best" drummers out there, then they are truly the best. You can take your lesser twitch and develop it to it maximum potential, but you should realize that if you are emulating a drummer and find there is something you just can't do, it's not because you suck. What you must do is figure out your own assets and use them. Let them make you an individual.

There are four ingredients necessary to have any kind of shot at making in the music business as a drummer:

**Practice.** You must practice. All the time. You will never know when you will be getting "the call." Your friend who went out to a club last night might come to you and say, "I saw this band last night and they were really good. Unfortunately for them, their drummer had to leave. They are looking for a new drummer. I told them about you and they want you to go down to audition today." You say, "Well I haven't played for about two months, I'm really out of shape. I don't think I should go today." If that band is good they will want to continue to work and they'll want to hire a drummer right away. They won't wait. Always be ready. I got the call in 1968 to play with Mitch Ryder. The tour manager called me and said their drummer was sick. They had heard I was good and wanted to know if I would be interested in the gig. I said, "When do I start?" He said, "Tonight." I didn't have my drivers' license, so I needed my dad to drive me to meet them. I was a big fan of Mitch and I had been playing locally with cover bands. So I was ready.

**Dedication:** You must be dedicated to your instrument and this form of lifestyle. Lots of kids ask their parents for a drum set for Christmas. Take one kid, he loves the drums and is in his room practicing all the time. At first he is way into it, but eventually he wants to hang out with his friends. The drums start to collect dust. Then he gets distracted by baseball season. His interest has fallen somewhere else. Now take the same kid, but he has committed to practicing. He is now in a band. They are writing and performing their own material. Soon they become very popular in their home city and the record industry is interested in them. Then one night as he is playing in a club, his eyes meet with a beautiful woman's. He's in love. They date for a while, then they start to live together. About six months into the relationship she says to him, "Do you have to play the drums? When you play the clubs you're always out so late, and when you come home you smell like smoke. Then, when you have your bowl of cereal, you put the TV on and it's so loud that it wakes me up. Whenever I go to see you play, the club is always so smoky and loud, and there are always girls talking to you. I've been thinking you should quit the drums and go to work for my father."

My advice to you is to dump her. No one can tell you when to quit. Only you will know if that time ever comes. One day you may say, "I need to eat. I have to think about doing something else." That will be your decision and your decision only. When I was younger, I wanted to marry my high school sweetheart. Her father told me that if I quit the drums and worked with him, I could marry his daughter. He worked for the telephone company. I didn't know what to do, so I went to the wisest person I knew for advice: my mother. She said to me, "If you quit the drums to marry her, and just one of your friends makes it, you will end up resenting her for the rest of your life, because you will always think that could have been you if she didn't make you quit." I broke up with her, and I was the one of all my friends to make it big. My mom was right.

**Staying one step ahead of the other guy**. Once a drummer plays something on a record, it is yours for the taking. Take it and make it your own. Think differently. The only difference between you and me is most likely the reason you're reading this paragraph, because I wrote it first. I do things on the drums that you would never think of, because I think differently.

**Being in the right place at the right time.** You can put yourself in the right place at the right time. This is part of the dedication and commitment to your passion. If you want to play country music, go to Nashville. In the nineties, if you wanted to play grunge, your best shot was to move to Seattle. For jazz, many aspiring pros go to New York City or Chicago. You have to put yourself where your music is. This might mean telling mom and dad you have to go and follow your passion. Don't rent out your room, in case you change your mind. I was fortunate to be living in the New York City, where it was happening in the seventies. I had moved to Baltimore to try something with a band. I lived there for six months. I should have gone further south at the time. Southern rock was becoming huge in the late sixties and early seventies. Once I did a clinic in Osh Kosh, Wisconsin, and was told to go check out this great drummer playing in a local club. When I saw the guy play, I thought he was great, but he had a really bad attitude. He told me he was upset because he hadn't made it yet. So I asked him, "When was the last time a famous producer or other great musicians came through Osh Kosh?" It was time for that guy to move. When someone's bio says, "He was born in Wisconsin, but now calls California home," there's a reason for it. Go where it's happening.

When dealing with music, you must have zero tolerance for the words "no" and "can't." When you have an idea in your head, you should never think "it can't work." Change direction to achieve your goal. No "ifs," "ands," or "buts." It's either great or it isn't. Music is not supposed to come easy. It is a hidden gift that you need to find.

# Album Credits & Liner Notes

## *Turnstiles*

Side One
1. Say Goodbye to Hollywood (4:36)
2. Summer, Highland Falls (3:15)
3. All You Wanna do is Dance (3:40)
4. New York State of Mind (5:58)

Side Two
5. James (3:53)
6. Prelude/Angry Young Man (5:17)
7. I've Loved These Days (4:31)
8. Miami 2017 (Seen the Lights Go Out on Broadway) (5:12)

All songs written by Billy Joel

Billy Joel – piano, electric piano, Moog synthesizer, clavinet, organs, harmonica, vocals
Richie Cannata – saxophones, clarinet
Liberty DeVitto – drums
Howie Emerson – electric and acoustic guitars
Russell Javors – electric and acoustic guitars
Mingo Lewis – percussion
James Smith – acoustic guitar
Doug Stegmeyer – bass guitar

Jerry Abramowitz – cover photography
Ken Ascher – orchestral arrangements
John Berg – cover design
Bruce Botnick – mixing
John Bradley – engineer, project supervisor
Jo Buckley – production coordination
Don Puluse – engineer
Brian Ruggles – basic track consultant
Lou Waxman – tape engineer

# *The Stranger*

Side One
1.  Movin' Out (Anthony's Song) (3:30)
2.  The Stranger (5:10)
3.  Just the Way You Are (4:52)
4.  Scenes from an Italian Restaurant (7:37)

Side Two
5.  Vienna (3:34)
6.  Only the Good Die Young (3:55)
7.  She's Always a Woman (3:21)
8.  Get It Right the First Time (3:57)
9.  Everybody Has a Dream (6:35)

All songs written by Billy Joel

Billy Joel – vocals, piano, keyboards, synthesizers, Fender Rhodes
Doug Stegmeyer – bass guitar
Liberty DeVitto – drums
Richie Cannata – tenor & soprano saxophones, clarinet, flute, organ, tuba
Steve Khan – six and twelve string electric guitars, acoustic rhythm guitar, high string guitar
Hiram Bullock – electric guitar
Patrick Williams – orchestration
Ralph MacDonald – percussion on "The Stranger," "Just the Way You Are," "Get it Right the First Time," and "Everybody Has a Dream."
Hugh McCracken – acoustic guitar on "Just the Way You Are," "Scenes from an Italian Restaurant," "She's Always a Woman," "Get It Right the First Time," and "Everybody Has a Dream."
Steve Burgh – acoustic guitar on "Just the Way You Are" and "She's Always a Woman;" electric guitar on "Scenes from an Italian Restaurant."
Phil Woods – alto saxophone on "Just the Way You Are"
Dominic Cortese – accordion on "Scenes from an Italian Restaurant" and "Vienna."
Richard Tee – organ on "Everybody Has a Dream."
Phoebe Snow – background vocals on "Everybody Has a Dream."
Lani Groves – background vocals on "Everybody Has a Dream."
Gwen Guthrie – background vocals on "Everybody Has a Dream."
Patti Austin – background vocals on "Everybody Has a Dream."

Recorded at A&R Studios, 799 7th Avenue , New York, NY.
Phil Ramone – producer, engineer

Jim Boyer – engineer
Ted Jensen – mastering at Sterling Sound, New York.
Kathy Kurs – production assistance
Jim Houghton – photography

Released 1977, #2 US, #25 UK, US Sales 10,000,000 Diamond
Hit Singles:
- 1978 Movin' Out (Anthony's song) #17 US #35 UK
- 1978 Just the Way You Are #3 US #19 UK
- 1978 Only The Good Die Young #24 US
- 1978 She's Always a Woman #17 US

## *Live At Carnegie Hall, June 3, 1977*
(Included with 2008 Legacy release of *The Stranger*)

Billy Joel – vocals, piano and synthesizers
Richie Cannata – saxophones and keyboards
Doug Stegmeyer – Fender bass
Howie Emerson – electric and acoustic guitars
Liberty DeVitto – drums
Recorded by David Hewitt Record Plant NY Remote Truck

## *52nd Street*

Side One
1. Big Shot (4:03)
2. Honesty (3:52)
3. My Life (4:44)
4. Zanzibar (5:13)

Side Two
5. Stiletto (4:42)
6. Rosalinda's Eyes (4:41)
7. Half a Mile Away (4:08)
8. Until the Night (6:35)
9. 52nd Street (2:27)

All songs written by Billy Joel

Billy Joel – acoustic piano, Yamaha CP-70 electric grand piano, Fender Rhodes, synthesizers, vocals
Doug Stegmeyer – bass, backing vocals

Liberty DeVitto – drums
Richie Cannata – saxophones, organ, clarinet
Steve Khan – electric guitar, acoustic guitar, backing vocals
Freddie Hubbard – flugelhorn and trumpet on Zanzibar
Mike Mainieri – vibes and marimba on "Zanzibar" and "Rosalinda's Eyes"
David Spinozza – acoustic guitar on "Honesty"
Donnie Dacus and Peter Cetera – background vocals on "My Life"
Russell Javors – acoustic guitar on "My Life"
David Brown – electric guitar on "My Life"
David Freidman – orchestral chimes and percussion on "Until the Night"
Ralph MacDonald – percussion on "Rosalinda's Eyes" and "Half a Mile Away"
Eric Gale – electric guitar on "Half a Mile Away"
Frank Floyd, Babi Floyd, Zack Sanders, Milt Grayson and Ray Simpson – background vocals on "Half a Mile Away"
George Marge – sopranino recorder on "Rosalinda's Eyes"
Hugh McCracken – nylon string guitar on "Until the Night" and "Rosalinda's Eyes"

Robert Freedman – horn and string orchestration on "Until the Night" and "Honesty"
Dave Grusin – horn orchestration on "Half a Mile Away"
David Nadien – concertmaster
Phil Ramone – producer, mixing
Kathy Kurs – associate producer
Carol Peters – associate producer
Jim Boyer – engineer, mixing
David Martone – assistant engineer
Ted Jensen – mastering at Sterling Sound (New York City, NY)
John Berg – cover design
Jim Houghton - photography

Released 1978, #1 US, #10 UK, US sales 7,000,000
1979 Grammy for Album of the Year
Hit Singles:
- 1978 "My Life" #3 US (1979 release UK) #12
- 1979 "Big Shot" #19 US
- 1979 "Honesty" #24 US

# *Glass Houses*

Side One
1. You May Be Right (4:15)
2. Sometimes a Fantasy (3:40)
3. Don't Ask Me Why (2:59)
4. It's Still Rock and Roll to Me (2:57)
5. All for Leyna (4:15)

Side Two
6. I Don't Want to Be Alone (3:57)
7. Sleeping with the Television On (3:02)
8. C'était Toi (You Were the One) (3:25)
9. Close to the Borderline (3:47)
10. Through the Long Night (2:43)

All songs written by Billy Joel

Billy Joel – acoustic piano, synthesizers, harmonica, electric pianos, accordion, vocals
David Brown – acoustic and electric guitars (lead)
Richie Cannata – saxophones, organs, flute
Liberty DeVitto – drums and percussion
Russell Javors – acoustic and electric guitars (rhythm)
Doug Stegmeyer – bass guitar

Phil Ramone – producer
Jim Boyer – engineer
Bradshaw Leigh – assistant engineer
Ted Jensen – mastering
Brian Ruggles – technician
Steve Cohen – lighting
Jim Houghton – photography
Michele Slagter – production assistant
Jeff Schock – product management

Released 1980, #1 US, #9 UK, US Sales 7,000,000
Hit Singles:
- 1980, "All For Leyna" #40 UK
- 1980, "It's Still Rock And Roll to Me" #1 US #14 UK
- 1980, "Don't Ask Me Why" #19 US
- 1980, "Sometimes A Fantasy" #36 US
- 1980" You May Be Right" #7 US

# *Songs In The Attic*

Side One
1. Miami 2017 (Seen the Lights Go Out on Broadway) (5:05)
   (Performed June 24, 1980 at Madison Square Garden, New York, NY)
2. Summer, Highland Falls (3:03)
   (Performed July 23, 1980 at the Bayou, Washington, D.C.)
3. Streetlife Serenader (5:17)
   (Performed July 20, 1980 at St. Paul Civic Center, St. Paul, MN)
4. Los Angelenos (3:48)
   (Performed July 10, 1980 at Toad's Place, New Haven, CT)
5. S he's Got a Way (3:00)
   (Performed June 1980 at Paradise Rock Club, Boston, MA)
6. Everybody Loves You Now (3:08)
   (Performed July 23, 1980 at the Bayou, Washington, D.C.)

Side Two
1. Say Goodbye to Hollywood (4:25)
   (Performed July 14, 1980 at Milwaukee Arena, Milwaukee, WI)
2. Captain Jack (7:16)
   (Performed July 5, 1980 at Spectrum, Philadelphia, PA)
3. You're My Home (3:07)
   (Performed July 23, 1980 at the Bayou, Washington, D.C.)
4. The Ballad of Billy the Kid (5:28)
   (Performed June 24, 1980 at Madison Square Garden, New York, NY)
5. I've Loved These Days (4:35)
   (Performed July 16, 1980 at the Horizon, Chicago, IL)

All songs written by Billy Joel

Billy Joel – vocals, pianos, synthesizer, harmonica
David Brown – electric guitar (lead), acoustic guitar (lead)
Richie Cannata – saxophones, flute, organ
Liberty DeVitto – drums, percussion
Russell Javors – electric guitar (rhythm), acoustic guitar (rhythm)
Doug Stegmeyer – bass guitar

Phil Ramone - producer
Ted Jensen at Sterling Sound, NYC - mastering
James Boyer - recording engineer
Bradshaw Leigh - recording engineer
Larry Franke - recording engineer

# *The Nylon Curtain*

Side One
1. Allentown (3:52)
2. Laura (5:05)
3. Pressure (4:40)
4. Goodnight Saigon (7:04)

Side Two
5. She's Right on Time (4:14)
6. A Room of Our Own (4:04)
7. Surprises (3:26)
8. Scandinavian Skies (6:00)
9. Where's the Orchestra? (3:17)

All songs written by Billy Joel

Billy Joel – vocals, acoustic and electric pianos, synthesizers, Hammond organ, melodica, Prophet-5 synthesizer, Synclavier II on "Pressure"
Liberty DeVitto – drums, percussion
Doug Stegmeyer – bass guitar
David Brown – electric and acoustic guitars (lead)
Russell Javors – electric and acoustic guitars (rhythm)
Dominic Cortese – accordion on "Where's the Orchestra?"
Eddie Daniels – saxophone and clarinet on "Where's the Orchestra?"
Dave Grusin – string and horn arrangements
Charles McCracken – cello on "Where's the Orchestra?"
Rob Mounsey – synthesizer on "Scandinavian Skies"
David Nadien – concertmaster on all except "Laura" and "Scandinavian Skies"
String Fever – strings on "Laura" and "Scandinavian Skies"
Bill Zampino – field snare on "Goodnight Saigon"

Phil Ramone – producer
Laura Loncteaux – assistant producer
James Boyer – engineer, remix
Bradshaw Leigh – associate engineer
Michael Christopher – assistant engineer
Larry Franke – assistant engineer
Andy Hoffman – assistant engineer
Ted Jensen at Sterling Sound, NYC – mastering engineer
Kenneth Topolsky – production manager
Paula Scher – artwork
John Berg – inner sleeve design

Chris Austopchuk – front cover design
Benno Friedman – back cover photo

Released 1982, #7 US, #27 UK US Sales 2,000,000
Hit Singles
- 1982, "Pressure" #20 US
- 1982, "Allentown" #17 US

# *An Innocent Man*

Side One
1. Easy Money (4:04) (Homage to James Brown and Wilson Pickett)
2. An Innocent Man (5:17) (Homage to Ben E. King and the Drifters)
3. The Longest Time (3:42) (Homage to doo-wop groups like Frankie Lymon and the Teenagers)
4. This Night (4:17) (Homage to Little Anthony and the Imperials; also to Ludwig van Beethoven's Pathetique sonata)
5. Tell Her About It (3:52) (Homage to Motown groups like the Supremes and the Temptations)

Side Two
1. Uptown Girl (3:17) (Homage to Frankie Valli and the Four Seasons
2. Careless Talk (3:48) (Homage to Sam Cooke)
3. Christie Lee (3:31) (Homage to Little Richard and Jerry Lee Lewis)
4. Leave a Tender Moment Alone (3:56) (Homage to Smokey Robinson)
5. Keeping the Faith (4:41) (Lyrical homage to pre-British Invasion rock 'n' roll)

All songs written by Billy Joel
except the chorus for "This Night" by Ludwig van Beethoven

Billy Joel – Baldwin SF-10 acoustic piano, Fender Rhodes electric piano, Hammond B3 organ, lead and background vocals
Liberty DeVitto – drums
Doug Stegmeyer – bass guitar
David Brown – lead electric and acoustic guitars
Russell Javors – rhythm electric and acoustic guitars
Mark Rivera – alto saxophone on "Keeping the Faith," "This Night," and "Christie Lee"; tenor saxophone; percussion; backing vocals
Ralph MacDonald – percussion on "Leave a Tender Moment Alone" and "Careless Talk"
Leon Pendarvis – Hammond B3 organ on "Easy Money"

Richard Tee – acoustic piano on "Tell Her About It"
Eric Gale – electric guitar on "Easy Money"
Toots Thielemans – harmonica on "Leave a Tender Moment Alone"
"String Fever" – strings
Ronnie Cuber – baritone saxophone on "Easy Money," "Careless Talk," "Tell Her About It," and "Keeping the Faith"
Jon Faddis – trumpet on "Easy Money"
David Sanborn – alto saxophone on "Easy Money"
Joe Shepley – trumpet on "Easy Money," "Careless Talk," "Tell Her About It," and "Keeping the Faith"
Michael Brecker – tenor saxophone on "Careless Talk," "Tell Her About It," and "Keeping the Faith"
John Gatchell – trumpet on "Careless Talk," "Tell Her About It," and "Keeping the Faith"

Tom Bahler – background vocals
Rory Dodd – background vocals
Frank Floyd – background vocals
Lani Groves – background vocals
Ullanda McCullough – background vocals
Ron Taylor – background vocals
Terry Textor – background vocals
Eric Troyer – background vocals
Mike Alexander – background vocals

Phil Ramone - producer
Laura Loncteaux - assistant producer
James Boyer - engineer, remix
Bradshaw Leigh - associate engineer
Michael Christopher - assistant engineer
Larry Franke - assistant engineer
Andy Hoffman - assistant engineer
Ted Jensen at Sterling Sound, NYC - mastering engineer
Kenneth Topolsky - production manager
Paula Scher - artwork
John Berg - inner sleeve design
Chris Austopchuk - front cover design
Benno Friedman - back cover photo
David Matthews – horn and string arrangements
Tom Bahler – background vocal arrangements
Billy Zampino – musical advisor

Released: 1983, #4 US, #2 UK, US Sales 7,000,000
Hit Singles:
- 1983, "Tell Her about It," #1 US, #4 UK
- 1983, "Uptown Girl" #3 US, #1 UK
- 1983, "An Innocent Man" #10 US #8 UK (1984 release}
- 1984, "The Longest Time" #14 US, #25 UK
- 1984, "Leave A Tender Moment Alone" #27 US #29  Double A- side with Goodnight Saigon in UK
- 1984, "Keeping the Faith" #18 US

## *Greatest Hits Parts 1 and 2*

Side One
1. Piano Man, *Piano Man*, 1973 (5:36)
2. Say Goodbye to Hollywood (live edited version) *Songs in the Attic*, 1981 (3:54)
3. New York State of Mind, *Turnstiles*, 1976 (6:02)
4. The Stranger, *The Stranger*, 1977 (5:07)
5. Just the Way You Are (radio edit), *The Stranger* (3:36)

Side Two
1. Movin' Out (Anthony's Song), *The Stranger* (3:28)
2. Only the Good Die Young, *The Stranger* (3:53)
3. She's Always a Woman, *The Stranger* (3:17)
4. My Life (radio edit), *52nd Stree*t, 1978 (3:51)
5. Big Shot (radio edit), *52nd Street*, 1978 (3:43)
6. You May Be Right, *Glass Houses*, 1980 (4:09)

Side Three
1. It's Still Rock and Roll to Me, *Glass Houses* (2:54)
2. Don't Ask Me Why, *Glass Houses* (2:57)
3. Pressure (radio edit), *The Nylon Curtain*, 1982 (3:15)
4. Allentown, *The Nylon Curtain* (3:48)
5. Goodnight Saigon, *The Nylon Curtain* (7:00)

Side Four
1. Tell Her About It (radio edit), *An Innocent Man*, 1983 (3:35)
2. Uptown Girl, *An Innocent Man* (3:15)
3. The Longest Time, *An Innocent Man* (3:36)
4. You're Only Human (Second Wind), previously unissued (4:48)

5.  The Night Is Still Young, previously unissued (5:28)

Some original pressings omit "Don't Ask Me Why" and place "Honesty" after "Big Shot," pushing "You May Be Right" to the beginning of side three.

Released 1984, #6 US, #7 UK, US Sales 21,000,000
Hit Singles:
- 1985, "You're Only Human (Second Wind)" #9 US

## *The Bridge*

Side One
1.  Running on Ice  (3:15)
2.  This is the Time (4:59)
3.  A Matter of Trust (4:09)
4.  Modern Woman (3:48)
5.  Baby Grand (duet with Ray Charles)  (4:02)

Side Two
1.  Big Man on Mulberry Street (5:26)
2.  Temptation (4:12)
3.  Code of Silence (backing vocals by Cyndi Lauper)  (5:15)
4.  Getting Closer (5:00)

All songs written by Billy Joel except "Getting Closer," music by Billy Joel, lyrics by Billy Joel and Cyndi Lauper

Billy Joel – piano, synthesizers, vocals, Fender Rhodes on "Getting Closer," electric guitar on "A Matter of Trust"
Liberty DeVitto – drums, percussion
Doug Stegmeyer – bass guitar
David Brown – guitars, acoustic 12-string and electric guitars on "Code of Silence," guitar on "Getting Closer"
Russell Javors – guitars
Mark Rivera – tenor saxophone on "Modern Woman," alto saxophone on "Temptation"
Peter Hewlett – background vocals on "Running on Ice"
Rob Mounsey – synthesizers on "Running on Ice"; orchestration on "This is the Time," "Modern Woman," and "Big Man on Mulberry Street"
Jeff Bova – synthesizers on "A Matter of Trust" and "Code of Silence"; orchestration on "Temptation"
Jimmy Bralower – percussion on Modern Woman

Ray Charles – vocals and piano on "Baby Grand"
Vinnie Colaiuta – drums on "Baby Grand"
Dean Parks – guitar on "Baby Grand"
Neil Stubenhaus – bass on "Baby Grand"
Patrick Williams – arrangements on "Baby Grand"
Ron Carter – acoustic bass on "Big Man on Mulberry Street"
Eddie Daniels – alto saxophone on "Big Man on Mulberry Street"
Michael Brecker – tenor saxophone on "Big Man on Mulberry Street"
Ronnie Cuber – baritone saxophone on "Big Man on Mulberry Street"
Marvin Stamm – trumpet on "Big Man on Mulberry Street"
Alan Rubin – trumpet on "Big Man on Mulberry Street"
Dave Bargeron – trombone on "Big Man on Mulberry Street"
Philippe Saisse – orchestration on "Temptation"
Cyndi Lauper – vocals on "Code of Silence"
Steve Winwood – Hammond B3 organ on "Getting Closer"
Neil Jason – bass guitar on "Getting Closer"
John McCurry – guitar on "Getting Closer"
Don Brooks – harmonica on "Code of Silence"


Produced by Phil Ramone
Engineer: Jim Boyer
Associate engineers: Steve Boyer, Fred Tenny, David Dickson and Bradshaw Leigh.
Technical support: Joe Salvatto, Gary Ciuzio, Joe Lopes, Frank Rodriguez, Peter Bergren, Bruce Howell, Cary Butler, Ed Evans, Mark Betts, Steve Buller, Ricki Begin, Audrey Tanaka, Billy Rothschild and Phil Vachon
Production coordinator: Joseph D'Ambrosio
Support system Jim Flynn, Barry Bongiovi and The Power Station staff
Digitally recorded at The Power Station, Chelsea Sound (North), RCA Studios, New York, NY and Evergreen Studios, Burbank, CA
Mixed at the Power Station, New York, NY
Direct metal mastering at Sterling Sound, New York, NY by Ted Jensen
Acoustic piano supplied by Yamaha
Design: Mark Larson
Cover painting: Brad Holland
Photography: Patrick Demarchelier
Sleeve photos: Larry Busacca, Phil Ramone and Charles Reilly


Released 1986, #7 US, #38 UK, US Sales 1,000,000

# *Kohuept*

Side One
1. Odoya (Traditional Rustavi Ensemble) (1:17)
2. Prelude/Angry Young Man (5:23)
3. Honesty (3:58)
4. Goodnight Saigon (7:20)

Side Two
5. Stiletto (5:09)
6. Big Man on Mulberry Street (7:17)
7. Baby Grand (6:09)

Side Three
1. An Innocent Man (6:09)
2. Allentown (4:22)
3. A Matter of Trust (5:09)
4. Only the Good Die Young (3:31)

Side Four
5. Sometimes a Fantasy (3:38)
6. Uptown Girl (3:08)
7. Big Shot (4:44)
8. Back in the U.S.S.R. (Lennon–McCartney) (2:43)
9. The Times They are A-Changin' (Dylan) (2:55)

Billy Joel – vocals, piano, harmonica, keyboards, electric guitar

Liberty DeVitto – drums, maracas, Simmons drums

Doug Stegmeyer – bass, electric upright bass

Dave Lebolt – keyboards

Russell Javors – acoustic and Electric guitars, harmonica, BVs

Mark Rivera – baritone saxophone, alto saxophone, BVs, keyboards, tambourine, lyricon

Kevin Dukes – electric and acoustic guitars

Peter Hewlett – background vocals, percussion

George Simms – background vocals, percussion

The Georgian Rustavi Ensemble of USSR–vocals on "Odoya"

Oleg Smirnoff – on-stage translation

Album Released : 1987, #38 US, US Sales 1,000,000

# *Storm Front*

1. That's Not Her Style (5:10)
2. We Didn't Start the Fire (4:50)
3. The Downeaster "Alexa" (3:44)
4. I Go to Extremes (4:23)
5. Shameless (4:26)
6. Storm Front (5:17)
7. Leningrad (4:06)
8. State of Grace (4:30)
9. When in Rome (4:44)
10. And So It Goes (3:38)

Billy Joel – vocals, acoustic piano (1, 4, 6, 7, 8, 10), clavinet (2, 3, 6), accordion (3), percussion (3), Hammond organ (4, 6, 9), harpsichord (5), organ (8), synthesizers (10)

Liberty DeVitto – drums (1–9), percussion (2)

David Brown – lead guitar (1–9), MIDI guitar solo on *Storm Front*

Joey Hunting – rhythm guitar (2)

Crystal Taliefero – backing vocals (1, 2, 5, 6, 9), percussion (2)

Schuyler Deale – bass guitar (1–9)

Jeff Jacobs – synthesizers (1–9), backing vocals (1), horn arrangements (6)

Don Brooks – harmonica on "That's Not Her Style"

Mick Jones – guitar on "Storm Front," guitar solo on "State of Grace," backing vocals on "That's Not Her Style," "I Go To Extremes," and "State of Grace"

John Mahoney – keyboards on "We Didn't Start the Fire," keyboard programming on "Leningrad"

Sammy Merendino – electronic percussion on "We Didn't Start the Fire"

Kevin Jones – keyboard programming on "We Didn't Start the Fire"

Doug Kleeger – sounds effects and arrangements on "We Didn't Start the Fire"

Dominic Cortese – accordion on "Leningrad"

Itzhak Perlman – violin on "The Downeaster 'Alexa'"

Lenny Pickett – saxophone on "Storm Front" and "When in Rome"

Andrew Love, Wayne Jackson – The Memphis Horns on "Storm Front"

Bill Zampino – choral arrangement on "Leningrad"

Chuck Arnold – backing vocals and choral leader on "Leningrad"

Arif Mardin – orchestral arrangement on "Leningrad"

Hicksville High School Chorus – backing vocals on "Leningrad"

Richard Marx – backing vocals on "Storm Front" and "That's Not Her Style"

Patricia Darcy-Jones – backing vocals on "That's Not Her Style," "Shameless," "Storm Front," and "When in Rome"

Frank Floyd – backing vocals on "That's Not Her Style," "Shameless," and "Storm Front"

Brian Ruggles – backing vocals on "That's Not Her Style"
Joe Lynn Turner – backing vocals on "I Go to Extremes" and "State of Grace"
Ian Lloyd – backing vocals on "I Go to Extremes" and "State of Grace"
Brenda White King – backing vocals on "When in Rome"
Curtis King – backing vocals on "When in Rome"

Produced by Billy Joel and Mick Jones
Mixed by Tom Lord-Alge (tracks 1–3) and Jay Healy (tracks 3–10)
Engineered by Jay Healy
Assistant engineers – Dana Becker, Tim Crich, David Dorn, Suzanne Hollander, Joe Pirrera and Gary Solomon
Mastered by Ted Jensen at Sterling Sound, New York, NY
Art direction – Chris Austopchuk
Back photo – Timothy White
Front photo – Frank Ockenfels

Released 1989, #1 US, #5 UK, US Sales 4,000,000
Hit Singles:
- 1989 "We Didn't Start the Fire" #1 US, #7 UK
- 1990 "I Go To Extremes" #6 US
- 1990 "And So It Goes" #37 US

# Liberty DeVitto
# Band Tree

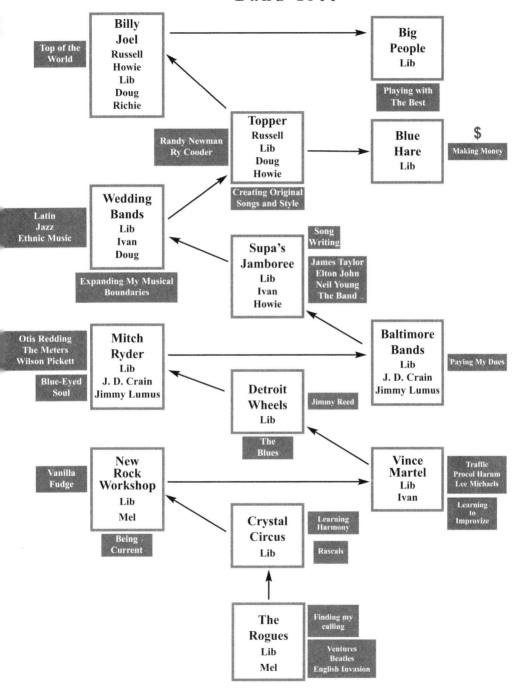

269

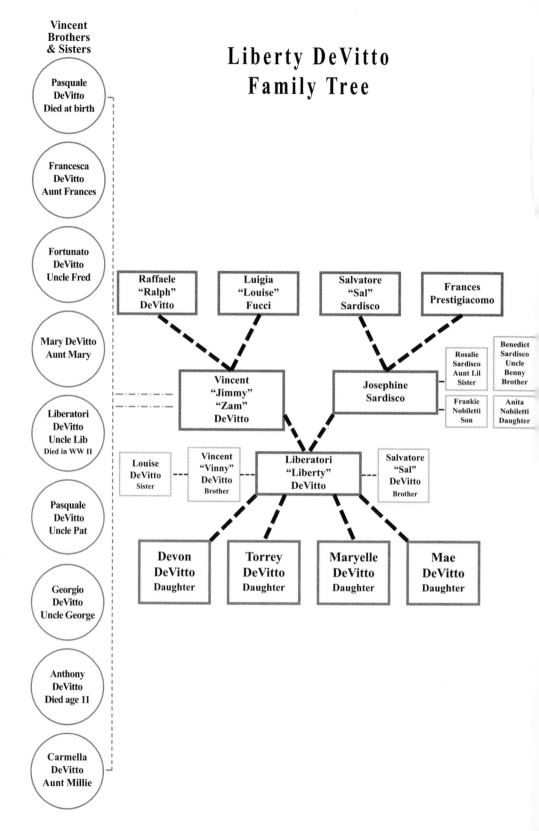

# Liberty DeVitto
# Family Tree

**Vincent Brothers & Sisters**

Pasquale DeVitto
Died at birth

Francesca DeVitto
Aunt Frances

Fortunato DeVitto
Uncle Fred

Mary DeVitto
Aunt Mary

Liberatori DeVitto
Uncle Lib
Died in WW II

Pasquale DeVitto
Uncle Pat

Georgio DeVitto
Uncle George

Anthony DeVitto
Died age 11

Carmella DeVitto
Aunt Millie

Raffaele "Ralph" DeVitto

Luigia "Louise" Fucci

Salvatore "Sal" Sardisco

Frances Prestigiacomo

Vincent "Jimmy" "Zam" DeVitto

Josephine Sardisco

Rosalie Sardisco
Aunt Lil
Sister

Benedict Sardisco
Uncle Benny
Brother

Frankie Nobiletti
Son

Anita Nobiletti
Daughter

Louise DeVitto
Sister

Vincent "Vinny" DeVitto
Brother

Liberatori "Liberty" DeVitto

Salvatore "Sal" DeVitto
Brother

Devon DeVitto
Daughter

Torrey DeVitto
Daughter

Maryelle DeVitto
Daughter

Mae DeVitto
Daughter

# MORE FROM HUDSON MUSIC
## IN-DEPTH BIOGRAPHIES FEATURING SOME OF THE BIGGEST HITTERS IN MUSIC HISTORY

### BUDDY RICH: ONE OF A KIND
**Pelle Berglund • Foreword by Max Weinberg**
A complete record of the life and career of Buddy Rich, still considered by many to be the greatest drummer ever to pick up sticks. A complete chronology of Buddy's life is presented, including never-before-seen photos of Buddy, add a new perspective and a glimpse into the mind of a musical titan who demanded greatness from himself and those around him, and became one of the most celebrated and controversial stars in music.

### BOBBY MORRIS: MY LAS VEGAS
**Bobby Morris/JJ Grant • Foreword by Steve Smith**
The incredible life story of Bobby Morris, who arrived in the U.S. from Poland at age ten and rose to become a music legend. Accompanying such artists as **Judy Garland, Barbra Streisand, Bobby Darin, Frank Sinatra, Eddie Fisher, Louie Prima, Elvis Presley**, and dozens of others. This is the inspiring and nearly unbelievable story of one man achieving his dreams and rubbing elbows with the greatest personalities of the twentieth century in the process.

### THE ROOTS OF ROCK DRUMMING
**Edited by Daniel Glass with Steve Smith**
A behind-the-scenes look at the origins of rock n roll drumming. Presented through the eyes of the players themselves, including **Bobby Morris, Dick Richards, Earl Palmer, DJ Fontana, JM Van Eaton, Buddy Harman, Jerry J.I. Allison, Hal Blaine, Idris Muhammad, Sam Lay, Bernard Purdie, Roger Hawkins, Sandy Nelson, Smokey Johnson, John Boudreaux, Brian Bennett, Bobby Graham, Clem Cattini, Jaimoe, Carmine Appice, Steve Gadd, and Jim Keltner.**

## LEARN MORE : **HUDSONMUSIC.COM**